D0783547

Living Strategy

FINANCIAL TIMES
Prentice Hall

In an increasingly competitive world, it is quality
of thinking that gives an edge. An idea that opens new
doors, a technique that solves a problem, or an insight
that simply helps make sense of it all.

We work with leading authors in the fields of
management and finance to bring cutting-edge thinking
and best learning practice to a global market.

Under a range of leading imprints, including
Financial Times Prentice Hall, we create world-class
print publications and electronic products giving readers
knowledge and understanding which can then be
applied, whether studying or at work.

To find out more about our business and professional
products, you can visit us at www.business-minds.com

For other Pearson Education publications, visit
www.pearsoned-ema.com

Pearson
Education

Living Strategy

PUTTING PEOPLE AT THE HEART OF CORPORATE PURPOSE

Lynda Gratton

FINANCIAL TIMES
Prentice Hall

An imprint of **PEARSON EDUCATION**

London · New York · San Francisco · Toronto · Sydney
Tokyo · Singapore · Hong Kong · Cape Town · Madrid ·
Paris · Milan · Munich · Amsterdam

PEARSON EDUCATION LIMITED

Head Office
Edinburgh Gate
Harlow CM20 2JE
Tel: +44 (0)1279 623623
Fax: +44 (0)1279 431059

London Office:
128 Long Acre
London WC2E 9AN
Tel: +44 (0)20 7447 2000
Fax: +44 (0)20 7240 5771
Website: www.business-minds.com

First published in Great Britain in 2000

© Pearson Education Limited 2000

The right of Lynda Gratton to be identified as Author
of this Work has been asserted by her in accordance
with the Copyright, Designs and Patents Act 1988.

ISBN 0 273 65015 7

British Library Cataloguing in Publication Data
A CIP catalogue record for this book can be obtained from the British Library

All rights reserved; no part of this publication may be reproduced, stored
in a retrieval system, or transmitted in any form or by any means, electronic,
mechanical, photocopying, recording, or otherwise without either the prior
written permission of the Publishers or a licence permitting restricted copying
in the United Kingdom issued by the Copyright Licensing Agency Ltd,
90 Tottenham Court Road, London W1P 0LP. This book may not be lent,
resold, hired out or otherwise disposed of by way of trade in any form
of binding or cover other than that in which it is published, without the
prior consent of the Publishers.

10 9 8 7 6 5 4 3 2

Typeset by Pantek Arts, Maidstone, Kent
Printed and bound in Great Britain by Biddles Ltd, Guildford & King's Lynn

The Publishers' policy is to use paper manufactured from sustainable forests.

Coventry University

About the author

 Professor Lynda Gratton is Associate Professor of Organizational Behaviour at London Business School and a global authority on the people implications of strategy. She writes, teaches and consults across the world on human resource strategy. At London Business School, she is Dean of the MBA Programme and Director of the executive programme 'Human Resource Strategy in Transforming Organizations'. Since 1992 she has directed the Leading Edge Research Consortium in partnership with companies such as Hewlett-Packard, Glaxo Wellcome and Citibank. Reflections on these companies formed the framework for *Strategic Human Resource Management: Corporate Rhetoric and Human Reality* published by Oxford University Press in 1999.

Dr Gratton has profoundly influenced the way managers think about human resource strategy. She is an active consultant working with some of the world's largest companies and has trained managers all over the world in her 'Living Strategy' process.

To my father and sons: David, Christian and Dominic

Contents

Part III

THE SIX STEPS TO CREATING A LIVING STRATEGY

Part IV

THE LIVING STRATEGY WORKBOOK

Acknowledgements

I really appreciate the wise counsel of my friends and colleagues Sumantra Ghoshal at the London Business School and Dave Ulrich of the University of Michigan, both of whom gave detailed comments at various stages of the book.

I would like to thank London Business School for the support it provided for the research. Under the successive guidance of Professors Nigel Nicholson, Rob Goffee and Paul Willman the School's Organisational Behaviour Group has been unstinting in its support. Since 1992 I have been joined by a group of research colleagues which has brought insights and ideas. I would like to thank Veronica Hope-Hailey, now at Cranfield Business School, Pat McGovern, now at the London School of Economics, Philip Stiles, now at the Judge Institute of Management Studies at Cambridge University, Catherine Truss, now at Kingston Business School, and Joanna Zaleska, a Research Fellow at the London Business School, each of whom has brought their unique insights into the unfolding story.

Many people have contributed to the thinking in this book. The 'Leading Edgers' have been an important thread since 1992. I would like to acknowledge Nick Savage from BT, John Kick from HP, Gillian Arthur from Citibank, Mike Anscombe from Kraft Jacob Suchard, and Bill Proudlock from Glaxo Wellcome, all of whom have made important contributions to my understanding of the realities of organizational life. The Leading Edge data on emotions and attitudes, trust, commitment and pride bring added insights to this argument. I am immensely grateful to these companies for allowing their data to be shared, and in the case of BT, Citibank, Glaxo Wellcome and Hewlett-Packard, for their stories to be told.

The six-steps process could be illustrated only through a real case example, and I am extremely grateful to the management team at Philips Lighting, in particular, John Vreeswijk and Hans van Reenen, for allowing me to recount their story.

I have been enormously grateful to the teams who have worked on editing this book. Cedric Crocker and six anonymous reviewers at Jossey Bass and my long-time editorial friend Simon Bird all provided insights and support to the earlier draft of the book. At FT Prentice Hall I would like to extend my thanks to my editor Richard Stagg and the editorial team of Jacqueline Cassidy, Vivienne Church, Linda Dhondy and Lisa Nachtigall. I have really enjoyed working with them and experiencing their enthusiasm and professionalism. Anthony Senior, my assistant at the London Business School, prepared the manuscript and has been a great colleague and support.

A final heartfelt thanks to my sons Christian and Dominic who saw me working in the study when they probably would have preferred us to be playing. My mother Barbara has been an enormous support and my father, now sadly gone, would have been proud of this book ... he too believed that people are at the heart of corporate purpose.

Preface

People are our most important asset. 'We are a knowledge-based company.' 'All we have is our people.' These are statements we hear more and more. Yet for many people the reality of life in an organization is that they do not feel they are treated as the most important asset, or that their knowledge is understood or used. The reality of working in contemporary organizations was starkly described in *Human Resource Strategy; Corporate Rhetoric and Reality*[1] which I wrote with the Leading Edge research team. I came away from this research with three messages. First, that in many companies people do not feel inspired, engaged or free to voice their opinion. Second, that there has been no uniform progress in people management over the six years of the study. The longitudinal nature of the research captured clearly that people practices and attitudes are just as likely to deteriorate over time as they are to flourish. And finally, that there are profound differences between companies in both the behaviours, skills and attitudes of their employees and in the rigour and appropriateness of people policies and practices, and that these differences have a significant impact on the long-term health of the company.

This has raised some crucial questions in my mind which I have sought to understand and answer in my research and consulting. This book is the culmination of my thinking. It is based on four propositions:

1 there are fundamental differences between people as an asset and the traditional assets of finance or technology;

2 an understanding of these fundamental differences creates a whole new way of thinking and working in organizations, a shift in mind set;

3 business strategies can only be realized through people;

4 creating a strategic approach to people necessitates a strong dialogue across the organization.

In essence, then, a new way of thinking and a new way of doing. A way of thinking that places the creation of meaning at its centre. A way of doing that builds a people strategy through visioning, through a deep understanding of reality, and through broad involvement of multi-functional task forces.

My aim is simple – to present an argument about *why* we need to think and act differently, and to provide a clear step-by-step guide to *how* we can make this happen. I believe that managers who follow these steps will significantly increase the performance of their business, and create organizations which have meaning and soul.

My journey began with my initial training as a psychologist. My doctoral study in 'Maslow's Hierarchy of Needs' attempted to understand the sources of motivation for people in organizations, and the factors which impacted on their motivation. I finished my dissertation greatly interested in the human side of organizations, with a profound belief that studies of organizations should work at the level of the individual in the organization. The experience also refined my position as a humanistic psychologist, with the belief that people have a soul and a spirit, that they are basically good rather than evil, and that they become engaged and inspired by their dreams. This humanistic perspective places the context as a critical part of the actualization, as Maslow called it, of human potential. As a committed humanistic psychologist, I joined British Airways for five years as one of their resident psychologists. Thus began my corporate life and with it a growing understanding of the challenges and the reality of day-to-day existence for employees throughout the organization. Seconded to the newly formed BA strategy team I worked with a group given the task of developing the policies and processes which began to change British Airways from a moribund public airline to the world-class company it is today.

After British Airways my understanding of corporate life grew when I joined PA Consulting Group, where I led the fledgling human resource strategy team. Again, I was seconded to the business strategy team, and we spent the next year developing an approach to strategy which held people at its core. There followed initial experimentation with business tools such as the risk matrix and forcefield analysis which are described in this book. These early attempts at creating a strategic approach to people were supported by a number of companies, in particular British Petroleum, the Prudential Insurance company, and Philips. In the case of Philips this support was to continue over more than a decade. I have chosen the work at Philips Lighting to illustrate how a strategic approach to people could be taken.

The experimentation with what was now termed human resource strategy continued when I joined the London Business School and engaged in people strategy development for a number of large international companies. Teaching and researching at the London Business School has been an enormously rewarding experience. From the outset I taught a course in human resource strategy to first-year MBA students. Many came to the school to increase their financial and strategic acumen as a prelude to joining a consultancy practice or banking. Like many managers they implicitly believed that financial capital is what really counts in corporations. After all, they would argue, it is obvious from the amount of space taken up in reporting the state of financial capital in any annual report. If human capital is really so important, they would continue, why do we know so little about it? A good point, and as I argue in this book, until that changes an interest in people will always remain simply the two-paragraph statement from the chief executive officer about the importance of people to the business. Working closely with successive groups of MBA students I have had to confront the rhetoric of people and create a personal philosophy about what we really mean. This personal philosophy is described in the three tenets which make up the first part of this book.

The industry experiences described in this book emerge from three sources – from my experience as a consultant to companies, as a member of the Leading Edge Research Consortium at the London Business School, and as a teaching faculty and director of the Global Business Consortium. The visioning and risk matrix work was developed over the past decade through working as a consultant with the senior teams of a number of companies including ABB, BAT, British Petroleum, BT, Northern Telecom, Philips, Unilever and Shell. During this time I was also privileged to work with a number of Shell strategists, in particular Arie de Geus and Jo Jawarski, both of whom reinforced my thinking about the human side of organizations.

My insights into the human side of the organization have been enormously enriched through the Leading Edge Research Consortium which I founded at the London Business School in 1992. Since that date we have collected in-depth data about the rhetoric and reality of people management in the payphones business of BT, Citibank, Glaxo Wellcome, Hewlett-Packard, Kraft Jacob Suchard (a Philip Morris business), Lloyds TSB and a National Health Service hospital. Using extensive survey data, interviews and focus groups, we have explored the human side of organizations. The mission of the research consortium was clear: to create a deep understanding of the reality of people management in contemporary organizations; to share this information, initially throughout the member companies of the research consortium and subsequently with a broader group; and to commit to a longitudinal study, so we could see how interventions played out over time.

The global forces operating in organizations have become ever more apparent. For four years my colleague Sumantra Ghoshal and I have directed and co-taught on the Global Business Consortium. Designed to explore the impact of the forces of globalization, the programme takes participants throughout Asia, South America and Europe. Since its inception we have seen the management teams of the consortium companies ABB, BT, Lufthansa, LG, Standard Chartered Bank and SKF facing up to the immense turbulence in their markets. I have become ever more convinced that the pulse of commitment, trust and inspiration must be the heartbeat of any company attempting to ride out these successive waves of turbulence.

Over the past 20 years I have developed a way of thinking about people in organizations and the central role played by dreams, hopes and aspirations. In this book I want to make the case forcibly that people really matter. I believe passionately that the reality in organizations falls well short of the rhetoric that 'people are our most important asset'. Until we face up to this gap, until we can stare reality in the face, and until we can care as much about feelings as about finance, we are doomed to create organizations which break the soul and spirit of those who are members, and which reduce rather than build human potential. In this book I make the case for the human side of the organization and how we can build processes within organizations which sustain the potential of people.

PART I

The new agenda: putting people at the heart of corporate purpose

Introduction

How has Hewlett-Packard sustained 20 per cent annual growth over a ten-year period, or Glaxo Wellcome brought its products to the market-place quicker by achieving significant reductions in its product development cycle, or Motorola kept its growth rate buoyant in China? These are examples from across the globe but united by a common thread. If we had asked a similar question of companies in 1900, the answer would have been that these companies achieve success because they have the financial capital to expand into new and emerging markets. In the fifties we could have spoken of their technological advantages, of the patents they hold and exploit. But in 2000, at a time when raising $1 million is a nanosecond away, when patents erode in months, the advantages of the past have little meaning. The new sources of sustainable competitive advantage available to organizations have people at the centre – their creativity and talent, their inspirations and hopes, their dreams and excitement.[1] The companies that flourish in this decade will do so because they are able to provide meaning and purpose, a context and frame that encourages individual potential to flourish and grow.

For some of us the idea that people are at the very centre of successful organizations is an overriding passion, for others it is something we feel deep down, at an intuitive level, or perhaps we believe that people are peripheral to success. Over the years I have become increasingly aware that it is people who make great companies. But with this awareness has come a growing realization that by putting people at the heart of corporate strategy we must acknowledge the very humanness of this resource.

My purpose in this chapter is simple: to share with you the experiences of three companies and to review the wider body of research which together have convinced me of the prime role of people in organizational success. But that only raises the 'so what' question ... so what if people are at the centre of organizational success? I believe that putting people at the heart of organizational success has implications on *how we think* about organizations and *what we do* within them. The first part of this book addresses the question of how we think about organizations if we put people at the heart of corporate purpose. For me it raises three basic tenets of being human: we operate in time, we search for meaning, and we have a soul. With this comes a set of nine organizational and managerial capabilities that support these tenets. The second part of the book addresses the question of what we can do to create living strategies that place people at the centre. Over the years I have refined a six-step process that puts people at the heart of corporate success. This, together with the workbook that follows, provides a frame for you to move from this as rhetoric to action-based reality.

People inspiration: some professional experiences

Each of us has our own set of stories about how people have made a real difference to our business. My set of stories has been built up over the past decade. Some have come directly from consulting experience where I have observed how people have impacted on the bottom line. Others have come from the programmes I have developed and run and the research in which I have participated, particularly in the Leading Edge Research Consortium.

There are examples from across the globe of how companies have created a human asset which is so intangible it cannot be easily described or imitated, but which is capable of accelerating the success of that company to bring competitive advantage. At Glaxo Wellcome the speed with which products are developed and brought to the market has been drastically increased by virtue of people working closely across functions and trusting each other. We see at Hewlett-Packard a company which has at its very core the notion of the 'HP Way'. This has created and sustained a level of commitment and inspiration which others can only observe and envy. At Motorola, we see a company which continues to flourish in China through the development of a Chinese workforce who are loyal, highly skilled, and, surprisingly for the super-mobile Chinese labour market, committed to staying with Motorola.

Accelerating product development at Glaxo Wellcome

In the early 1990s, Glaxo Wellcome, the world's largest pharmaceutical company by sales and the largest company in the UK, has a combined 5.1

per cent of the fragmented world market. Since the eighties Glaxo Wellcome had been faced with the need for radical changes because of cost cutting in drug purchases, and the introduction of 'managed care'. The consequence of the squeeze of costs had been a shrinking of profit growth for the pharmaceutical companies. With the imminent expiry of patents on the blockbuster drugs such as Glaxo's Zantac and Wellcome's Zovirax, and major rises in the cost of research and development, particularly in the emerging biotechnology field, the race for product innovation was on.

In 1988 Glaxo chairman Richard Sykes and his team looked at how they could remain successful in this increasingly competitive marketplace. In reviewing their business strategy, two challenges became clear – to move away from a single product focus to the concept of disease management, and to develop a closer partnership with their customers and speed the delivery time of new drugs. In the past, one of the core competencies of a pharmaceutical company such as Glaxo Wellcome was its research and development capability. But the senior team concluded that this was no longer sufficient. While financial investment in the research and development capability would continue to play a necessary part in the long-term success of the company, it would not be enough to bring sustainable competitive advantage. They determined that the necessary leap in reducing product time to market, creating a world-class product portfolio and focusing more on the needs of customers would come in part from research-based innovation, but more importantly from the way in which the functional teams deep within the company could work together. All this hinged on the abilities of the research and development teams to share ideas and inspiration, to establish trust and reciprocity between the development teams and the marketing groups, and on the success of the sales team rapidly to bring information from the doctors and patients back into the research and development teams. This would require a radical move away from providing not simply products (in the form of drugs) but also services (after-care, diagnosis) to form a complete disease management system.

The intention was to break down the strong internal barriers caused by rigid functional silos and replace them with horizontal working practices, capable of transferring knowledge and encouraging entrepreneurial behaviour. In other words, to fundamentally transform the company from a functional, hierarchical structure and culture to one which was process driven, customer focused and multi-disciplinary. Capital investment and technological innovations were necessary, but they would not bring Glaxo Wellcome the competitive edge it required.

From 1988 the senior team began to concentrate on the creation of a new way of working across functional silos. This resulted in training managers in team working, restructuring work flows, and creating a team-based performance management process. From 1990 the company began to see significant differences in the speed to market. At the same time the organization was beginning to create a stable of potential drug winners which would form the basis of its continued success over the coming decades.[2]

What we saw at Glaxo Wellcome was the capacity to create cross-functional team working and this ensured that products were brought to the marketplace more rapidly. The groups' ability to work together, to share knowledge and to trust each other was of immense value to the business, resulting in a real impact on performance and on the bottom line. This capacity to create value raises a number of questions to which we will return:

◆ How was Glaxo Wellcome able to realign the practices and processes to deliver the business goal of rapid product creation?

◆ More broadly, how is value created in organizations, what are the attitudes, behaviours, skills and capabilities which underpin value creation?

◆ It took Glaxo Wellcome more than ten years to create cross-functional team working. What does this tell us about human and organizational timescale? What might be the broader aspect of time in people-centred organizations?

Developing an inimitable culture at Hewlett-Packard

Many people have testified to the strength of human potential and culture at Hewlett-Packard (HP). The difficulty of imitating this formula was highlighted in my own work. The Leading Edge Research Consortium which compared HP and six other companies with significant business operations in the UK.[3] This study used a complex triangulated methodology to dig deeper into the inner workings of these organizations and to identify the means by which they created competitive advantage in their marketplace.

What is fascinating about the way in which human potential is created and developed at HP is the subtle combination of the 'soft' and the 'hard'. The 'hard' which forms the process backbone of the company is a performance management process which creates a shared set of strategic objectives and constantly aligns and realigns the behaviour of every individual to the business goals. This cascading of business objectives, termed the 'Hoshin', creates a relentless focus on growth and profitability. This focused performance management process brings short-term competitive advantage. In fact, many companies benchmark against HP and share information with them in the hope of imitation. However, what we saw clearly in our study was that HP is able to balance this tight, highly focused and driven performance management process with the 'soft' of a value set the 'HP Way' which places dignity and respect for the individual employee at its centre.

The interview and survey data we collected highlighted this unmistakable source of competitive advantage. The HP employees we surveyed and spoke to are highly committed (of the many hundreds of employees we surveyed, 80 per cent described themselves as very committed), they trust their managers (only about 20 per cent said they did not trust their managers) and they have pride in their company (about 90 per cent said they were proud to be part of HP). These commitment and trust levels are significantly higher than those in many of the other companies we studied. Commitment, trust and pride are critical to sustaining ongoing change at HP and senior executives believe these are major factors in the ability of the business to remain flexible and to increase turnover and profitability at a rate of 20 per cent per annum, year on year, without significantly increasing employee numbers.

We may believe, like the team at HP, that commitment, pride and trust are critical to long-term success. But do we really understand the complexity of creating organizational trust and commitment, and the time it takes to do so? It is not difficult to describe and benchmark against the strength of the HP culture. But ask those companies which have benchmarked HP whether they have been able to imitate it. The answer is a resounding no! It would take a company years of focus, senior management commitment action, and skill to create what HP has. This brings sustained competitive advantage precisely because it is near impossible for competitors to imitate these core elements of commitment, pride and trust, and hence the goodwill and flexibility that have allowed the company to flourish and grow.

Hewlett-Packard's capacity to create a deep sense of meaning and commitment again raises a number of questions to which we shall return:

◆ What is the role of meaning in the organization? How was this deep sense of meaning created at Hewlett-Packard?

◆ What role do emotions play in organizations? How is emotional resilience built, and what destroys it?

◆ What are the means by which managers can build capacities such as trust and pride which are difficult for competitors to imitate?

Creating a Chinese management cadre at Motorola

In the Asia-Pacific region the explosive growth of the economy and the political and cultural history are placing particular strains on the way in which people are recruited and retained. Nowhere is this more apparent than in China. During the mid-eighties I, like others working with the senior teams of European and US multi-national companies, heard of aspirations to create, by the end of the decade, a significant proportion of company profits in China and the rising tiger economies of South-East Asia. While many companies may not have had a highly articulated strategy for the people side of the business, the general view was that there were two options. At the right time, competent Asian managers could be bought from the external Asian labour market; alternatively, Western managers from these companies could be expatriated into China to build the business.

The predicted growth occurred, and China is set to become a dominant world economic force within the next decade. But for many the dream has turned sour. The Chinese cultural revolution created a 'missing generation' of people. That cadre of Chinese who should now be taking senior roles often have limited education and limited experience in Western business practices. The salaries commanded by that small group of experienced Chinese managers are way in excess of predictions, and more importantly the turnover rates of skilled employees in many sectors are so high that it is almost impossible to keep competitive knowledge within the company – it walks out with the people who leave. Repeated surveys of businesses operating in China have shown that the primary problem they face is the retention of skilled people. Their priority challenge is to attract, recruit and retain management talent; the option of 'buy-in' from the external labour market is unfeasible.[4]

However, in China, the US multi-national Motorola continues to grow and remain profitable at a time when other Western companies are struggling. In the eighties the senior team participated in long-range scenario planning for Asia and from this created a long-term people strategy for the region. At the heart of this strategy was the creation of strong links with local Chinese universities; the development of the 'Motorola University' in Beijing committed to educating and developing young Chinese talent; the provision of coaching, mentoring and management support; and a fundamental commitment to grow Chinese talent through the company – there would be no 'glass ceiling' for Chinese nationals.

By 1996 many Western businesses were reporting that the lack of management talent was severely hampering their ability to grow. Yet Motorola continued to attract young Chinese talent, was seen as an employer of choice in the region, and had a turnover rate which was one of the lowest of the multi-nationals in China. The company's early commitment to people and understanding of what worked in the Chinese market created the basis of long-term success in a way which has been difficult for other companies to catch up with or imitate.

What we saw at Motorola was the capacity to build a Chinese management cadre at a time when very few other multi-nationals were attempting this. What they had was something that was rare and of value. And the combination of rarity and value brought competitive advantage in the region. This raises the following questions to which we shall return:

◆ Motorola's capacity to move faster than other Western multi-nationals in part reflected the visioning capability created within the organization. How can visionary capacity be created and sustained within an organization?

◆ The decision to create the Motorola University in Beijing was taken long before such ideas became fashionable. How can management commitment to large projects such as these be created?

People are at the centre of business success

At the heart of business success at Glaxo Wellcome, Hewlett-Packard and

Motorola are the skills and behaviours of groups of talented people. But these are simply three companies. How do we know the impact of people on the financial performance of a business can be generalized into other companies and industries? Making the link between people and the financial health of the organization was an act of faith for inspirational leaders such as Richard Sykes at Glaxo Wellcome or Lew Platt at Hewlett-Packard. But over the past five years a series of European and US studies have brought greater clarity about how the behaviour of individual employees impacts on financial performance, and what influences individual behaviour. At the heart of this is the simple causal model shown in Fig. 1.

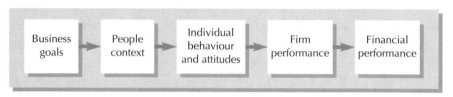

FIGURE 1 ◆   **The link between individual behaviour and financial perfor-**

High-performance companies are created by focusing on a number of appropriate business goals, which are translated into an appropriate context in which people work. Employees behave in a way which meets the business goals and this impacts on firm performance and ultimately financial performance. At Glaxo Wellcome, changes in the business goals – to become closer to the marketplace and faster to market – were translated into a changed context for people. Jobs were restructured, performance management and pay realigned, training programmes created to emphasize cross-functional working. Over time these changes in the context of the workplace influenced the behaviour of individuals and this impacted on the speed to market and the profitability of the organization.

At HP we saw how attitudes of trust and pride have sustained 20 per cent per annum growth in financial performance. The crucial part of this relationship is that it places the *behaviour of individual employees* at the centre of wealth creation. I return to this simple model throughout the book – as we see how Citibank linked the business goals to the context, how Hewlett-Packard linked the people context to individual behaviour, how Philips developed a strategy for the people context.

Over the past five years a series of large-scale research projects has tracked the impact of the context in which people work and their behaviours and attitudes on the financial performance of the business. Each of these projects has demonstrated that people are indeed at the centre of business performance. When companies adopt certain people practices, they experience significant increases in shareholder wealth.[5]

There is also growing evidence of the impact of individual employees' attitudes on the performance of the business. A significant number of changes in productivity over time can be explained by the culture of the organization and individual employees' commitment to the business.[6]

The message from the growing body of research and corporate experience of companies such as Glaxo Wellcome, Hewlett-Packard and Motorola is clear: the attitudes, skills and capabilities of people have the potential to create sustainable competitive advantage.

The firms in the US and UK research study were able to build financial performance because the resources which brought sustained competitive advantage were rare or difficult for competitors to imitate. Financial capital brought advantage in the last century because it was a relatively scarce commodity; technology later brought advantage because the patents protecting a technology rendered it difficult for others to copy. But financial capital is no longer scarce, and technology can be easily imitated. These resources continue to bring advantage, but they are no longer capable of *sustaining* this advantage.

In this decade it is only people who can sustain the competitive advantage of a company. This is because people potentially have three aspects which can bring sustainable competitive advantage: the ability to create rarity, value and inimitability.[7]

TABLE 1 ◆ **When does a resource create sustained competitive advantage?**

When it is rare ... so that all competitors do not have it	For example, the Motorola University in Beijing, through training and mentoring, has created a Chinese management cadre whose commitment and loyalty ensure that skills and knowledge remain within the firm
When it is valuable ... so that it impacts on the bottom-line performance	For example, Glaxo Wellcome's creation of cross-functional teams has significantly reduced product time to market
When it is inimitable ... so that it cannot be easily copied or substituted by competitors	For example, the HP Way and HP's strong culture of commitment and involvement has proven to be very difficult for competitors to imitate

What Motorola built in China was *rare* – a cadre of Chinese managers at a time when no other Western multi-national had achieved this. The cross-functional teams at Glaxo Wellcome created *value* for the business as they accelerated the time to market of the key products. What Hewlett-Packard has is a culture that *cannot be easily imitated* by competing companies. Many have tried to imitate the HP Way by producing plastic-covered cards with their own value statements. But often employees view these with suspicion or good humour, just another example of management rhetoric. What the creators of these value statements have failed to grasp is that the rhetoric of the HP Way statement is not the source of competitive advantage for HP. It is the everyday actions of managers and the thousands of decisions taken every year that fuel the advantage the HP Way has brought.

As the challenge shifts from managing capital and technology to managing people, so this requires a fundamental shift in the way we consider resources. At the centre is the notion that people are uniquely different from capital and technology. This uniqueness flows from the very 'humanness' of this resource. While it creates the possibility, as HP has done, of building a unique and long-term advantage, it brings with it challenges, the need for very different ways of thinking, and a new set of managerial competencies. These new ways of thinking rest on the deep-rooted characteristics of people. To disregard this is to create an organization with no hope of success; to create a workforce dissociated from the general business needs and aspirations of the company; to develop a pool of people whose personal identity rests outside the organization, who direct their considerable talents outside rather than inside; to develop individuals who are continuously engaged in short-term tactical behaviour. This creates an organization with little regard for longer-term development, and as a consequence leads to a fundamental schism between the goals of the company and of the trust and commitment of individual employees.

The three tenets of the new agenda

People are fundamentally different from capital and technology, and the shift of sources of competitive advantage across these resources has profound implications for the organizations in which we work. If we place people at the centre of sustained competitive advantage then we have to take full account of the fundamental characteristics of human capital.

What are these fundamental characteristics? What separates us from money or machines, and what are the implications of these differences? My view of this comes essentially from the perspective of an individual psychologist and from my experience in organizations. For me the question of time is crucial, both because we humans operate in time with the past, the present and the future assuming importance; and because there are phases, sequences of time and rhythms, which are essentially human. Like many other psychologists, I have been influenced by the notion of meaning and of soul. Both are deeply philosophical terms, with roots as old as mankind. They are soft, perhaps even flaky, notions, but I believe to deny them is to create organizations fit for machines, not people. They may not be the terms with which you are most comfortable, perhaps other words suit you better, but somewhere within our views of organizations we need to acknowledge the difference between machines and man.

The first tenet: we operate in time

Human time is felt in two ways. First, by the ticking of the human clock, by the stages of human development, by the time it takes to build commitment and inspiration. Second, by our deep immersion in time, in the memories and commitments of the past, in the excitement of the present, and in the dreams and hopes of the future. We are not creatures of the moment. On the contrary, each of us has our own personal history and memory of our past, a history and memory which influence the way we see our world and the expectations and hopes we have for it. The past is continuously with us. But so too is the future. Our memory of the past is balanced by a 'memory of the future', captured in our daydreams and the vignettes we paint to think through our options and the way we would like to see our life develop.

Our development follows the ticking of the human clock. We grow from childhood through to adolescence and then to adulthood in a predictable, staged sequence. In a similar way our ideas and skills grow and develop in a predictable and staged manner. Many of us have experienced the shock of the death of a loved one. The sequence of grieving is predictable. We do not move from despair to acceptance, but instead go through a time-dependent sequence, beginning with shock which moves to anger, then to denial, and finally we come to accept that our loved one is no longer with us. We all experience this sequence, and this unfolding of events is part of the human condition. The same is true of the formation of teams. Over the years I have watched the MBA study groups at the London Business School as they go through the sequence of forming, storming, norming and performing in a relatively predictable way. Few groups move from forming to being high-performing groups without going through a time when the potential leaders are jockeying for position. The passage of time is a crucial part of the unfolding of this sequence.

What we see in our reactions to bereavement and the formation of high-performing teams are the natural sequences of human life, which unfold in a predictable way and over a predictable timescale. The same is true of the sequences and timescales at work. We do not change our emotions and values or skills overnight. Instead, we have a rhythm which is essentially a human cycle. The team at Glaxo Wellcome realized this when they saw the time it took for people to move from suspicion to acceptance and then to positive working with those from different functions. Our attitudes and values are resilient. They are part of us, the very essence of what we are.

The second tenet: we search for meaning

We are not simply passive recipients of all that life offers us. On the contrary, we actively engage in our life. We strive to create meaning from the many signals and cues we receive and to understand the contradictions with which we are faced. For most of us the companies of which we are a member are a crucial part of our life. We seek to understand and to create meaning from our work, to understand the purpose of the organization and the role we play, to select organizations with the same values as our own. We listen carefully to what those around us say. We are sensitive to the statements made by the founding members and senior team – the statements made by Bill Hewlett and Dave Packard in the fifties are still remembered at HP and form a real part of the meaning that people create. We also closely observe how others behave – at Glaxo Wellcome the behaviour of managers to colleagues from outside their immediate work group was watched with great interest as the cross-functional team working plan unfolded.

We may note the expressions of company policy in the manuals, the handbooks and the policy statements. But more importantly we listen to and ask questions about the history of the place, the myths and reputations, how the company behaved in the past, the heroes and the villains. We are profoundly influenced by our colleagues and work groups. Their social cues help us to understand how people behave around here, and provide impressions about the organization which guide us in our understanding.

As a consequence, one of the great challenges in organizational life is to create cues and processes which are mutually aligned and coherent with the goals of the business. When this alignment is weak we receive conflicting messages about what is important and what we have to do to be successful, and we become confused and distrusting.

The third tenet: we have a soul

Finally, we are not machines, programmed to deliver in a rational and predetermined manner. We have hopes and fears, we laugh and cry, we have a soul, and we engage in our dreams. The notion of the soul captures the emotional side of the organization, for with it comes trust and commitment, inspiration and exhilaration. The trust and commitment which HP has created stems from an unwavering belief in the soul of the organization. People are not interchangeable parts. To engage at the emotional level can profoundly influence the relationship between the individual and the organization.

Unlike machines, we can choose to share or withhold our knowledge, ideas and creativity. In an environment in which our emotions and feelings are allowed to flourish, where we trust and feel commitment, we will choose to share our knowledge and ideas. In an environment of mistrust, where our emotions are blocked and disregarded, we will keep our knowledge and creativity to ourselves. But if our excitement is captured, if we can dream, if we work in an organization which has a vision for the future which we find compelling and exciting, then we are capable of bringing ideas and creativity beyond our wildest imagination.

This trust and commitment proves difficult for competitors to imitate. It takes a senior team with their fingers on the pulse of this precious commodity. It takes a profound understanding of how trust and commitment can be built, and destroyed. It takes an unflinching dedication to creating a workplace in which justice and fairness flourish. And it takes real insight into the nature of the relationship between the organization and the individual, an understanding not only of the financial aspects of the contractual relationship but also of the psychological contract, what has been promised and what is assumed. Without this understanding of the nature of the soul of the organization we will never create the inspiration and vitality which is so hard for others to imitate.

These three tenets should exist at the very core of the philosophy of an organization. An understanding of human time frames should be a part of the way we look at human potential and the speed at which it can be transformed. An acknowledgement of memories of the future should be part of the way we consider the longer-term development of people. In creating transforming organizations we should be continuously aware of the need to create an organization in which the messages are aligned, where there is a shared sense of meaning. We should be sensitive to how meaning is created and the role which symbols play. At the heart of the human side of organizations are people with a soul and feelings and emotions. The feelings and emotions we bring to work are as important as those we bring to our personal life. Trust and commitment are as important inside work as they are outside.

TABLE 2 ◆ The three tenets

First tenet: we operate in time

◆ Past beliefs, hopes and commitments influence our current behaviour: the 'memory of the past'.

◆ Current behaviour is influenced by beliefs about what will happen in the future: the 'memory of the future'.

◆ Skills and knowledge take many years to develop.

◆ Human development progresses through a shared sequence.

◆ Attitudes and values are resistant to rapid change.

Second tenet: we search for meaning

◆ We strive to interpret the clues and events around us, we actively engage with the world to seek a sense of meaning, to understand who we are and what we can contribute.

◆ Symbols, which may be events or artefacts are important in creating a sense of meaning.

◆ Over time groups of people create collective viewpoints, a sense of shared meaning.

Third tenet: we have a soul

◆ Each of us has a deep sense of personal identity of what we are, and of what we believe in.

◆ We can trust and feel inspired by our work – and when we do we are more creative.

◆ We can dream about possibilities and events.

◆ We can choose to give or withhold our knowledge – depending on how we feel.

Yet for many organizations these three basic tenets are disregarded. We may believe that people operate on a human timescale, but so much of management thinking and action remains resolutely focused on the short term; we may believe that people strive for meaning, but we continue to create working environments which are pitted with mixed messages, where managerial rhetoric falls sadly short of organizational reality; we may acknowledge that we have feelings, emotions and a soul, yet we fail to create balance or engage in building trust, commitment and dreams.

The nine capabilities of the new agenda

These three basic tenets pose a real challenge for organizations to develop the organizational and managerial competencies capable of acknowledging and nurturing people.

The capabilities of the first tenet: we operate in time

Balancing the short term with the longer term is at the heart of acknowledging that people, and the knowledge and inspiration they bring to an organization, are a key source of building and sustaining competitive advantage. The creation of human potential spans decades, and we engage in this by having a memory of the past and the future, and attitudes and characteristics that remain remarkably stable over time.

Putting people at the centre demands a view of the future and an ability to respond to changing circumstances across the decades. This shift from the short term to the longer term is predicated on three organizational and managerial capabilities: the capability to build compelling and engaging visions, to develop capabilities to sense the future, and to create a strategic approach to the management of people which is capable of bridging from the realities of the present to the aspirations of the future.

1 *Build visioning capabilities*: the capacity to create and develop a vision of the future that is compelling and engaging, and provides a shared view of what could be possible and how this could be achieved. This is at the very centre of creating a human approach to organizations.

2   *Develop scanning capabilities*: the creation of a compelling and engaging vision is predicated in part on an organizational capability that scans what the future may bring.

3   *Create strategic capabilities*: creating people-centred strategies is one of the means by which the organization balances the needs of the short term with those of the long term, as well as balancing financial capital with human potential. Creative and engaging people strategies have, at their core, an understanding of how the vision and business goals can be delivered through people, and of the specific actions which need to be taken in the short and longer term to bridge from reality to aspirations.

The capabilities of the second tenet: we search for meaning

We search for meaning and actively seek to bring understanding and clarity. This search comes from what we hear from others, how we see others behave, and the symbols and myths that surround us. While the creation of meaning is an essentially individual pursuit, yet it is one in which organizations can play an important role. The creation of a context in which the goals and visions are known to all, and in which there is alignment of goals and processes, is the basis on which enduring competitive advantage can be created. There are three capabilities here.

4   *Develop diagnostic capabilities*: working at the level of meaning in an organization requires a new way of thinking. To understand meaning it is not sufficient to simply consider what the organization is doing with regard to its tasks, the reporting structure or the policy statements. We have to understand how the organization is perceived by its individual members. Working at the level of the 'unwritten rules of the game' provides us with such an opportunity. This level of analysis begins to answer questions about what is important around the organization, what people have to do to get on, what really motivates and excites individuals, and which factors send the most positive messages.

5   *Create systemic capabilities*: the creation of meaning in organizations is complex and difficult. At the heart are inter-related elements which can work together to create a context in which the processes, policy statements and realities are aligned with each other and with the goals of the organization. The challenges of creating vertical and horizontal alignment

between these elements and the business goals is immense. A comprehension of these elements and the ways in which they work together requires employees who are capable of thinking systemically, of seeing the organization in its totality rather than focusing on specific areas.

6   *Build adaptive capabilities*: learning to adapt means building the capability for incremental and transformational change, and establishing change competencies which have at their core an understanding of the human time frame of change, from the past into the present and the future. It is important to view change as realignment across the vertical, horizontal and temporal axes of the organization, and to build the capability for renewal and adaptation.

The capabilities of the third tenet: we have a soul

Placing people at the centre of a strategy to create and maintain competitive advantage requires an understanding of the resource we are working with. Unlike technological and financial capital, people have a soul. We have hopes and aspirations, we can trust and feel committed, and the trust and commitment we feel profoundly influence our propensity to give 'beyond the call of duty'. Organizations do not need inspiration and innovation if jobs are centrally managed, clearly defined and relatively straightforward. All they need is a small carrot and a large stick. But how many of us work in a company that can make that claim? The roles we play are ambiguous and often unsupervised. Our success depends on trusting our colleagues and sharing ideas, and on our inspiration and entrepreneurship. We work in companies where the management of knowledge is key. And in these companies, individuals who do not feel committed, and who do not trust, may choose to withhold their knowledge, or they may be too fearful to take the risks which form the basis of creativity and innovation.

7   *Develop emotional capabilities*: understanding and developing emotional capacity is an essential part of the new agenda. Diagnosing the level of trust and commitment in any group of people produces a key measure by which the general health of the company can be assessed. It is possible to see over time the impact that certain decisions are having, and to create an early warning system.

8 *Create trust-building capabilities*: a crucial aspect of the creation of trust and commitment is the justice and fairness with which people are treated. Justice and fairness can be played out at many levels in an organization. Here the emphasis is on the impact that the key people processes (selection, objective setting, performance measurement and reward, training and development) can have on notions of fairness and justice. We know that the manner in which these processes are developed and rolled out can create deep feelings of injustice and unfairness, and that these have a significant impact on trust and commitment.

9 *Capability to build the psychological contract*: building an appropriate psychological contract becomes a fundamental organizational and managerial capability as structural and technological changes rip apart the old notions of the relationship between the individual and the organization. The stability of the past has been replaced with rapidly changing individual needs and what the organization offers in terms of employment stability, skill development and remuneration.

Accommodating these changes in the working model requires a respect for the past and the capability to build bridges to the future. It requires an understanding of the meaning in the organization and how this meaning can be created and leveraged. And it requires a finger on the pulse of emotional capacity and the realignment of key processes in a manner which provides a voice to individual employees, gives choice and ensures people are treated in a fair and dignified manner.

Figure 2 has at its centre the three fundamental shifts: that people operate in time, we search for meaning, we have a soul. Against each of these are the managerial and organizational capabilities which are crucial to this new agenda. The arrows encircling the areas signify that companies should be working on all these capabilities as they are self-reinforcing. For example, the building of visioning capability will be reinforced by managers who are capable of thinking systemically rather than sequentially. Similarly, the creation of a process for a strategic approach to people is reinforced through process discipline and the capability to truly embed people processes. Understanding the 'unwritten rules of the game' provides a backdrop to creating measures around trust and inspiration and to understanding and creating process fairness.

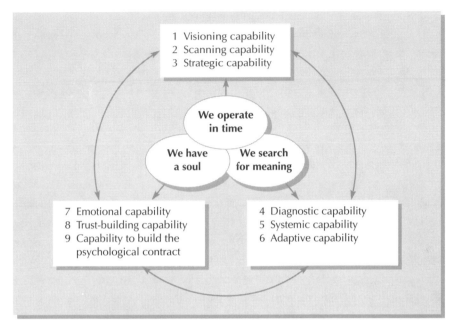

1 Visioning capability
2 Scanning capability
3 Strategic capability

We operate
in time

We have
a soul

We search
for meaning

7 Emotional capability
8 Trust-building capability
9 Capability to build the
   psychological contract

4 Diagnostic capability
5 Systemic capability
6 Adaptive capability

FIGURE 2 ◆ **The new agenda: the tenets and capabilities**

Taken together, these three fundamental shifts and nine managerial and organizational capabilities represent a new agenda. The new manager-ial agenda emphasizes the ability to think in a visioning and systemic way. The new organizational agenda supports this through the creation of people strategies, focusing on process fairness and creating process disci-pline to embed people processes. The challenge is to understand the 'human' side of our organizations by understanding the 'unwritten rules of the game' and creating organizational metrics around 'softer' issues such as trust and commitment.

This book is about the 'why' and the 'how' of putting people at the centre of corporate strategy. I have led in Part I with the 'why' because I believe that unless we understand why this is crucial, the 'how' will never become embedded. The question of 'why' reaches deep into the funda-mental tenets of humans. These tenets are explored in Part II of this book.

In Part III, I focus on how you can create a living strategy and by doing so put people at the centre. Building on the experience of the many companies with which I have worked, I have developed a six-step process which goes from building commitment to moving into action.

For each of the six steps I describe why the step is important (the guiding principles), the tools you can use for each step, how you might expect to benefit, and what it means for the competencies of line managers and the human resource professional. This is a question I return to in Part IV, the workbook, where I summarize what it means and provide a diagnostic check to help you consider where your company is in the six-step process.

I am very conscious that the questions of why and how are distinctly different, requiring rather different styles. The why is essentially a philosophical question while the how is practical and pragmatic. I have tried to unite the two by bringing as much company experience as possible to the question of why, and using a series of diagnostic questions to help you and your peers build deeper understanding. You may at this stage be turning rapidly to Part III to get straight into the how and the six-step process. By all means do so, but later reflect on why this approach makes sense, take a look at Part II, and re-examine your own and your company's mind set on the questions of time, meaning and soul.

The three tenets: the philosophy of the living strategy

We operate in time

L iving in a world where financial and technological capital has dominated, what are our assumptions about the nature of time? I believe there are two implicit assumptions. Changes in performance can take place within a relatively short time frame. Consider, for example, the time it takes to raise financial capital or to put a new piece of technology into operation. Second, the present dominates the past and the future. Consider the emphasis on immediate, short-term performance.

These two assumptions have profoundly influenced the way in which organizations have been created and are run. In part this short-term approach is driven by the perceived short-termism of the financial capital markets which emphasizes immediate results. This demand for short-term performance then drives the way in which the achievements of managers are appraised and rewarded and the relatively short-time horizons of job tenure. The domination of the present is reflected in the prevalence of tactical, fire-fighting issues and the denial of the past. But just how appropriate are these assumptions and are there opportunities to consider time in a more extended perspective?

Business leaders in the West may believe that while they would like to develop businesses by making long-term investments, the financial markets drive them to a short-term attitude in investment opportunities. The argument goes that the money providers are pressing hard for immediate results, frustrating their ability to build for the longer term. Managers in the Anglo-Saxon world often look enviously at what they perceive to be a much longer-term attitude to financial capital in Germany and Japan. But what capital markets demand is simply value through performance. Value is created through current surplus for shareholders, or in the form of expectation among shareholders that a surplus will be generated in the future. Managerial short-termism is the result of a low expectation of future value generation. If the promise of profits is great enough, markets are prepared to wait, a fact that is demonstrated by numerous new businesses which are financed by venture capital on the basis of the promise of future returns. For Amazon, Yahoo and E-bay, this financial capital time frame has been broken, their market valuations rest on anticipated lifetime customer relationships.

Capital markets demand performance, but they do not force managers to take a short-term view. Rather, it is managers who fail to appreciate that people and customers operate in a different time frame than financial capital, and require a longer time frame and continuum of resources and commitment. If management complains about short-termism it means they have a different perception of the possibility of future value creation than the market. To build an expectation of growth is to create a strong and compelling vision of the future and to engage and excite employees and shareholders in this vision.[1]

Managerial short-termism is emphasized by the reward and development processes, the domination of short-term tactics, and the emphasis on the present. Managers understand both formally, via performance management objectives, and informally, through the demands of their superiors, that their main priority is the short-term 'hard stuff', the numbers, the monthly sales targets, while the 'softer', longer-term people issues are less significant. As a result they have little incentive to invest in long-term planning or career development which has limited pay-off.

Similarly, in many organizations time horizons for jobs are short – high-potential people remain a maximum of two or three years in each job and therefore the emphasis is on delivering short-term results rather than building for the future. The complexity of senior roles creates a race to develop high-potential people with sufficient cross-functional and cross-national experience to deliver. This has necessitated accelerated fast-track career development. While the benefits are obvious, the costs are clear: it discourages people from building for the future, from really engaging in the development of people in their own team, and from working with the dreams and aspirations of those around them.[2]

The tactical, fire-fighting issues are at the fore, and the concerns of the present overwhelm the future. Many managers have diaries which are full months in advance, often with tactical actions. As a consequence they focus overwhelmingly on the short term, and the consequences of this short-termism are clear: managers have no time to think about the future ('we do it on the plane', they say optimistically) and do not allow for the unanticipated thought or unplanned action which could result in breakthrough thinking.[3] We must provide the space, time and competence in long-term thinking and visioning to counter the seduction of tactical fire-fighting.

In the rush to change there is an overwhelming desire to start again, to deny the past, to continuously look for the new formulae – consistency and continuity are destroyed. Employees are the victims of a stream of new initiatives and management despair when the quick fix fails to materialize. The key is to go to selective parts of the past and to build from them, to incorporate history and to create a future which has cohesion and meaning.

The reality of a human perspective on time

The assumptions about the nature of time in organizations may have held when financial or technological capital dominated. As we see they have been influenced by the nature of the financial capital markets and these in turn have driven managerial reward and development processes. The focus on the present is seen by the speed with which initiatives are created and then disbanded and the tactical nature of many managerial roles. Our assumptions about dominant time cycles and a focus on the present may have served well in the past. But how appropriate are these assumptions at a time when it is human endeavour which will be the key to success? I believe the old assumptions of the nature of time no longer hold in the new world in which people are at the heart of corporate strategy, and the changing of these old assumptions has profound implications on organizational processes and managerial capabilities. Let us take each of the assumptions in turn.

Cycle times for changes in human attitudes and performance

Consider the time frame for financial capital. How long would it take any company to raise substantial funding from the capital markets? My guess is that your answer could be calibrated in minutes or possibly hours.

Consider the time frame for technological capital. How long does it take the production team at ABB's Baden plant in Switzerland to put on stream the robots in their turbine factory?[4] A highly complex piece of machinery, with a development and introduction phase which can be measured in months. The timescale for technological capital is calibrated in months.

Now consider people. How long does it take ABB to create an international cadre of managers? Or Motorola to develop managerial skills in Chinese nationals? Or Glaxo Wellcome to create a networked organization capable of rapidly sharing ideas and innovations across functional teams? We are creatures of time, and the clock which marks the passage of time ticks slower than the financial or technological clock. Are we sensitive to the human clock? Probably not – for most companies the dominant clock is a financial one and reward structures and career development are tied into the ticking of this clock.

It is only when we can observe organizations over time that we can calibrate the speed of the human clock. There have been relatively few such studies of change in practices and processes and in the attitudes and behaviours of people in organizations. However, since 1992, the Leading Edge Research Consortium at the London Business School has provided us with an opportunity to observe six large companies: Hewlett-Packard, Glaxo Wellcome, Lloyds TSB (the major UK retail bank), Kraft Jacob Suchard, the payphone business of BT and Citibank. In all cases we studied their European operations. Over time, we have been able to shed light on two questions about the nature of time in organizations:

- How long does it take to implement and embed changes in people processes?

- How fast do the attitudes and behaviours of people change?

Certainly over the time frame we saw profound changes in the policies relating to people. For all the companies there was a renewed emphasis on performance-related pay; policies of employability as the primary contact between the employer and employee; policies of self-directed learning, where employees are encouraged to learn more about themselves; policies of career development supported by management mentoring and coaching; and broad policies designed to encourage innovation and entrepreneurship.

How long did it take those companies to actually implement these people policies? From 1992 onwards we have surveyed a representative

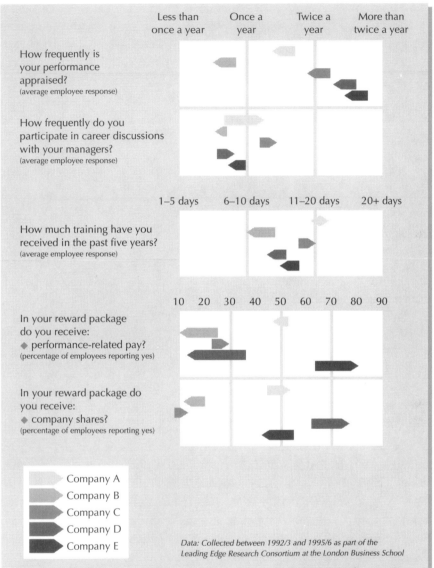

For each of the five companies we prepared case studies every three years by interviewing more than 30 managers and employees and surveying at least 10 per cent of employees (200–600 employees in each business at each time). So we conducted in-depth interviews with more than 400 people and surveyed another 3000 employees.

The data from the 1992/3 and 1995/6 employee surveys are shown in above. Because of the confidential and sensitive nature of employee response, the company names have not been used and instead are assigned letters from A to E. The data presented show the average response for the employee we surveyed in each of the five companies. In the case of the questions about company shares and performance-related pay, it is the percentage of employees responding yes to the question. The direction of the arrows shows the changes over time. Arrows pointing to the right show greater frequency of the practice over time. Arrows pointing to the left show a deterioration in practice over time. The length of the arrow represents the extent of change across the three-year time period.

FIGURE 3 ◆ **Changing people policies across a three-year period** sample of employees from these companies. I have chosen two sets of data, 1992/3 and 1995/6 and four survey items from five of the companies to illustrate the operationalization of two policies – a focus on performance management and performance-related pay, and the policy of career discussion and development. The policy on performance management and pay and reward is illustrated by two survey questions: *'How frequently is your performance appraised?' 'In your reward package do you receive performance-related pay and/or company shares?'* The policy on career discussion and development is illustrated by two survey questions: *'How frequently do you participate in career discussions with your managers?'* and *'How much training have you received in the last five years?'*

There are clearly differences in some people processes between the five companies. For example, employees in Company A participate more frequently in training and career discussions, while in Company B, employees are less likely to be appraised, trained or developed. Remember that in all these companies policies had been devised to increase performance management practices.

The underlying message from this data is clear. It may be fashionable to speak about how a certain CEO changed the context of the company over a three-year period. As a senior manager you may believe the policy to which you put your signature a couple of years ago has now been embedded throughout the company. But the reality is that it is extremely difficult to support the development of people policies and to gain traction deep in the organization. In fact, as we saw in companies B and E, practices can actually deteriorate over time. If companies began 1993 with managers who failed to speak to employees about their career development, they were likely to end 1996 with managers behaving in much the same way. I believe the question of traction is crucial and one that we return to with hard action points in step six of the six-step process.

But what of the attitudes and aspirations of employees? How do they change over time? I have selected a number of survey questions which capture the basic attitudes and values of employees.

'I really care about the fate of this organization.' 'This organization really inspires the best in me in the way of job performance.' 'Senior management are well informed about what people at lower levels think and feel.' 'People work together as a team.' 'I find my values and the organization's values are similar.' 'I'm proud to tell others that I am part of this organization.'

Figure 4 covers 1992/3 and 1995/6 and is the average response for the employees we surveyed in each of the five companies. Again, these survey items show the limited extent of changes in these fundamental attitudes

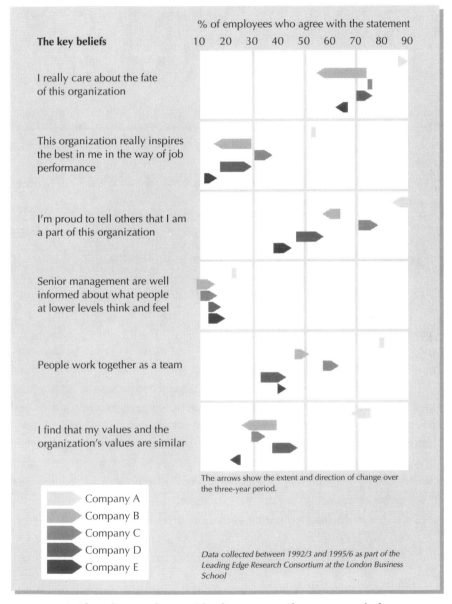

FIGURE 4 ◆ **Changing employee attitudes across a three-year period**

over time. As companies differ in people policies and practices, so too do they differ in the attitudes and values of their employees. Moreover, we saw no radical change over the three-year period.

However, these survey items can provide only a glimpse of the human time frame for change. A deeper understanding of the human time cycle comes from looking at these companies in more detail. I have chosen Glaxo Wellcome to illustrate the cycle time for changes in performance, and BT's Payphones business to illustrate the role of the past, present and future in representing time. In the course of our research we were able to observe the endeavours of the senior team at Glaxo Wellcome to create an organization prepared to share ideas and innovations. It emerged as a well-run organization, with the ability to leverage as many resources as possible to achieve change. In fact, the time frames at Glaxo Wellcome are probably shorter than those of other companies without the same calibre of managers or access to resources.

Cycles time for changes in performance at Glaxo Wellcome

Earlier we considered the competitive advantage Glaxo Wellcome had created through the development of multi-functional team working. However, the feelings of trust and reciprocity which underlay the team working were not developed overnight. The concept of team-based working was first discussed among the senior team members in early 1988. They outlined the behaviours needed to support this change and discussions continued during 1989, with a series of workshops being developed to support the move. From 1991 to 1994, greater use was made of projects and team work. In late 1993, a more formal structural redesign was undertaken, with the creation of a new organizational structure in which the old hierarchies were replaced with teams to create a single commercial entity with self-managed teams at the point of sale.

This change in the structure was accompanied in 1994 by the overhaul of the performance management process. Greater use was made of performance data from the immediate team and from colleagues in boundary teams. This was supported by computer software which enabled individuals to give and receive feedback from named employees. Appraisal forms were dispensed with and replaced by employees collecting information about their own performance on an ongoing basis. At the same time, the reward mechanisms were redesigned, and went from being functionally structured and heavily reliant on job families, to being less complex, reinforcing working across functional boundaries and pay for performance. The need to create team working was also supported by a move away from a portfolio comprising off-the-shelf, generic training programmes to customized and focused programmes, such as the provision of coaching and counselling within the teams. This was accompanied by a renewed effort to break down the well trodden functional career paths and replace them with development opportunities gained through project work and secondment to other functions and project teams.

During the implementation of the new organizational structure the company announced its merger with Wellcome with the intention of controlling a sizeable chunk of the pharmaceutical market.

By 1996 the senior team at Glaxo Wellcome had done almost everything in their power to create a team-based organization. They had realigned the structure and processes to the new business goal by creating strong, self-managed teams; they had realigned performance management by moving from hierarchical to collegiate feedback; and they had provided coaches to support team performance.

What was the impact of this change in context on the behaviours and attitudes of people working in these teams? As part of the Leading Edge Research Consortium we surveyed a sample of employees in 1993 and again in 1996, and more recently in 1999 (*see* Fig. 5 overleaf). I have selected a small number of questions from the survey to illustrate the extent of change. These look at the 'hard wiring' – whether the team processes themselves had changed – and the 'soft wiring' – whether the attitudes to teams had changed.

One of the strong signals for employees would be the involvement of their team members in describing and appraising their performance. Prior to the change programme, the boss was the sole appraiser of performance. The policy of appraisal by colleagues was introduced in 1994, but by 1996 not much had changed. The rhetoric was strong, but individual managers still sought sole responsibility for performance appraised. It took until 1999 for there to be any real shift, by which time peer-based performance appraisal was the norm. It was not until the senior team received appraisal data from their team members that others were prepared to move in this direction.

The three tenets: the philosophy of the living strategy

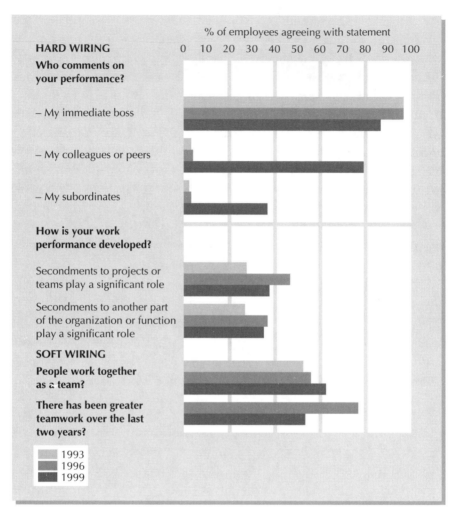

FIGURE 5 ◆ Developing teams at Glaxo Wellcome from 1993 to 1999

Creating a team-based structure also requires that development is seen to be taking place within the team rather than simply through vertical progression. From 1996 we saw that project teams and cross-functional development were playing an increasing role in employees' development experience.

So from 1996 the context within which people worked was changing, with clear realignment of the 'hard wiring' of appraisal and development. But what of the 'soft wiring'? Did people believe that teams were central to the way in which work took place? In fact, this 'soft wiring' of attitudes and values proved much more difficult to change. While the context of team work had altered dramatically, the beliefs about team work were much slower to change, although from 1996 people reported that team working was greater.

Could the changes at Glaxo Wellcome have been achieved more quickly? I believe not. Glaxo Wellcome has a highly regarded team of change agents working within the company, and as one of the most profitable companies in the world it was able to focus enormous internal and external resources on the issue, for example by supporting many of the cross-functional teams with facilitators skilled in team development and processes. Therefore one could argue that the changes we have seen in Glaxo Wellcome are actually faster than for most companies attempting this type of change.

The Glaxo Wellcome timeline for team development demonstrates two critical aspects of people. Perhaps most importantly it shows the speed at which fundamental change in human behaviour and attitudes takes place. It may be fashionable to speak about how organizations have changed overnight, of how a poorly performing company was turned around by a charismatic and dynamic chief executive, but the longitudinal research from the Leading Edge Research Consortium gives no hint of sudden transformation. We saw no examples of workforces suddenly changing their skill sets or attitudes. Instead we noted a gradual change, reinforced by changes in management attitudes and behaviours, and by the creation and embedding of processes to support these changes.

The Glaxo Wellcome timeline also shows the sheer complexity of realigning the processes so that they support the changes in business goals. This realignment began with a structural redesign of the team functions, continued with the overhaul of the performance management process and the creation of team-based metrics and feedback, before finally team training was introduced. This process had a natural sequence and rhythm which could not have worked if all stages had been introduced simultaneously. The sequencing gradually built a coherent message about the importance of team working, creating the framework for new business goals and a new meaning through realigning the key structures and people processes.

This discussion of the time frames of human capital underlines the difficulty of imitating this precious resource. Many companies face the challenge faced by Glaxo Wellcome: to create strong horizontal working practices, to create sharing and reciprocity, and to destroy the old functional chimneys. And what we learn from their experience is the huge amount of time and effort required.

The relationship between the past, the present and the future

Let us now turn to the second aspect of the human time frame, the relationship between the past, the present and the future. Anthropologists such as Hofstede described cultural differences in this time dimension with the use of three circles representing the past, the present and the future.[5] The size and proximity of the circles represents the relationship between these dimensions of time. I believe the behaviour of many organizations suggests the dominant perspective is that shown in Fig. 6 where the present is at the fore with a disconnected and much smaller past and future.

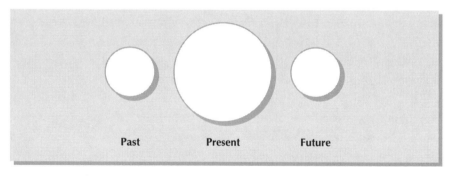

Past   Present   Future

FIGURE 6 ◆ **The organization's perspective on time**

Yet for the individual member of the organization the past assumes a much more important role in terms of memories and commitments to the future, or what Arie de Geus has termed 'the memory of the future'. As Fig. 7 shows, the past, present and future are connected. They 'run into' each other and are seen simultaneously.[6]

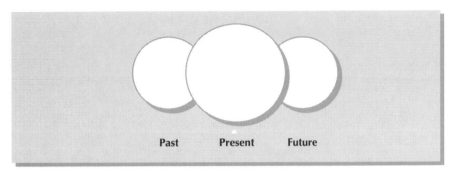

Past   Present   Future

FIGURE 7 ◆ The individual's perspective on time

While the past is important, individuals also continuously strive to create possible futures. These sets of alternative futures about what might happen are based in part on what has occurred in the past. These scenarios, or vignettes, contain both cognitive schema to interpret and explain the situation and a behavioural script which can potentially guide the behaviour. In a sense we rehearse our future and think through what will happen, what we will feel and what we will do.

To ignore the commitments of the past and to deny the aspirations and hopes of the future, is to build an organization which is outside of time. I believe that to really develop the potential of people in organizations, we have to acknowledge the individual perspective on time.

The heritage of HP is a deep commitment to people built initially by Bill Hewlett and Dave Packard and continued with an unswerving commitment by future generations of managers. A commitment to the past which the current CEO, Carly Fierina, is taking very seriously as she reminds the company of its entrepreneurial and dynamic roots. A commitment to the promises of the past, to the realities of the present, and to the excitement of the future. Given this heritage, you may say, it is easy for HP to build through people. But what of companies born without this silver spoon? For me, that is the fascination of BT Payphones.[7] Here is a company, a relatively recently privatized utility, which was born at a time when capital was king and where protected markets had allowed the talents of people to be squandered. Yet what we see is a leadership team who have had a significant and positive impact on the trust and pride of the employees throughout the business. How did they do it?

The relationship between the past, the present and the future at BT Payphones

The telecommunications industry is highly dynamic, reflecting in part the forces of deregulation, increased competition, advances in technology, growth of multi-media and increased convergence. Deregulation in the UK began in 1984 when the British government sold 51 per cent of its shares in BT and issued Mercury with a licence to operate a fixed network. Five years later, the Department of Trade and Industry removed the final barrier to full competition by taking away the duopoly's hold on the provision of international telecommunications facilities. In 1984, BT had a workforce of 250 000; ten years later the figure was down to 150 000, with 100 000 by the end of the century.

BT was restructured in 1991 into five broad business units, of which BT Payphones was one. The Payphones business is the 'front line' in terms of customer perceptions, but its history has not been without turbulence. Seen as the problem child of BT, its image was badly tarnished due to faults and vandalism that drew vitriolic press attention in the mid eighties. From 1991, the management team sought to rebuild the reputation and profitability of the business. As a result of rapid reduction in employee costs, and a renewed focus on quality and customer care, the Payphones team were able to reverse an operating loss of £40 million to a profit of £60 million in 1993. Accompanying this phenomenal recovery was a renewed focus on building human potential, with two major initiatives in 1993. Yet the 1993 employee survey we carried out for the Leading Edge Research Consortium showed that while employees understood what they needed to do, commitment, pride and inspiration were low – fine if BT remained in the same marketplace with similar competitive pressures; not fine if the competitive environment changed and innovative, risk-taking behaviours became necessary.

During 1993, the management team gained a deeper insight into the soul of the organization through employee surveys and focus groups. In our own research interviews at the time the message from employees was clear. As one manager said: 'The overall motivation and commitment of our people can block initiatives. As long as we have insecurity hanging over large numbers of people, can we really expect them to give of their best?' For many employees at BT Payphones, the pull of the past was strong, with deep collective memories of being survivors through the successive waves of redundancies. Interestingly, however, the concept of the future was weak. People knew it would be different from the past, but there were no collective 'memories of the future' or shared purpose.

Faced with the uncertainty of the future, employees fell back on the assumptions of the past to guide behaviour. A past of lifetime employment; of slow, predictable, vertical progression; of strong and autocratic managers; of deep paternalism. As a number of employees said at the time: 'I'm waiting for my manager to promote me. BT is just not using my skills in the way it should be.' Or: 'My hope is that I'll be promoted like we always were. First, I'd like to move to a middle-level job and then upwards from there.' Because this pattern had been shattered, employees felt anxious and mistrustful.

Unfortunately, the written policy for the future did little to allay these fears. The career policy document put it this way: 'BT can no longer offer lifetime employment, but we shall ensure a contract of employability. We will increase the worth of every employee during the time they are employed.' By 1994, the way forward for BT Payphones was less clear, and the avenues for expansion of its traditional business were increasingly limited. There was an urgent need to build brand image while continuing the cost reduction strategy. Until they addressed the long-term future, the present would continue to suffer.

BT began to plan for the future between 1994 and 1997 through the inspiration of Stafford Taylor, the head of the personal communications business. Under the banner of 'For a Better Life', his ideas and inspirations gave people the opportunity to dream about the future. He said: 'It is a crusade to change the company culture from reactive to proactive, encouraging people to take personal responsibility, decisive action and considered risks, and transform managers from cops to coaches.'

In a portfolio of workshops, employees learned about their skills and abilities, and created career maps to give a broad view of how they could develop in the future. The UK Olympic athletic coach was engaged to help team leaders understand that coaching was what they did naturally at the weekends with their kids. Teams across the country worked closely with their communities to explore where BT could provide support. Other teams made videos about how customer needs were changing and how they could support these changes.

Here, the details are not as important as the absolute clarity that individuals do operate in time, that the future is important, and that BT could make the decision to be part of individuals' dreams of the future, or they could deny their role. Either way, their employees would continue to dream. By understanding the temporal dimension of human potential, by engaging people's dreams, BT embarked on a journey of supporting a group of people to become the best they could be.

Building on the human perspective on time: the three core capabilities

The changes in the sources of competitive advantage from capital and technology to people demand that we continually strive to operate within a time frame which is appropriate to the development and maturation of people, measured in years rather than days or months.

One of the great challenges contemporary organizations face is to acknowledge that people operate in time, that the pacing and cycles which were appropriate to financial capital are not appropriate to people. Yet many organizations were built when capital or technology was king and the shared sense of time is the time of capital or technology. Short-term tactical actions were tolerated and rewards reinforced short-term actions, often at the expense of the longer term. Waves of initiatives broke over the organization, with limited understanding of the heritage of the past or the promise of the future. There was deep anxiety when initiatives and pro-grammes failed to create immediate improvements in performance.

The challenge is to create harmony between the short term and the longer term, to acknowledge the past, yet create a compelling and involving vision of the future. Those companies which strive for short-term results at the expense of building long-term capability fail to capitalize on human potential. This may be of limited concern for those companies where people are simply interchangeable parts, easily trained and replaced. But these companies are not representative of those which will flourish now or in the future. For more and more companies, success lies in the innovation of their people, in their ability to demonstrate commitment and personal inspiration.

I believe that a profound acknowledgement of the human perspective of time is built from three organizational and managerial capabilities.

◆ *Capability 1: visionary capability*
If we are to build successful, profitable organizations then the human perspective on time demands that our dialogues about the future are as rich and as inclusive as possible. These visions must be capable of drawing people into them and of portraying a future which is meaningful and exhilarating for people across the organization.

◆ *Capability 2: scanning capability*
Building on the human perspective of time demands an understanding of what the future may bring: a broad, shared understanding of the key trends.

◆ *Capability 3: strategic capability*
Working with human time frames requires the breadth of planning we saw earlier in the Glaxo Wellcome timeline. This demands a strategic capacity to develop clearly articulated steps which bridge from the present to the future.

Capability 1: build visioning capabilities

Consider the experience of Motorola in China. Compared with many of its competitors in the Chinese market, the company made significant early investments in the Motorola University in Beijing and in the development of local Chinese managers. This was at a time when other multi-national companies believed that skilled Chinese managers could be bought from the Chinese labour market as and when they were needed. Motorola was an early mover in the Chinese labour market for high potential managers, and as a consequence established an employee brand before others were able to do so.

Why did Motorola act ahead of others? How did it understand the phases of human development in China? How did it realize that 'buying in' talent was not an option and that it would take at least ten years of investment to 'grow' a committed Chinese cadre of managers? The answer in part rests in the way the senior team at Motorola thought about the future, and their understanding of human time frames.

Ten years beforehand the senior team at Motorola had imagined what it would be like to have a significant operation in Asia and what this would mean for the structuring of the company, the type of managers it employed and the way it would reward and develop people. This vision sustained the development of the Motorola strategy in China before the successes became apparent.

The same is true of Glaxo Wellcome, where the management team committed themselves to creating a team-based culture and understood it would take a decade of resource focus to deliver. They imagined and discussed a future for the company and described the key role the teams would play.

For both Motorola and Glaxo Wellcome the ability to create sustained competitive advantage through people rested in part on the ability to imagine a future and describe what this would mean for people and the organization. The time frames for people cannot be understood in minutes or days, they span years and decades. As a consequence we must develop mental models and ways of looking at the future which span these time frames. Without the creation and embedding of a visioning capability, the long-term investment in building people will fail to materialize and the organization will simply engage in continuous tactical and short-sighted actions.

These conversations about people can take one of the two routes, as illustrated in Fig. 8. In Route 1, we start from a conversation about the

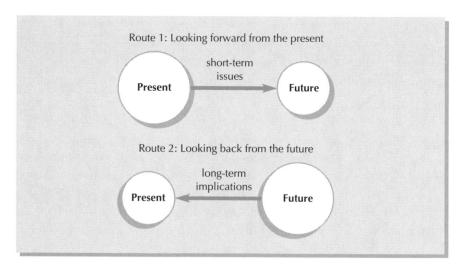

FIGURE 8 ◆ **The routes of the strategic discussion**

present situation, the here and now. From this analysis of the present the most pressing short-term issues are identified, and a plan created with a set of sub-plans and actions which solve these short-term issues. Thus, the primary driver for actions are the short-term tactical issues of the present. But we must remember that in taking this route there is a danger that the urgent may drive out the important.

The timeline for the development of cross-functional teams at Glaxo Wellcome showed the processes required to realign the organization from a functional, hierarchical one to a horizontal structure and this spanned the decade from 1988 until 1998. Was this the most pressing problem for the CEO in 1988? Probably not. At that stage Glaxo Wellcome was still an immensely successful company with a number of block-busting drugs. Without some understanding of what the company could be in the future, and an understanding of future competitive pressures, it would have been enormously difficult to justify the upheaval and stress associated with the intermediary steps as the organization and the associated processes became 'unfrozen'. Route 1 has the advantage of solving the short-term problems, but it fails to focus on the broader, longer-term issues which can be key to building human performance and an organization capable of being a marathon runner rather than a sprinter.

In Fig. 8 Route 2 the concerns of the present are important, but this is balanced with a vision of the future. In building a compelling vision of the future we are identifying now what needs to be achieved to build for later. I believe the second route, starting with a view of the future, is fundamentally more compelling and engaging. It has the power to make many people in the organization think about the future, to place themselves in that future, to walk around it and look at the organizational structures, culture and values, the skills and aspirations of individual company members, and the way in which senior managers behave. In building a shared vision of the future it is possible to view the present as a pathway to the future and to build the channels and roads capable of bridging from the realities of the present to the visions of the future.

People are more excited by visions which balance the new and the old or sustain ideas, values or perspective, which have sufficient roots in the current organizational mental models to make them plausible, yet which contain an element of novelty in the directions in which the vision of the organization needs to be stretched.

Capability 2: develop scanning capabilities

The past, the present and the future have meaning to us and are the foundations upon which great companies are built. The gravitational pull of the past is strong. But in building on the past we face a double challenge: not simply to deny it but to retrieve from it those jewels which create inspiration and excitement, and to jettison those orthodoxies which are no longer appropriate.

Operating in time demands a deep understanding of our heritage, but also a rich understanding of what is possible within the organization, and of a wider context outside the organization. The future is essentially unknowable. But if we are to create time frames in organizations which mirror human time frames, we must have a broad, informed view of what the future could be – not a detailed and exhaustive list of possible futures, but a broad and shared articulation of how the world could change and the impact this could have. We need a view of the broad social and demographic trends which could impact on the type and quantity of people entering the workforce, so that the company can prepare for potential skills shortages and plan for the effects of work or lifestyle changes. We need to consider the impact of technological trends and how political and economic activity could influence our visions for the future. These scanning tools include trend analysis and environmental scanning of demographic, socio-cultural, political and legal trends.

Motorola invested in developing people capability in China because the analysts focusing on the region were aware that the educational infrastructure was poor and the indigenous businesses unlikely to develop an entrepreneurial skills base of sufficient depth. This information about the probable shortfalls in managerial resources was available to other companies in China with growth aspirations but they did not collect this data, or chose not to listen, or the knowledge was held by the wrong people, or perhaps some managers listened but could not influence the investment strategies. Whatever the reasons for inactivity, the facts remain the same: the sensing capabilities which Motorola had developed were the eyes of the organization – they warned of the challenges and opportunities of doing business in China.

Capability 3: create strategic capabilities

Visioning and scanning are part of a larger capability to develop an understanding of what the organization could be in the future, what the critical external factors will be, and what needs to happen to create a bridge between present realities and future visions. These are the foundations for a strategy about people. Putting people at the heart of corporate strategy enables senior teams to discuss the future, to heart timelines which have a human element to them, to understand where they need to make significant investments to build for the future, and to maintain inspiration through engaging in future visions.

The focus has been on the content of strategy, about the importance of people being at the centre, and of bridging from the present to the future. This content is crucial, but just as important is the process of strategy, how a strategic conversation occurs within an organization, who becomes involved in these discussions of the future, and how the plans are created, communicated and put into action.

Consider your own mental models about the process of developing and implementing a people-centred strategy. Three possible approaches are shown in Fig. 9 (see overleaf).

◆ *Top down*: Here the assumption of strategy creation is that it occurs in a rational, planned fashion in which business strategy and a people strategy are linked in a logical manner. We assume that both occur in a purely top-down way. Senior management formulate a broad strategy approach and this is cascaded down through successive management layers and subsequently implemented through line management and the operating core in a portfolio of separate activities.[8]

◆ *Bottom up*: In the middle model, people-centred strategies are not specifically formulated through rational processes but emerge through dialogue and discussion which can take place at various places in the organization. So, conversations and ideas can emerge from the core of the business and are communicated upwards to become part of the broad strategy of the organization. This model rests on the notion of an empowered employee group and highly developed communication and information channels capable of moving ideas up the organization as rapidly as they are moved down.

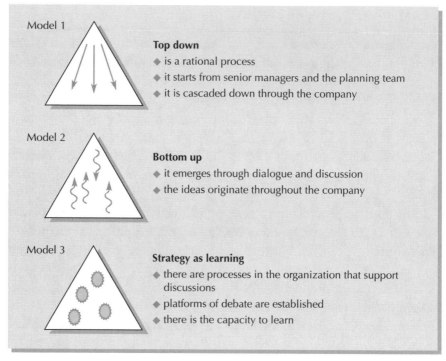

FIGURE 9 ◆ The strategy creation process

◆ *Strategy as learning*: The lower model tells a more complex story. While it is not possible to work out optimal strategies through rational thinking processes alone (as the first model suggests), managers can create processes in the organization that make them more flexible and adaptive and capable of learning, and that encourage a strategic debate.[9] These strategic processes support people coming together to visualize the future, to consider the options they face and the decisions they should take. These shared visions are capable of creating strategic conversations which are rich, deep and engaging.

In Model 1 we are essentially viewing the organization's decision making as machine, in which rationality and causality can be understood and codified. But does this really take account of organizational realities? This rational approach to strategy is based on the tacit assumption that there is only one best answer to the strategy question, everyone in the organization thinks rationally, and implementation follows the discovery of strategy. In reaction to the arguments against this rational view, the evolutionary or emerging view of strategy, shown in Model 2, came to the fore. This emphasizes the complex nature of organization behaviour and sees strategy as a perspective on emergent behaviour, the metaphor here being one of ecology. So does strategy simply 'emerge', as the second description would suggest? Model 3, the 'processual' view, takes a middle stand, suggesting that while it is not possible for managers to work out optimal strategies through a rational thinking process alone, they can create processes within the organization which guide the emergence of strategy, and make the organization more flexible, adaptable and capable of learning from its mistakes. The foundation of these processes is an individual's reflection on events and strategic conversations, their cognitive maps and sense making, and the notion that managers and the organization of which they are a part engage in active learning and a process of adjustment and reorganizing through double loop learning.[10]

In my experience, the creation of a people-centred strategy is predicated on a process and the creation of process skills in which a language is developed which engages groups as a whole to become skilful observers of the business environment, and to create and communicate this information in such a way that the organization is able to act upon it. This requires knowledge to be shared by a critical mass of people, who together are able to create action on the basis of their 'consensus' view. This way of thinking should become embedded and be a key aspect of group learning, not a new management fad, or an episodic special activity, or a disruption of the normal flow of activities, but a way of thinking that penetrates the institutional mind and eventually affects all activity.

We have considered the first tenet that we operate in time. Let us move to the second tenet, that we search for meaning.

We search for meaning

Let me share with you an insight from the Leading Edge Research Consortium. I first came across the concept of written and unwritten rules in 1985 when I met Peter Scott Morgan who at that time was beginning to develop a process which he called 'the unwritten rules of the game'. Briefly his thesis was that within organizations there are 'written rules' in the policy statement – management communications – and 'unwritten rules' – the rules of the game which are understood by employees and rapidly learned in the socialization process by new employees. I was intrigued by Peter's work and in the subsequent years he and I collaborated and introduced the 'rules of the game' methodology into the Leading Edge research. As a consequence, we were able to collect many examples of the written and unwritten rules of the game in the companies we studied.[1]

Below are some examples where the written and unwritten rules are aligned and others where there is misalignment.

What does it matter if in organizations there is a gap between the business goals of the organization and the perception of individual employees about the meaning of their work? I believe that lack of clarity of business goals and mixed messages have a profound influence on performance.

In the Leading Edge Research Consortium we were able to consider the creation of meaning through three key statements. First, the clarity of business goals. Second, through the alignment of processes such as performance appraisal and rewards. Finally, through shared meaning. As

Table 3 shows, organizations differ enormously in their capability to create a meaning and values that are shared by individual employees. At the most obvious level, employees either have similar values to those of the organization or their personal values are dissimilar. As we can see in Table 3, in one of the companies we have studied almost 90 per cent of employees say that their own and the organizational values are similar. For this company there is a clear sense of meaning and this is something people buy into. But this is not true in all cases. In most of the companies studied fewer than half the employees felt in line with the corporate values. We know that the *espoused values* of all five organizations are very similar – in each the corporate credo speaks of teams and innovation and entrepreneur, trust and professionalism, values that most individual employees would salute. But it is not the espoused values that employees are commenting on, it is the *values they see enacted* every day – the daily actions of managers and the many thousands of decisions taken every year, the stories and myths about the leader.

Business goal	Unwritten rules of the game
To be customer focused	'I know that what is really important around here is the customer. If you don't understand this then you really never get on.'
To build a global network	'You have to really take control of your own career. Networking is crucial – you have to ensure that you meet people in your business stream from across the world. Without this it is impossible to build credibility with your customers.'
To innovate	'The most important thing around here is don't take any risks, don't put your head above the parapet. If you do you'll have it knocked off.'
To build human performance	'Just focus on the numbers, that is what really counts.'

I cannot seem to get into a Virgin Airways car to drive from my home in central London to Heathrow airport without the driver regaling me with stories about the chairman, Richard Branson. About what he did on the last flight, about the parties he has in his house for employees, about the last conversation the driver had with 'Richard' (and remember that the Virgin Airways drivers are subcontracted employees). The same is true when I stumble across an Amazon.com employee. One gets a real sense that they feel part of an e-business vanguard, when in fact their competitive advantage is simply our old friend customer obsession. This is illustrated every time, and by every person, with the tale of the founder Jeff Bezos buying cheap second-hand furniture for his office in order to spend more on the customers. Such is the power of these stories that this business has deeply embedded an Amazon way in only a few years. And having spent many years wandering around Hewlett-Packard, I think I would be a millionaire by now if I had a dollar for every story I heard about 'Dave and Bill'.

It is often in these stories that we embrace collective memory. It is this multiplicity of action that creates a sense of what the organization is about, and potentially a sense of shared meaning. In the wider context, coherent corporate voice (internal and external, from ad campaigns to internal e-mails) will matter more and more to the corporate personalities.

Meaning is also created through the business goals, through what individual employees believe the business is about, and what they have to do to support these goals. Again as we see in Table 3, organizations differ in their ability to create a shared sense of the goals of the business. In some of the companies we researched the majority of people understand what the management is trying to achieve, the strategy of the corporation and what they personally have to do to reach these goals. Yet in others less than half have this clarity. In some of these companies the performance appraisal process is in place, and managers are required to meet their team members to talk about their performance and business goals. But this alone will not bring clarity of purpose and meaning. Meaning is created when managers and leaders talk about the goals of the business and act in a way that reinforces these goals.

Take any great leader – Jack Welsh at GE, for example, or Percy Barnevik at ABB. What you see is a relentless communication of their vision of the purpose and goals of the business, and an underscoring of this with their behaviour and the behaviour of those around them. It

TABLE 3 ◆ **Creating meaning in the organization**

	30	40	50	60	70	80	90	100
Clarity of business goals								
◆ I know what management is trying to achieve		*		***	*	*		
◆ My organization has a clear corporate strategy				*	**		*	**
◆ My work goals are clearly defined	*		*	**	*	*		
Alignment of people context								
◆ I understand the basis on which my performance is appraised				*	*	***	*	
◆ The rewards I receive are directly related to my performance at work				*	*	***		*
Shared meaning								
◆ There is a clear set of corporate values		*	*		**		**	
◆ I find that my values and the organization's values are similar		*	*			**	**	

* Percentage of surveyed employees in each company who strongly agreed or agreed with the statement

Companies: BT Payphones, Citibank, Glaxo Wellcome, Hewlett-Packard, Kraft Jacob Suchard (Philip Morris), Lloyds TSB. Each is represented by an asterix. Collected in 1995/96.

Data from Leading Edge Consortium

brings to mind the apocryphal tale of Percy Barnevik who, when asked what kept the complex businesses of ABB together, replied 'overheads'. Unusual, thought the interviewer, in a company with so small a corporate head office and minimum overheads. 'No, no,' said Barnevik, *'these* overheads,' pointing to the pilot case of many hundreds of transparencies he took with him to use as a 'show and tell' of the strategy of business goals in the many ABB businesses he visited. It was this that brought coherence to the ABB business.

You know yourself, and we have seen through the surveys in the research consortium, that companies do indeed differ in their capacity to create contexts of shared meaning. The question is, why is it that in some companies the meaning is shared, while in others employees are bombarded with mixed and confusing messages?

So why are there mixed messages?

If the cues and messages to employees – via people policies and processes, communication and management behaviour – lack integration and cohesion, people will create a sense of meaning which is far removed from the aspirations of the organization. And if these frames and meanings are removed from the business goals, the performance of the business will suffer.

There are many possible reasons for these mixed messages, but three in particular are influential:

◆ *Organizations create multiple or conflicting business goals* which may not be coherent. For example, there are messages around the importance of delivering long-term customer service, yet the predominant goal is to maximize short-term profits, at times at the expense of what is best for the customer and the longer-term relationship with that customer. Alternatively, as we saw earlier the need to innovate and be creative is a key business goal, while at the same time people are punished for taking risks and encouraged to be 'right first time'. These multiple strategies need not be in conflict, but if they are not resolved at a corporate level, the dilemmas they create are played out at an individual level.

◆ *The heritage of process* is at any one time inherent within the life of an organization. The key processes such as selection, reward and development may be vestiges of past systems, processes and structures which have been developed at different times in the history of the company. I live in a house which has a structure dating back to 1860, a plumbing system which was updated in about 1920, primary decorations some of which date back to 1960, and a voice and data circuit which was installed in 1996. Each of these systems is a vestige of the past, but when I look at my house I see it as a whole rather than a collection of period items. In the same way, in the organizations of which we are members, we attempt to create a total meaning of 'what this organization is about'.

In some companies these processes and systems have been updated over time, in others this has not occurred – the reward system may still reflect a time when hierarchical power structures dominated, when managing your boss was more important than working collectively as a team; the promotion system may still reinforce and reward individual excellence and accomplishment even as the current goals are for excellent team performance and collegiality.

◆ *The complexity of creating consistent meaning.* Meaning is created in organizations from many sources – what senior managers say; how colleagues and peers behave, their values and norms of behaviour; the expressions of the organizational policy on matters such as reward and appraisal, and how these work in reality; and the understanding of the history and reputation of the organization. As business goals change, so the meaning of the organization changes. Thus at any one time there is ample opportunity for the messages of senior managers, or the behaviour of colleagues and peers, or the processes such as reward and career development, to be misaligned with the business goals and aspirations.

John Kotter uses the analogy that realigning processes and structures is like moving the furniture around in a room where all the pieces are attached to each other with elastic bands. Pulling a chair in one direction pulls with it, for example, a table and a sideboard.[2] In the same way, the processes and structures in complex organizations are not independent but interdependent. Realigning the reward system to be more customer-focused simply puts pressure on the metrics around customer satisfaction and the development of customer skills. Therefore, working to create a shared and coherent meaning in line with corporate aspirations demands an understanding of the current meanings within the organization. It requires the ability to view the organization in its complexity and to understand the symbols, the linkages and the relationships, to think systemically.

Why is meaning important in organizations?

I have shown that the gaps between rhetoric and reality, the misalignment of business goals and processes, and contradictory business goals can be damaging to the overall performance of the business. In understanding why this is the case, we have to consider the role of meaning in the organization, and the role of meaning to the individual.

We operate in time, constructing vignettes of the future and rehearsing the behaviours which would accompany these scenarios. In constructing these vignettes we are not simply passive recipients but actively strive to engage, interpret and create meaning, a belief that we are making a personal contribution to something which is meaningful. As we saw at BT Payphones, the active interpretation spans the past as well as the future. We strive to interpret our world, not simply by imposing structure but by translating events and developing frameworks for understanding. These cognitive models of the world form the basis on which we notice and construe meaning and the basis on which we act.

This interpretation is highly individual, yet the people and groups of which we are a part influence and shape the meaning we create. We do not work in isolation but become members of what have been termed 'cognitive systems' of shared patterns of beliefs, symbols and myths. It is these shared patterns of belief that allow groups in organizations to create and engage in collective viewpoints and to drive for high performance.[3] Our individual frames of reference exist within a collective frame. Our conversations and discussions with colleagues – the sharing of experiences over time – create a cognitive consensuality, a dominant logic, or reality of the group of which we are a member, of what needs to be achieved and how it can be achieved.

We consider not only the 'written rules of the game' but also the 'unwritten rules of the game', the cues and messages we receive from all aspects of the organization to create an understanding of 'what do you have to do around here to get on'. This understanding comes only partly from the corporate messages and videos. It arises largely from the very fabric of the organization: from who gets rewarded, and what they get rewarded for; from the way in which people and customers are treated; from who gets promoted; and how senior managers behave. It is these unwritten messages which create the frame for interpretation.

The implications of this second tenet are clear. We should view organizations as complex cognitive systems, made up of people who see and interpret the world around them, and who strive to create values which have meaning to them and coherence with the group. Our corporations are populated with individuals who are striving for meaning, trying to understand what the company is about and what they have to do to succeed. If we view organizations in this way, we must have an acute awareness of how we create meaning in our organizations, of the messages which are sent, the symbols which define our organizations, and the cues given by the policies and practices. We should be sensitive to the reality for individuals and of what is espoused in strategy, policy statements, and the reality as perceived by individuals.

Yet consider your own work and experiences. Even the most casual observer of organizational life will find examples of a lack of integration and cohesion between what the company espouses through its business goals and the meaning and understanding of these goals as created and shared by employees. How often do corporate plans and mission statements remain simply that: senior executive rhetoric with little meaning to those people whose job it is to deliver customer satisfaction or bring complex products rapidly to the marketplace? Employees may hear corporate mission statements extolling the virtues of customer satisfaction or product innovation, but when the communication fanfare is over, the customer-focus workshops completed, and the lights dim on the business video, what is left? A group of employees trying to make sense and create meaning from the many messages and cues they have received.

Too often these messages contain fundamental paradoxes: people try to understand the underlying message of customer satisfaction when no attempt is made to provide them with the skills necessary to deliver this satisfaction; or they are encouraged to think long term but are rewarded and promoted for delivering short-term financial targets; or they see those who try hardest to understand customer needs penalized for the time they take to do so. Faced with this plethora of contradictory messages the employee, in their quest for 'sense making', looks at which behaviours are rewarded, what skills are promoted, and who is developed. It is the messages from many sources – not simply corporate rhetoric which form the basis of sense making and which give the indication on meaning and hence on how to behave.

Therefore, the quest is to understand the way in which meaning is created, to take account of the symbols created and to strive for cues and messages which are integrated and have a cohesive meaning. To do this requires a fundamental shift from thinking in 'bits' to thinking systemically – to go from ad hoc initiatives to thinking about organizations and transformation in an integrated and cohesive manner. In the work of the Leading Edge Research Consortium we saw two companies, Citibank and Hewlett-Packard, which have created a relatively strong sense of meaning around the dominant business goals. At Citibank, the refocusing of the business goal to a global network shows the performance impact of realigning processes and behaviours. The experiences of Hewlett-Packard give real insight into how a business can keep employees' eyes on the business goal while making ongoing adjustments with changes in the business context.

Creating meaning through alignment at Citibank

The Global Finance business of Citibank operates in a high-velocity environment, characterized by increasing integration of financial services and globalization of the world markets, disintermediation of banks from their traditional areas of expertise in lending, and increasing levels of liquidity in the financial system.[4] In addition, the revolution in technology has meant that the information advantage that banks once had in product knowledge and tracking movements in the market is fast disappearing. As John Reed, the chairman of Citibank, put it: 'Banking could be replaced by one line of code of Microsoft.' The rise in technology, combined with the disappearance of the regulatory barriers which separated national financial markets, has created a global financial market. To gain competitive advantage Citibank has sought to increase focus and leverage global capabilities in order to provide a unique service. Within each country the bank aims to create a strong local relationship management while leveraging the skills and product capability of the global network.

In the early nineties, John Reed set the Global Finance business a challenge: to compete by creating global networks which would serve customer needs through a flexible and rapidly changing product portfolio. It was understood by managers throughout the business that this was a complex and challenging goal in terms of both geographic spread and product portfolio. Clearly the attitudes of Citibank employees to the customer, their ability to build long-term relationships and to sell a wide portfolio of products would be a critical part of the business success.

When I spoke to the management team of Citibank during this period it became clear that this goal had been achieved in part through the creation of a strong sense of shared meaning. At the centre of this meaning was a global network which spanned customers and products, reinforced by structures and processes strongly aligned to the new meaning. The key processes and practices aligned to the global networks business goal are shown in Fig. 10.

The network flexibility was created through a matrix structure in which ten functional 'activity centres', such as financial institutions, derivatives and capital markets, were headed by an activity centre manager, each acting as an autonomous business unit. In addition, each country had its own management structure, responsible for overseeing all operations there. Therefore, while an individual may be located within one activity centre, they may work closely with individuals of other centres and have a dotted line responsibility to them, in addition to their immediate manager and country manager. The complexity of the matrix is compounded by the highly variable lifespan of the products. The shelf life of some products is extremely short, so teams are brought together or disbanded at great speed. Therefore, it is particularly critical that structural alignment is retained through the capability to rapidly create and disband teams of experts.

The business goal was also supported by realigning and 'hard wiring' two key processes: the career and reward systems. In the past, Citibank employees could be assured of a relatively straightforward vertical career movement through the organization. This was misaligned with the need for a global networked organization made up of rapidly forming, high-performing teams and a relentless push for individual performance. By 1994 the career management structure was being realigned to emphasize the informal network at Citibank and the importance of building performance

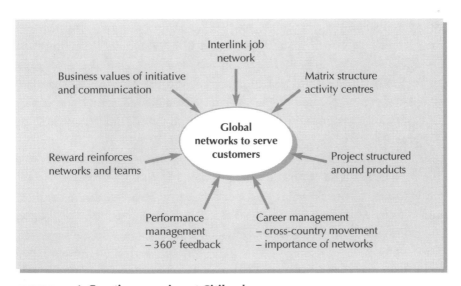

FIGURE 10 ◆ **Creating meaning at Citibank**

through making contacts with key people. The chance to pursue a career was supported by an internal job advertisement system called Interlink which allowed individuals to apply for vacancies across the company.

Realigning the reward processes at Citibank proved complex and time-consuming. Prior to the networked business goals, individual performance was reinforced through reward mechanisms which were individually focused. With the goal of creating global networks the reward mechanisms had to be realigned to take into account performance across a number of teams, products, locations, the internal equity between individuals and departments, and external market rates. In 1993 Ernst Brutsche, the CEO of the European business, complemented the business performance goals with three management goals: managers were appraised on their ability to give feedback and communicate and build a common understanding of the Global Financial goals; their retention of high achievers in their teams; and the development of their team members by revitalizing the career development discussions and identifying successors for critical roles. This appraisal was carried out every year and supported by a system of cross-evaluation from peers and subordinates. As Fig. 10 shows, at Citibank a whole raft of processes and structures reinforced the central business goal of creating global networks.

How was Citibank able to reach its goal of creating a global network so swiftly and effectively? In part it was through the clarity of purpose which Ernst Brutsche and his team communicated and lived by and through their relentless push to create a context in which building global networks became the dominant goal, the shared meaning. This shared meaning was created through the alignment of processes and practices to reinforce and support this core meaning, which encompassed shared values and aspirations. The challenge was not simply to see this fit as static and fixed, but rather as dynamic and capable of building from the past into the future.

At its simplest this relationship can be expressed as the dynamic *vertical alignment* between the business goals and aspirations of the organization and individual behaviour (*see* Fig. 11A).[5] If the shared meaning of the organization is to be embedded in the past, yet sufficiently adaptive to the present, the goals and the aspirations must be capable of being rapidly deployed. This deployment of strategy takes place through vertical alignment of the processes and practices of the organization which ensures that the pulse and energy of the business strategy is felt throughout the organization.

Around vertical alignment are the clusters of processes and practices which reinforce the goals and the underlying meaning of the organization, the *horizontal alignment* (*see* Fig. 11B). This captures the level of cohesion and coherence, the capability of the processes and practices to work together to create consistency and resonance. When as at Citibank all the processes are aligned, this creates real synergistic benefits.

Vertical and horizontal alignment are essentially static concepts, expressing the alignment between business goals and people processes. Yet if people processes and behaviour develop over an extended period of time, the challenge is not simply to create alignment around the current values, meaning and goals, but also to prepare for and adapt to future goals. I have termed this type of linkage *temporal alignment* (*see* Fig. 11C).

FIGURE 11A ◆ **Vertical alignment**

FIGURE 11B ◆ **Horizontal alignment**

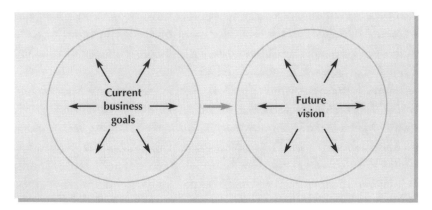

FIGURE 11C ◆ **Temporal alignment**

Temporal alignment is an essential part of the ongoing balancing between building on the past and creating the future. It is about making constant adjustments, linking the current processes to the vision of the future. The notion of temporal alignment is crucial for those processes which have long time frames of creation and development. At Citibank some of the reinforcing people processes could be developed within a relatively short space of time. Creating colleague and peer-based 360-degree appraisals and developing team-based reward mechanisms, though both difficult, could essentially be performed within a year. However, the structural realignment around the creation of a matrix and the facilitation of cross-country development moves took many years. For Ernst and his team, the vision of the future was critical and this temporal alignment ensured that what was achieved now would be capable of meeting future needs.

Renewing meaning at Hewlett-Packard

The Citibank experience demonstrates the bottom-line impact of a shared sense of meaning through aligning processes around business goals. But business goals can change relatively rapidly, posing the challange of sustaining a sense of shared meaning over time. Table 3 provides an overview of the success of these companies in creating a shared sense of meaning both in terms of awareness of the goals of the business and between the individual and organizational values. Hewlett-Packard employees consistently report high clarity around the business goals, and a strong sense of shared meaning. How have the management teams at HP achieved this? In the description which follows we look at both the way in which broad alignment is created, and the development of an organization which has significant adaptability and the flexibility to meet the needs of the rapidly changing marketplace in which it operates.

Certainly the performance management process has been a central plank of the creation of vertical alignment between the business goals and individual performance. As Dave Packard has said: 'No operating policy has contributed more to HP's success than the policy of management by objectives.'[6] But where the HP team has been particularly strong is in developing vertical alignment which reinforces corporate goals yet creates sufficient space for individual responsibility and innovation. When this is taken against HP's impressive performance of 20 per cent growth per annum in recent times, the exact nature of these systems is worth considering. Recall that in this highly turbulent sector, HP was the only major computer manufacturer to remain profitable during the last recession. It is an impressive organizational skill to implement such a battery of planning processes and at the same time create a culture which encourages individual freedom and innovation.

The processes which create vertical alignment between the business goals and individual performance have been in place for many years and their continuity and consistency has brought profound employee awareness of the principles and linkages, and a deep sense of shared meaning. Reflecting the engineering and systems heritage of the company, as Fig. 12 shows (see overleaf), the processes are closely vertically aligned from the business goals of the corporate group down to the individual business units, and through to the personal objectives of the individual members of the company, while feedback loops and monitoring keep the whole system in a dynamic state. The raison d'être behind such detail is, paradoxically, the promotion of individual freedom, innovation and entrepreneurial spirit. As Dave Packard wrote:

> '*Early in the history of the company, while thinking about how a company like this should be managed, I kept getting back to one concept: if we could simply get everyone to agree on what our objectives were and to understand what we are trying to do, then we could turn everybody loose and they would move along in a common direction.*'

As a result, individuals have their personal objectives defined with them, but how they achieve those objectives in terms of innovation activity or specific behaviour is a decision which they take. The establishment of the 'what' through clear targets and objectives does not mean that the 'how' is prescribed. Yet the company is not an 'adhocracy', or a free for all. Targets and objectives are co-ordinated globally in such a way that the entrepreneurial spirit and innovation can flourish within sound business parameters.

Every year the broad corporate aspirations and the impact on the individual objectives are agreed at a number of levels. At the corporate level the 'ten-step approach' creates a statement of purpose, five-year objectives, business goals for customers, product and services, a development plan, financial analysis, potential problems, recommendations, and the first-year plan. The annual plan has two components: the 'Hoshin Plan'

The three tenets: the philosophy of the living strategy

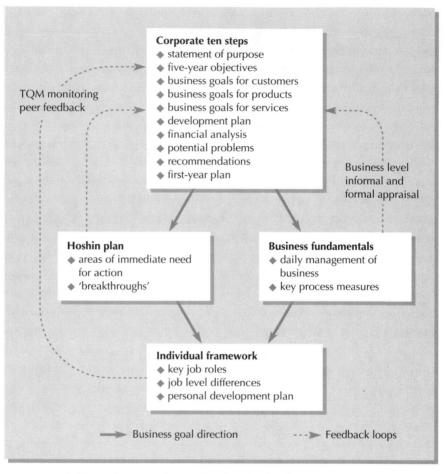

FIGURE 12 ◆ Renewing meaning at Hewlett-Packard

and the 'business fundamentals'. The Hoshin identifies those areas which need immediate and substantial attention because they are critical for business success and require 'breakthroughs'. For example, the then CEO Lew Platt sought to extend the frame and meaning of HP for many years by embracing a diverse workforce which reflected the diversity of the customer base. The 'business fundamentals' focuses on the daily management of the business and the key process measures. The performance of the business is vigorously monitored with the established total quality control system and its accompanying business and quality performance measures.

The feedback loops in the system are strong – for example, there is an informal, day-to-day appraisal of performance by team leaders. This might not be a formal mechanism, but it is well understood that an essential part of the meaning of HP is clarity, understanding and open sharing of business performance achievement. This is reinforced by highly developed and public monitoring processes, the rapid and open communication of performance targets and the unrelenting ranking of employees' performance to create a clear sense of performance stretch.

The cascade from the annual plan to the Hoshin and individual personal objectives creates the strong vertical alignment between the business goals and individual performance. The horizontal alignment between these interrelated processes is orchestrated through 'framework'. This integrating mechanism brings clarity of meaning by clearly integrating the key elements of the role, the criteria against which the individual ranking takes place, the key differences between the job levels, and the elements of the personal development plans. What we see at HP is a clear explanation of the meaning of the business place and how this is supported by the context of the processes. Individuals are therefore able to view the link between their job, the key elements of the job, how they will be evaluated, and the development activities they need to increase their performance. Great care is taken to support the central meaning of HP. Take the rewarding of performance, for example: this is absolutely integrated with the core meaning of HP as a single-status company. As one manager commented to us:

'HP is very single status, so that the only different benefits are where the company car cuts in. I think it's one of the strengths of HP to know that the Managing Director in theory is not getting a hugely different package from the other employees.'

Our in-depth, 'unwritten rules of the game' interviews across HP's UK business showed clearly how the processes had created a clear and shared meaning of what was expected in the company. People spoke about the importance of getting involved in task forces or projects which added value to the overall company. As a sales person put it: 'You have a day job and what I call an "evening job" where you get involved in extra-curricula activities such as task forces.' They spoke of sharing ideas with peers, supporting and coaching team members, taking risks in things you believe are important and becoming inspired and excited.

John Golding, CEO of the UK operation, described managing HP like driving a high-performance car along a road with unexpected twists and turns. The business is moving at terrific speed, the competitive landscape changing rapidly. The role of the team is to keep this high-performing car on the road by anticipating what may be ahead, and by creating a strong drive shaft between the steering wheel of the business goals and the wheels of performance. This drive shaft is the explicit discussion of the business goals, a climate of open feedback, and a continual push for high-performance. The strength of this ensures that even fine-tuning adjustments of the steering wheel are captured through the drive shaft into the wheels.

There may have been a time when ad hoc, poorly designed and integrated processes could be tolerated. Poor planning and implementation may have made it more difficult to raise financial capital. But the past can be forgotten – money does not have a mind or a memory. Clumsy implementation and support may slow the advantage gained by technological capital but past mistakes can be remedied – machines do not have a soul. People have minds and memories, are active rather than passive, they strive to make sense of their environment, to understand the unwritten rules of the game and to work to create a shared sense of meaning. To gain sustained competitive advantage through people demands an environment which has integrity and coherence, where reward, selection and development processes are integrated and the unwritten rules of the game are in harmony with corporate rhetoric.

Building on the human perspective of meaning: the three core capabilities

People in organizations feel more committed and work in a more focused manner when their sense of meaning fits with what the organization is striving to achieve. Citibank has created processes and structures which serve to create a coherent sense of meaning, while at Hewlett-Packard the meaning of the place is well understood. How do organizations arrive at this coherence?

If we believe that the creation of meaning is a prerequisite to being people centred, this poses a number of challenges. How do individual members of the organization view its collective meaning? What do they see as the central aim and purpose of the organization? How does this fit in with their values and the need to make a personal contribution to something they believe is important? Only when this alignment happens can human potential be released. But the greatest challenge is to rejuvenate, to keep fresh and exhilarating the meaning of the organization, yet at the same time to build from the meaning and symbols of the past and to do this in a way which is dignified and meaningful.

Creating organizations with meaning builds from the understanding of human time scales; it adds to the capabilities of visioning, scanning and strategy, the capabilities to diagnose, think systemically and build adaptive capabilities.

◆ *Capability 4*: *diagnostic capability*
The capability to understand how meaning is created in organizations and the role played by the alignment and readjustment of processes and practices.

◆ *Capability 5*: *systemic capability*
The capability to use systemic thinking to view organizations as complex and dynamic systems in which shared meaning is created.

◆ *Capability 6*: *adaptive capability*
The capability to build on the history of meaning in the organization, yet create adaptation and flexibility.

Capability 4: diagnostic capability

If we believe that the creation of meaning in an organization is central to an understanding of human performance, we need a view of how meaning is created, and how it changes over time. As we saw earlier, the central meaning of Glaxo Wellcome in the late eighties was as a traditional pharmaceutical organization dominated by strong 'chimney stack' functions. The flow of ideas took place in a sequential manner as the product development moved from one function to the next. This strong functional meaning was reinforced by many of the key organizational practices and processes. People developed within these strong functional chimneys, functional excellence was rewarded, and cross-functional experience was given little value.

The strong functionalism was reflected in the roles and responsibilities of individual members of the organization. Functions dominated the struc-

ture and, to an extent, the meaning of Glaxo Wellcome. The cues from job
design, the dominant career paths and the reward structures were clear. In
terms of the unwritten rules of the game there was a strong shared understanding of 'what you have to do around here'. The message was to create
functional excellence through dedicated functional experience and professionalism. But as the marketplace in which Glaxo Wellcome operated
became more volatile and competitive, the core meaning was no longer
appropriate. In fact, the meaning of Glaxo Wellcome was creating barriers
to rapid product innovation. Ideas were stuck in the research function, the
functional barriers slowed the development process, and the customer
remained at the end of the chain. The organization had to change and enter
a period of transformation which would break the meaning of the past and
recreate the context for the creation of a shared new meaning.

What we saw at Glaxo Wellcome was that to capture and understand
the 'humanness' of organizations depends on an awareness of many levels
of meaning. These levels include what drives the company, the visions,
aspirations and business goals that make the company what it is; the business goals, processes and systems that value certain behaviours and skills
and reinforce a set of attitudes and expectations; and at the deepest level,
the meaning that individuals create about what is important, how they see
the organization and what motivates and excites them. It is these aspects
which, as we saw earlier, link the business goals to firm performance.

One of the most visible signs of the state of human performance within
an organization are the aspirations, commitments, behaviours and performance of every member of that organization. These individuals or groups
add value by bringing skills, motivations or attitudes which are unique,
and knowledge, networks or contacts which cannot be imitated by competitors or substituted by another resource.

I believe that your ability to put a mirror up to your organization and to
face up to what you see is a crucial capability. In step 3 of the six-step process,
I describe how we can create an understanding of the current situation.

Capability 5: systemic capability

The fifth capability is to use systems thinking to build a shared understanding of what the organization could be. This is crucial, for example
one of the most overwhelming impressions left by the experiences of

Citibank is the complexity of continuously realigning the key structures and processes as the competitive environment changes and with it the business goals. What becomes apparent is that the processes and structures are not independent. Rather, they are part of a complex web of interdependencies, where realignment of one element has an immediate impact on the other elements. Vertical, horizontal and temporal alignment captures something of this, but at any one point in time there are specific factors which could have a disproportionate impact on the creation of shared meaning.

When developing organizational processes the tendency is to perceive processes such as reward and development, training and career management as isolated tools and techniques. In many cases these processes are designed over time in a relatively ad hoc manner, each reinforcing a different and potentially confusing message. Yet individuals in organizations experience all these processes simultaneously. In my own home the elements were created at different times, to suit different needs. Yet as I live in my home, I perceive these elements simultaneously: the plumbing, the lighting, the sound system are seen together. They have some cohesiveness. The same experience takes place in organizations, we see all the elements simultaneously and so can be deeply aware of the contradictions between them.[7]

Since these elements are not independent, changing any part of the context has an impact on the totality. As the team at Citibank found, the business goal of a global customer network required the realignment of the system to reward people for being more focused on these global customers. But they found that people cannot be rewarded for being customer focused until there are measures in place which are capable of reliably and fairly measuring key aspects of customer focus such as customer satisfaction. However, to create greater customer satisfaction requires people to spend more time in some customer-facing roles. Therefore, they have to spend less time in other roles and the profile of the job has to change, meaning the role itself must be redefined and a new set of competencies outlined. As a consequence, the old career development tracks are no longer adequate to develop and support this new set of competencies. This sequence is shown in Fig. 13, where the development of customer measures, new job profiles and the realignment of career paths are unplanned consequences of changing the reward structure.

Figure 13 is the beginnings of a map of the system, a figurative description of the major elements at play within the systems, their interdependencies and how they relate to each other.

To create a notion of the complexity of meaning we must view the organization not as independent processes and systems but as a dynamic, interrelated, complex system.[8] At the centre of the creation of meaning and transformation are three elements: the *key themes* which portray and capture the business goals of the organization; the *process levers* which are sensitive to the themes and capable of reinforcing them; the *dynamics* of the system and the actions and feedback loops which impact upon these dynamics. We need to understand the meaning that is currently in operation, where the power is coming from, what the primary feedback loops are, and how processes cluster together to reinforce a particular goal. Through modelling the system and the feedback loops we are able to understand the messages these processes send and isolate the potential contradictions between them, and the sources of leverage. These three parts of systemic thinking are described through the activities of Philips Lighting in step 4 of the six-step process.

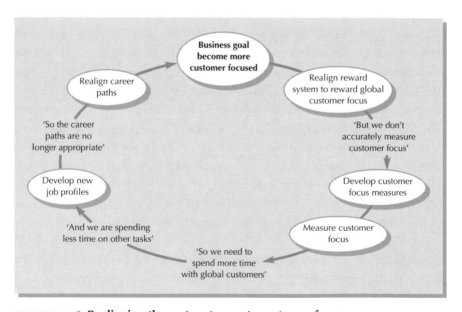

FIGURE 13 ◆ **Realigning the system to create customer focus**

Capability 6: adaptive capability

Creating a context which has at its core a strong and shared sense of meaning which is supported and reinforced by closely aligned processes and practices is complex and difficult in times of stability. The challenge becomes greater when core aspirations and goals change. Yet for many managers the challenge they face is not simply to create alignment in times of stability, but to ride the waves of turbulence in their high-velocity environments. Over the years of the Leading Edge Research Consortium we have witnessed BT Payphones restructure from a district-based organization into business units, and Glaxo Wellcome move from a traditional functional organization into ad hoc teams. Downsizing and delayering were also on the corporate agendas: Citibank reduced the number of its European employees, HP engaged in a voluntary severance programme in 1992 and restructured in 1999, and BT made significant reductions in employee numbers over the same period. These structural changes in many cases were the result of increasing strategic focus and business goals associated with product or service quality.

Business goals and visions for the future are not simply pieces of corporate rhetoric, they must be deep-seated views about how competitive advantage will be sustained. But goals and visions become rhetoric if they are not supported by the realignment of organizational processes to select people who have the capacity to excel, create an understanding of what they must achieve, provide targeted performance feedback, and increase skills through training. The challenge is not simply to create selection and performance management processes capable of supporting ossified business goals but to develop policies capable of adapting to meet the needs of the future and the changing competitive market. Nevertheless, the balance between ossification and adaptability is difficult. Too much change in these processes leads to common themes and meanings being lost, and people become overwhelmed by discontinuities or, as one manager put it, 'death by a hundred initiatives'. Too little flexibility and the processes become solidified and ossified, impervious to changing circumstances.

If we place individuals and their creation of shared meaning at the centre of organizational transformation, two broad propositions about the nature of change follow. First, as we have argued earlier, the timescales for the creation and transformation of meaning are longer than those associated with capital and technology. Second, we must be aware that the transformation of shared meaning may simply be the emphasis on a cluster of levers, or it may be more profound, based on the realignment of the whole system. The first requires a particular angle on transformation, the second the capability to think systemically.

Changes within a human time frame

As we have seen, the shared meaning in organizations and the behaviours associated with them are relatively slow to change, necessitating a compelling reason to kick-start the process. The same is true of the processes and structures, the 'hard wiring', within the organization. Processes such as career tracks and reward structures over time become ossified and resistant to change. This resistance is in part the result of an accumulation of resource commitments and institutionalized routines which create commitment to the status quo.[9] This inertia grows as more detailed, routine policies and procedures are developed to increase reliability, and the organization begins the process of institutionalization. At BT Payphones, for example, the career paths were highly institutionalized, having been established over the previous 30 years and providing a well defined and clearly understood path up the organization. With career moves from assistant to senior assistant to manager, these career paths were ingrained and well trodden. By 1994, managers who had moved up these career paths had invested in their development and were resistant to change. People entering BT Payphones learned very quickly how progression took place and where the 'launching pad' jobs could be found. The destruction of these pathways had enormous organizational implications, for while the career paths were indeed ossified, they were reassuring for people. Once destroyed, employees grew anxious and concerned about the future.

At BT Payphones, as in other companies, employees resist change in part because it becomes increasingly time-consuming to abandon complex activities such as career paths or reward structures. As these become more formal and satisfactory results are more predictable, so people are motivated to work with what has been inherited. What we see in both the behaviour and attitudes of employees and in the processes and systems of the organization is the notion of homeostasis, the tendency of a system to maintain its internal stability.

Change as realignment

As visions and values and the meaning associated with these visions evolve, so too do the processes and practices which create and support these visions. This realignment may involve one or more elements of the organizational system and processes or, as we saw at BT Payphones, a more fundamental questioning of the basic premise of the organization, which would affect all the key elements. When British Telecom moved from a state-controlled monopoly to a publicly listed telecommunications company in a highly competitive marketplace, it was decided that incrementalism, where one part of the system is changed, would not be sufficient. It would not address the fundamental changes in the business, the shifts in power, and the consequent alterations to the culture. For BT, privatization represented a change which addressed the whole system and meant breaking the pattern of alignment and developing a completely new configuration. The challenge the management team faced was to move BT Payphones to a new configuration and a new definition of alignment. In doing so they had to manage the political dynamics associated with change, motivate constructive behaviour in the face of the anxiety created by the change, and actively manage the transitional state.

For other organizations, transformation of meaning is part of a broader agenda of renewal and adaptation. Take HP for example, where the broad changes are primarily adaptive and iterative. At HP the Hoshin process is a crucial part of how managers communicate the challenging goals and agree the areas which need renewed focus, resources and energy. As importantly, the discussion processes create an opportunity to consider those areas of leverage which may have been important in the past but will be less crucial for the future. In many cases these goals focus on individual components of the system, for example the realignment of the reward system to emphasize customer focus or bottom-line profitability. The goal is one of maintaining or regaining congruence through incremental changes.

We strive for meaning, to create a shared understanding of the goals of the organization and how to achieve these goals. In this section I have argued that this search for meaning is underpinned by understanding the meaning of the organization, thinking systemically and creating adaptation and flexibility. In Steps 4 and 5 we consider how meaning can be understood, and how systemic thinking can reinforce this understanding.

We have a soul

S uccessful businesses are created by excitement and inspiration, innovation and ideas, the emotion which every member of the organization feels towards their team members and colleagues and to the goals of their group and the purpose of the company. Strip out the emotion, the ideas and the inspiration and a cold, empty shell remains. The financial capital bank may be full to capacity at that moment, but the reserves of emotion are at an all-time low – the 'pool of goodwill' has been destroyed.

In this chapter we consider why the emotional part of organizations gets pushed into the corner and how we can create a deep understanding of the soul of the organization. We also consider how to create a relationship or contract between the individual and the organization which encourages our emotional lives to flourish. Understanding the soul of the individual is critical to organizational performance, particularly to that growing number of companies which have knowledge at the centre of their strategy to create competitive advantage.[1]

Do our organizations inspire us, engage our emotions of commitment of trust, and encourage ideas? Figure 14 gives a snapshot of the soul in the seven organizations who participated in the Leading Edge Research Consortium, showing employee attitudes in 1996.

For me there are two striking features of employee responses. First, there are significant differences between companies in integrity, pride and inspiration. Second, asked whether 'my company inspires the best in me', in many companies less than 20 per cent of the many thousands of people we surveyed agreed with this statement. Since we collected the data, I

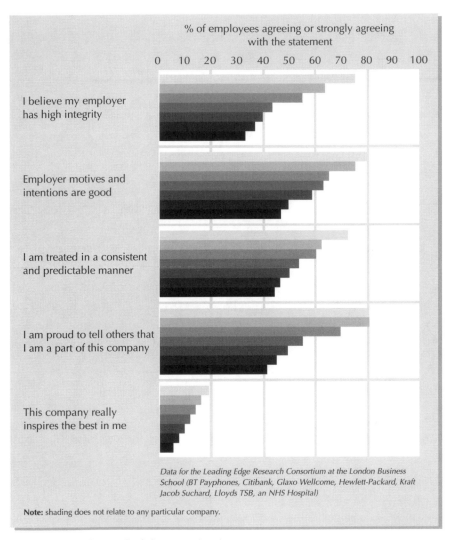

% of employees agreeing or strongly agreeing
with the statement

0   10   20   30   40   50   60   70   80   90   100

I believe my employer
has high integrity

Employer motives and
intentions are good

I am treated in a consistent
and predictable manner

I am proud to tell others that
I am a part of this company

This company really
inspires the best in me

*Data for the Leading Edge Research Consortium at the London Business
School (BT Payphones, Citibank, Glaxo Wellcome, Hewlett-Packard, Kraft
Jacob Suchard, Lloyds TSB, an NHS Hospital)*

Note: shading does not relate to any particular company.

FIGURE 14 ◆ **The soul of the organization**

have asked managers all over the world: 'How many of the people in your
company feel inspired?' Most are remarkably accurate, saying 'about
15 per cent'. So while we may extol the precision of our strategy creation
processes, or the exuberance and strength of our leaders, or the profound
ability of our company to create shareholder value, the hidden, dirty secret
is that many of us are working, and know we are working, in companies
where neither we nor our colleagues feel inspired.

Should we care? I believe that we should not only care but should strive with all our energy to develop organizations which are inspirational and engage our emotions in order to build organizations in which we can believe and from which we can profit. We want to be treated with respect, have our ideas taken seriously, and believe that we can make a difference. Our behaviour and performance is profoundly influenced by how we feel. Unlike the other sources of competitive advantage such as capital and technology, knowledge is a resource locked into the human mind. Creating and sharing knowledge are intangible activities that can be neither supervised nor forced out of people. The robots at the ABB plant in Switzerland can be switched on, but we cannot switch on the knowledge, creativity and ideas of the engineers who designed those robots. People can choose to give and to withhold their knowledge. The ABB engineers will give their knowledge only if they choose to. If they feel uncommitted, disrespected, or treated unfairly they have the option of withholding their knowledge and skills. Unlike machines and capital, we have a notion of what is right and wrong, and are sensitive to injustice and unfairness. As a primary focus for many people, work is a crucial part of the landscape of justice and fairness.

So are all of us uninspired most of the time? Are we uninspired at home, with our children, when we are on holiday? Some people are, but others are deeply inspired. Witness the team leader, an adequate performer at work, who shows immense leadership capabilities and inspiration out of work running a youth club for delinquent adolescents. Why is there no link between the two parts of their life? Ask them, and they will say that work is not challenging, they are not given sufficient responsibility to make a difference and there are too many political issues. They have separated and compartmentalized their work and life, and tacitly (probably unconsciously) withdrawn their knowledge and capability from work.

But this is not a zero sum game. Creating inspiration, hope and excitement at work does not reduce our inspiration out of work. On the contrary, inspiring work helps us to build inspiring lives. BT Payphones understood the link when it created the 'For a Better Life' programme. For years the senior team had encouraged the team leaders to coach and develop their people, but in the main this message had fallen on deaf ears. Enter the coach to the UK Olympic team. Coaching, he said, is about the field of play, it's about being off the field but assisting on the field, it's about creating winning teams, and it's about success. 'Ah,' said the BT Payphones managers. So what they were doing at the weekends with their kids on the football and baseball grounds was coaching, and they enjoyed it and felt inspired. If some of that excitement could be replicated at work, we would have the beginnings of great coaches.

We can create inspirational companies which build hope, trust and excitement.

Why is so little attention paid to the soul of the organization?

Why is it so difficult for some companies to engage the hearts and souls of people, to create a workforce which is inspired and committed? I believe the answer lies in part in our fundamental notion of what an organization is and in the sheer complexity of understanding soul concepts such as trust and inspiration.

There are two dominant organizational metaphors of man – man as a machine, where people are interchangeable parts, and will perform equally well across a range of circumstances; and homo-economicus, man as a rational; economic maximizer who will behave in a rational manner and make choices which maximize the results of his or her labour. These metaphors dominated our early thinking on how organizations were structured, how jobs were assigned, and how performance was encouraged through reward and punishment. They failed to capture the complexity of individuals, by assuming everyone was the same when in fact they were very different, and by overestimating rational behaviour and underestimating the part played by our will and emotions. Yet to move from the machine and economic metaphor is to create a more complex world, where factors such as emotions and hopes are intangible and inordinately complex, where the relationship between these factors is complex and the interdependencies understood only over time, and where people are seen as individuals rather than 'the workforce'.

The strength of the economic machine metaphor

There has been a fundamental shift in the sources of competitive advantage, from competitive advantage gained through financial and technological capital to that gained through people and their knowledge. But while the source of advantage may have shifted, in many organizations the fundamental model remains the machine metaphor. If we view the organization as a machine, then people are interchangeable parts. So just as a faulty piece on a machine can be replaced by an identical piece, so a manager who fails can be easily replaced by a successful manager. Also, machines are essentially black boxes – we may not understand the mechanisms deep within the robots at ABB, or the financial programmes Citibank uses in its global trading, but we do not need to understand what is in the black box, all we need to grasp is the input and the output. The machine metaphor places great emphasis on what is done and seeks to create uniformity around tasks. The concept of overhead value analysis, for example, is an aspect of the machine metaphor. Value can be created by studying inputs (rather than outputs) and by simply reducing or eliminating tasks. The machine metaphor emphasizes rationality and causality. Outcomes occur in a predetermined manner and there is little space for emotion or motivation, or for understanding what is within the black box.

Given the management rhetoric of 'people are our most important asset', why has the machine metaphor remained the dominant way of thinking about the organization and the people within it? If it is seen increasingly as an outdated notion, the new metaphors are only just beginning to have an impact. Arie due Geus describes organizations as living entities and Peter Senge's work on complex systems, makes the connection with biological, living systems.[2] Why has the impact of this metaphor been so slow? In part, the reason lies deep within the metaphor of the living organization: within the complex biological system – the simplicity of the machine metaphor; the simplicity of predictability and interchangeable machine parts, and the complexity of emotions and values, hopes and dreams. The complexity of this new metaphor operates at a number of levels, most obviously because emotions such as trust and hope are elusive and difficult to grasp, but it is also the complexity of measuring and substantiating 'hard' measures of profitability and financial growth, and 'soft' measures such as trust and commitment.

Emotions are complex

The obvious difficulty comes in creating clarity around the concepts of trust, commitment and inspiration and what they actually mean. How can they be accurately and reliably measured, and in what ways are they developed in organizations? More and more organizations are trying to grasp some understanding of these concepts, most obviously through employee surveys, thus allowing managers to keep their finger on the emotional pulse of the business.

But how do we interpret trust, inspiration and commitment? If 20 per cent of employees report that they have no pride or do not trust their managers, is this high or low? How do these measures change as the company grows and downsizes, or when there has been a change of CEO? In the financial market we are very clear about what a return on expenditure (ROE) of 5 per cent means and can calibrate it against our expectations of a company in that particular sector and point in its life cycle. When it comes to measures of emotion and attitude, however, we have limited shared calibration. Therefore managers become dispirited with the results, and the employee survey becomes another piece of corporate bureaucratic ritual with limited impact on organizational life.

The relationship between emotions and financial results

What does it matter if trust and commitment are low? What impact does this have on the financial positioning of the business and the ability to deliver business goals? What of the impact of caring about emotions and attitudes to the extent that hard business decisions are made on the basis of them, that much-needed resources are focused on them and that managers talk about the emotional capital of the organization as they now talk about the financial capital? To achieve this is predicated on a thorough understanding of the impact of trust, commitment and inspiration on business performance. For some managers, such as David Packard and Bill Hewlett, this was a leap of faith they were willing to take. The notion of the HP Way did not arise from a well understood relationship between the emotion of trust and company performance but from the beliefs of the founding members and a set of values about the nature of people and the way in which organizations flourish.

For some managers this act of faith is not sufficient. They want hard evidence that focusing on the soul will increase company performance. As we saw earlier, managers and academics are beginning to understand the impact of a company's emotional and financial strength. What we need now is the fine-tuned calibration of the relationship developed in other areas of organizational life. For example, the relationship between customer satisfaction and organizational performance is well understood by the world's leading service providers.

At the telecommunications company BT, the marketing team have plotted over a number of years the relationship between customer satisfaction and incremental revenue increases (*see* Fig. 15). What they have learned is that there is a complex relationship between customer satisfaction (measured on a ten-point scale) and incremental revenue changes. Customer satisfaction scores below a scale of seven result in decreases in revenue, while those over 7.5 are associated with increased revenue. Customer satisfaction ratings above nine are associated with revenue increases of up to 24 per cent. This graph allows the senior team at BT to make the hard management decisions, to understand the true implications they make in trade off, and the resources necessary to increase customer satisfaction to levels of nine or ten. Most customer-orientated organizations will have developed similar graphs for their own marketplace.

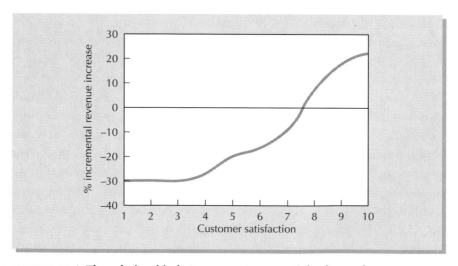

FIGURE 15 ◆ The relationship between customer satisfaction and revenue

Source: BT marketing group 1996

Few, if any, companies have such a finely calibrated understanding of the relationship between increases in revenue and employee emotions. As we will see in Steps 5 and 6, sharing the knowledge of this calibration is an essential part of seeing the organization as a complex system and describing the feedback loops. Yet despite all the difficulties of understanding the soul of the organization, some companies have continued to believe that this capital is as important as the financial capital. This belief has acted as a touchstone to managers as they make the difficult journey through turbulent times. HP is one such company where a belief in the soul of the organization has been a crucial part of the ethos.[3]

Placing the soul at the centre at Hewlett-Packard

At the heart of HP is an organization that cares deeply about people and for whom the rhetoric of people is a reality experienced by every employee, every day. In the thirties Dave Packard and Bill Hewlett agreed a fundamental dictum about what an organization should be:

> *'We made an early and important decision: we did not want to be a "hire and fire", a company that would seek short-term contracts, employ a great many people for the duration of the contract, and then let these people go ... we wanted to be in the business for the long haul, to have a company built around a stable and dedicated workforce.'*
>
> *Dave Packard, The HP Way: How Bill Hewlett and I built our company. 1996; page 129.*

Since 1994 we have interviewed and surveyed employees of the UK operations of Hewlett-Packard. I am conscious that survey data provide only a glimpse of organizational life, but nevertheless this provides some insight into the reality of individuals. Of the many statements we used in the survey, there are a number of questions which illustrate the collective soul.

During the time of the survey the company had operated an increasingly turbulent competitive environment, culminating in the restructuring of the business and the loss in the UK of a significant number of jobs. One might expect this to have a major impact on the feelings and attitudes of the remaining employees. Recall, for example, that at BT Payphones the downsizing had a negative impact on employees' morale. But the employee responses presented in Fig. 16 tell a very different story. There is no doubt that the basis of the soul of HP has changed since 1994. But even in 1999, most employees are positive about the organization (contrast this to the wider company data shown earlier in Fig. 14). These feelings are remarkably resilient over time. Even during 1999, when the very basis of the HP Way was being rocked, people continued to hold on to their beliefs about themselves and the company.

I believe the HP experience, sustained through times of extreme competitive turbulence, brings real insights into the nature of the soul of the organization and how this soul can be nurtured and sustained. The nurturing of the soul takes place in many ways and at many levels in HP. It can be summarized around three fundamental concepts:

◆ People at Hewlett-Packard have a voice – in general they are involved and consulted and their views considered and acknowledged.

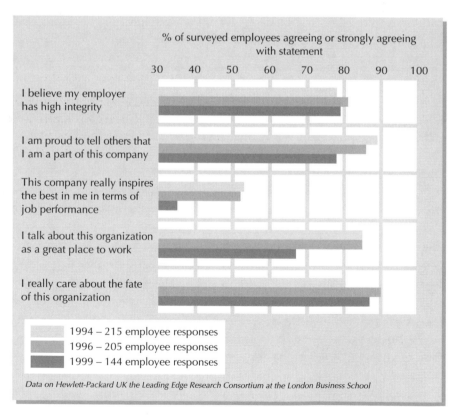

FIGURE 16 ◆ **Building the soul at Hewlett-Packard**

◆ They have a choice – they have the opportunity to influence how they are treated and what happens to them.

◆ They are treated, and treat others, with dignity, politeness and respect.

It would be wrong to assume that as a consequence HP is a soft, flaky organization, as we saw earlier there is a hard, performance-orientated edge. However, this is balanced with the creation of trust through treating people in a just and fair manner.

The development of the soul at Hewlett-Packard reflects the fundamental beliefs of the founding partners about people and the way in which they should be treated. Over the past eight years, I have seen many examples of understanding this essential humanness of the workforce. People are intimately involved in decisions about themselves and the organization. It is a relatively transparent organization in which the roles and responsibilities are clearly stated, and this transparency creates an environment in which people can engage and make their own decisions. People are sensitive to the signals conveyed through decision-making processes. I believe the transparency at HP signals the willingness to trust people.

There is also a profound interest in the well-being of individual members of the community. It is clear that people are absolutely not interchangeable pieces. Rather, each is unique, and this uniqueness should be cherished and developed. This notion of the unique individual is seen in the diversity programmes which has attempted over the years to create a workforce which more accurately reflects the diversity of the customer base. It is reflected in the wide portfolio of working arrangements which encourages mothers to spend time with their children and people to care for their ageing parents. The notion of uniqueness is reflected in the basic egalitarianism of the organization.

A particular example of this egalitarianism philosophy is the selection and development of talent. For many multi-national companies the choice is clear: recruit from the most prestigious universities and place people on a fast-track programme. These programmes are designed to accelerate career development by moving people every couple of years (sometimes even months) and providing cross-country work experience. These 'tournaments' are likely to create people who are well versed in managing their own image and their boss, but often sadly lacking in the skills of creating and developing high-performance teams. Perhaps more importantly, they dis-enfranchize those people who did not go to the prestigious universities and who do not have the high-potential 'stamp'. While fast-tracking pro-grammes have drawn some criticism, they remain intact in many multi-national organizations for the fundamental philosophy is that there are 'haves' and 'have nots', and separating the two is crucial.

Unlike the majority of multi-national companies, HP has never had a fast-track career scheme. It has never marked people with the high-potential stamp early in their careers, and it does not give preferential treatment to certain people early on. Also, it does not focus recruitment on a small number of prestigious universities. Why has HP remained alone in this? John Kick, a senior manager at HP, explained:

> *'It goes against the very grain of HP. We believe that every member of HP has potential and our job is to create a stretching context and environment which allows people to flourish and grow.'*

Everyone is given a choice: the internal job market is open, anyone can apply for the majority of jobs, and job responsibilities and skills are posted on the internal net informing everyone what training they need to be able to develop. In addition, training budgets are held by the individual and everyone is trusted to make the right decision.

The cycles of hope and despair

Over the past decade, Hewlett-Packard, like many other businesses, has had to reduce costs primarily through rationalization, yet at the same time build and revitalize the business. It is a balance which my colleague Sumantra Ghoshal has referred to as 'cooking with the sweet and sour'.[4] The sour focuses on the cost reduction and rationalization which brings short-term profitability by squeezing costs out of the business. Long-term success comes from the sweet, the building, revitalizing and entrepreneurship which creates new products, pushes into new markets, and explores unforeseen customer aspirations. This revitalization comes from employees who are energized, have hopes and dreams, are prepared to be flexible and adaptable, and are creative and risk taking.[5] And here is the rub. In the reduction and rationalization of the sour, it is so easy to treat employees in an unjust manner, and perceptions of injustice reduce commitment, lower flexibility and self-esteem and sap the energy and hope which are crucial ingredients for the sweet. Without this energy and hope to build and revitalize, the company sinks into a neverending cycle of cost reduction, and in doing so destroys any long-term advantage it may have hoped to gain. 'The cycle of despair' is illustrated in Fig. 17.

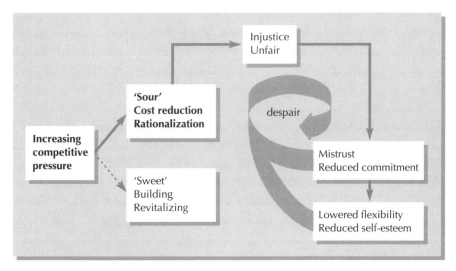

FIGURE 17 ◆ **The cycle of despair**

The breaking of these old contracts and implicit promises can potentially create feelings of anger and injustice. What makes us feel angry at work are the same situations in which we feel angry in our private lives: we feel we have been treated unfairly; we have no opportunity to make our needs understood; we are treated in a disrespectful manner. When we are angry and we feel we have been treated in an unjust manner, we feel less inclined to put extra effort into our work, to really push our ideas, or to use our imagination to let our creativity flourish. People who distrust the organization are less flexible, less willing to change the way they work, and more likely to argue for the status quo. Yet it is exactly this flexibility which is at the heart of realignment and change. Focusing on continuous, radical rationalization squeezes the costs out of the business and increases short-term profitability. But cost reduction eventually cuts deep within the emotional reserves of the organization and drains it of hope and energy. To build and revitalize needs goodwill, commitment and trust to encourage innovation and the acceptance of the risks which go hand in hand with innovation.

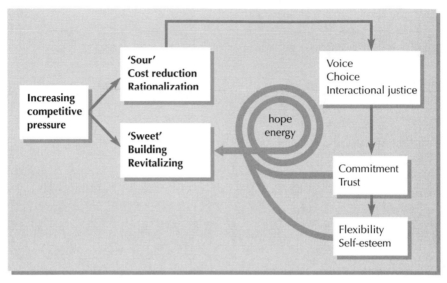

FIGURE 18 ◆ **The cycle of hope**

Yes surely cost reduction and rationalization always create emotions of mistrust and lowered self-esteem – the cycle of despair? It does not have to be so, but to keep from the centrifugal forces of despair requires a deep understanding of the soul of the organization and how it can be developed and built upon. An alternative cycle is the one I have observed at HP, the 'cycle of hope'. As before, faced with competitive pressure, HP has had to cook with both the sour of cost reduction and rationalization, and the sweet of building and revitalization. But over the past five years cost reduction and rationalization at HP has been treated in a just and fair manner, by providing people with a voice and an adequate explanation of why certain decisions are taken. This dignity is underpinned by managers who are skilled in dealing with people and who listen and treat them in a dignified manner.

The pool of goodwill which is created has allowed HP to build greater trust and from this comes the flexibility, self-esteem, hope and energy which are so vital to building and revitalizing the business. Creating this cycle of hope – this reservoir of positive emotion – has been an essential element in revitalizing HP.

Engaging with the soul of the organization: the three core capabilities

Trust, inspiration and commitment may represent the soul of the organization, but too often this soul lies buried and overlooked. The difference between our understanding of this aspect of people and our in-depth understanding of financial capital is striking. We may be able to debate at length the impact of a particular exchange rate on the profitability of an organization but have limited shared and agreed understanding of the impact of low levels of trust on profitability. We may have clear models to predict return on capital at a particular time in the economic cycle but hold little understanding of how trust and commitment declines with company downsizing, and how long it takes to build up to former levels.[6]

Until these issues are addressed, human performance will never have the same resonance in organizations, the same ability to influence managerial decision making, and the same impact on resource allocation. A company with low levels of trust and commitment is as bankrupt as one with low levels of financial capital – it is essentially a dying company.

Creating organizations with soul builds from the capabilities of the first and second tenet, of visioning, scanning and strategy, the capability to diagnose, to think systemically and build adaptive capabilities. To this is added emotional capability, trust-building capability and the capability to build the psychological contract.

◆ *Capability 7: emotional capability*
  The emphasis must be on the creation of a portfolio of measures which accurately and systematically reflect the emotional health of the organization. Until this is achieved, these emotions and attitudes will remain opaque and their relationship with long-term business performance unclear.

◆ *Capability 8: trust building capability*
  Unjust practices create schisms in trust and commitment which can be felt for years. Therefore, it is essential that we understand what makes for fair processes, and how trust can be built.

◆ *Capability 9: capability to build the psychological contract*
There must be greater clarity about the broad relationship between the
organization and its individual members. The concept of the psychological
contract captures the breadth and depth of this relationship. It is an inte-
gral part of the creation of trust in an organization. The emphasis here is
on developing an awareness of individual expectations (and organizational
expectations of the individual), understanding when the old psychological
contract is changing, and how best these changes can be supported.

Capability 7: emotional capability

Building the soul of the organization means keeping your finger on the
pulse of employee commitment and trust, really understanding hopes,
dreams and aspirations. Without these measures we are in danger of letting commitment slip away without even realizing. Companies such as 3M
and HP measure these softer aspects year after year. Their managers are
sensitized to the emotions of employees and are aware when stress levels
rise or commitment drops.

In many organizations, while the business goals may refer to customer
focus, innovation or the use of people as a source of competitive advantage, financial performance metrics predominate. The challenge is to
create metrics which value the 'softer' aspects such as building high-
commitment workforces, developing creative teams, or creating a culture
of innovation and entrepreneurship. Initiatives which create a stronger
emphasis on the non-financial measures include the active use of the balanced scorecard where the financial perspective (shareholder value) is
balanced by the internal business perspective, the innovation and learning
perspective, and the customer perspective. As a reporting mechanism this
has the potential to create greater balance. Some companies are working
on initiatives and pilots to bring in stronger measures of softer outcomes
such as skills in managing and developing team members. For example,
schemes to use upward feedback to accurately measure team-building
behaviours and project management skills met with enthusiasm at
Citibank and Glaxo Wellcome. At Citibank, the performance appraisal for
some senior directors is linked not only to financial targets but also to
their achievements in people management (measured through retention
and the effective development of team members).

Developing a stronger understanding of the role that trust and commit-ment play in creating business performance, and building strong and well understood measures of the softer side of the organization, should begin to balance the enormous power financial measures hold within the business. But we also need a shared understanding of how trust and commitment are created, and particularly the central role played by process fairness.

Capability 8: building trust

For many organizations the need to understand and build the emotions of trust and inspiration is increasingly important to their success. Yet this has never been more difficult. The rollercoaster of change demands a robust and emotionally strong workforce, the fundamental schisms in the old paternalistic contract demand a more mature employee relationship, and as we saw in the cycles of hope and despair, the need to manage the 'sweet' and the 'sour' demands resilience and commitment.

If organizations are changing and success requires flexibility and adaptability, then building trust matters, and if building trust matters, then justice at work is a crucial concept. In the past we have viewed this primarily in terms of distributive justice. For example, if we distribute rewards fairly and comparatively across a group, these people will feel sat-isfied and will believe they have been treated fairly.[7] The focus here is on the outcome and on the amount. Fairness is judged by the allocation of the resources, and the basis of individual satisfaction is the amount they receive. Distributive justice is essentially short term, transactional and occurs on a case-by-case basis.

Yet we are beginning to understand that while distributive justice is important, the way in which the process occurs is equally, if not more, important. Therefore, it is not simply the amount of pay an individual receives, but also the way in which the reward processes are enacted, and the way in which this enactment is perceived. Thus, it is possible to sepa-rate distributive justice from procedural justice, and it is the latter which most crucially impacts upon the emotions of trust and commitment. Fairness of process is broader than fairness of distribution: it is part of the long-term relationship with the employee. When people are treated fairly they feel wanted and valued, they are more accepting of mistakes and misalignment, and the pool of goodwill is replenished.

The arguments for fairness in the workplace are strong: being treated fairly increases self-esteem and therefore the capability to accept change; it builds trust and creates an environment in which people are prepared to be creative, to experiment and to take risks. But how fair are organizations? Earlier in this section we looked at perceptions of integrity, consistency and pride. Why do so many people in so many companies feel their employer does not have high integrity and does not treat them consistently and predictably? Fair process resides in three factors: the capability of individuals to have a voice, and for their voice to be acknowledged; an individual's capacity to exercise choice at work; and the fairness of those making the decision, termed interactional justice. Some survey questions about these three aspects of process fairness are shown in Fig.19. They refer to the three aspects of process fairness: voice, choice and interactional justice.

Voice

People feel they have been treated fairly if their voice has been heard. If they are allowed an input in decisions, they are more able to air their aspirations and grievances, to acknowledge their self-interest, and to come to a decision which they feel is fair. People believe a process is fair, and are more content with the results if they are given a chance to present their opinions. Even when they do not exercise the final authority, the provision of voice means they have an opportunity to convey a message about their interests to those who are making the decision. If their views are heard, they feel valued and their self-esteem grows as they believe their views are taken into consideration.

Nowhere is the issue of the voice more important than in changes to career structures. Having a voice becomes ever more important as organizations abandon the old 'paternalistic' contract of the manager as parent and the employee as child, which set the agenda for the top-down communication senior managers adopted in the paternalistic role. The realignment to employees taking responsibility for themselves and their career development demands the provision of a stronger voice. If we want people to take responsibility, they need to know about job opportunities as soon as they occur, they need their aspirations to be heard, and they need a voice.

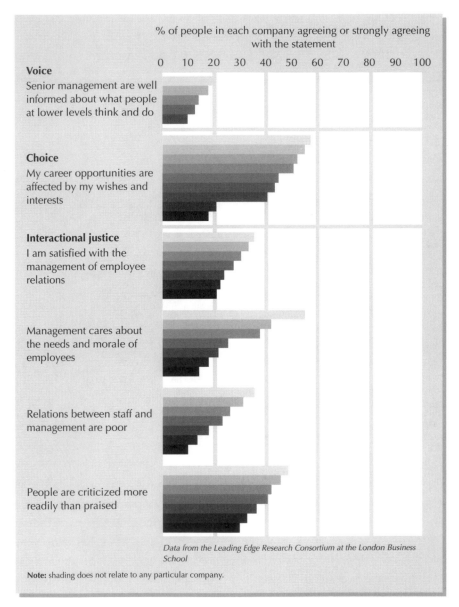

% of people in each company agreeing or strongly agreeing with the statement

Voice
Senior management are well informed about what people at lower levels think and do

Choice
My career opportunities are affected by my wishes and interests

Interactional justice
I am satisfied with the management of employee relations

Management cares about the needs and morale of employees

Relations between staff and management are poor

People are criticized more readily than praised

Data from the Leading Edge Research Consortium at the London Business School

Note: shading does not relate to any particular company.

FIGURE 19 ◆ Process fairness

As the Leading Edge Research Consortium data show, having a voice and being heard is a major problem for the employees in all the companies we studied. In none of these companies do more than 20 per cent of the employees we surveyed agree with the statement 'Senior managers are well informed about what people at lower levels think and do'. Clearly, if process fairness is central to the dynamic, revitalized organization, more needs to be done to create channels and processes which let employees' voices be heard throughout the organization.

Choice

People believe they have been treated fairly if they have been given a choice and can exercise this choice. Choice is about the opportunity to make decisions, for example about the type of reward package and the proportion of remuneration accounted for by stock options. If the choice is made and subsequent events create negative outcomes, such as the company stock price falling, then individuals have no one to blame but themselves. However, if they had no choice, and a proportion of their remuneration had to be paid in stock options, they can blame this negative outcome on others.

I have chosen one statement from the survey to capture the notion of choice: 'My career opportunities are affected by my wishes and interests.' Although the proportion of people agreeing with this statement is higher than the results of the voice issue, still the data show that for many the concept of choice is not operating strongly. If we are to value the creation of trust and resilience in organizations, we must become more sensitive to how people are given a choice and must increase the opportunities for them to become involved in these key decisions.

Interactional justice

Perceptions of fairness are profoundly influenced by the way we are treated, the manner in which information is given, and the means by which views are heard. If individuals are treated with politeness and respect, and explanations are given about why decisions are taken, people are more likely to feel they have been treated fairly. This notion of interactional justice is crucial since it is cumulative and builds goodwill and the reputation of fairness within the organization. This reputation acts as a buffer for the times the policy is wrong, or managers behave unjustly. People are willing to overlook individual instances of injustice if they have sufficient goodwill. This emotional reserve becomes crucial as rapid changes in business goals create glaring misalignment with the hard wiring, policies and processes.

Of the four survey questions used to illustrate interactional justice, two are positively scaled and two are negatively scaled. Again, we see the spread of beliefs across the companies, but it also illustrates that building an environment of fairness is not simple. Many people are dissatisfied with the management of employee relations in their organization. For more than half the companies we surveyed, less than 30 per cent believe management cares about the needs and morale of employees. The two other scales provide some insight into this issue. On average, across all employees surveyed, about 25 per cent describe the relationship between staff and management as poor, while more than 40 per cent believe people are criticized more readily than praised.

The message is clear. The emotional capital of a company is crucial, and to deny it is to be pulled into a cycle of despair, distrust and disinterest. Yet in cooking with the sweet and the sour, we are creating situations which are capable of destroying the core of trust. However, it does not have to be like this. If we can acknowledge the emotions of the organization, and treat people in a fair, honourable and dignified manner, we can create a pool of emotional resilience, reputation and goodwill which will carry us through the times when mistakes are made, when processes are broken and misaligned, and when individual managers behave in a less than dignified manner. But without this pool, each individual occurrence of injustice or unfairness results in another push towards dissatisfaction, distrust and disaffection.

Capability 9: capability to build the psychological contract

Cooking with the sweet and sour brings with it the challenge of retaining and building trust and resilience. The underlying changes in the technology, structure and processes of the business bring renewed stresses to the relationship between the individual and the organization. This is played out within a broader context of expectations: both those which the employee has of the organization, and those which members of the organization have of the individual employee. These expectations are rarely formally stated but are created as soon as the individual is attracted to joining the organization, and continue to be refined and shaped as they remain a member of this community.[8]

This unwritten or psychological contract is important here since it expresses the emotion of the implicit rather than the rationale of the explicit. It is the 'working model' of what is given to the organization and what can be expected in return. This working model changes with the transformation of individual or organizational needs. For the individual this may include changes in working hours, expectations of pay, the type of supervision, recognition and feedback they need, the degree of autonomy and flexibility to which they aspire, and expectations of the personal growth the job can provide. From the organizational perspective, changes in the psychological contract may include an increase or decrease in the hours of work, the need for flexibility, creativity and loyalty.

The unwritten contract is established relatively early on and is modified over time. The underlying expectations are influenced by an individual's understanding of the industry in which they work, by the messages they receive from those at work, and from their own predisposition and interpretations.

Until the nineties, there was a relatively stable alignment between business goals and employee expectations as expressed in the psychological contract. This was built on a deep acceptance of paternalism: that decisions would be made by the employer and accepted by the employee, and that the employer would look after the employee. Now there are few companies which display this stable alignment. The old paternalistic model where top management is invested with the knowledge and decision making no longer holds. We judge organizations on their ability to create horizontal team working, to build lateral communication, to encourage individuals to take control of their work lives, to build human performance, and to become individualized.

What we know about the nature of people can give us insight into the nature of the changes in the psychological contract and how these changes can be supported and reinforced. Earlier we saw how HP, over a six-year period, modified employee expectations of the company and their role. During this period the hours of work increased for most employees, primarily through the extensive use of task forces as people met early in the morning or later in the day. Perceptions of performance-related pay were also modified as HP struggled to remain profitable in an increasingly competitive and volatile marketplace. During 1999 HP employees faced the greatest change in the psychological contract as the policy on redundancies began to change. During the nineties HP made a significant reduction in the workforce and by doing so cut away a crucial part of the HP Way. Yet this had limited impact on trust or commitment.

How did HP achieve this? In part it came from an organization with an established and shared belief about human potential, and about the role played by trust and fairness. The downsizing programme was handled in a just way, with employee numbers reduced across the board and managers just as likely to leave as engineers. Discussions about career options were open, people were able to voice their opinions, and were given a choice about retraining within HP or leaving. Most importantly, the bank of emotional resilience built up over the years and the sense of trust within the company created an atmosphere of joint problem solving and decision making.

At BT Payphones the changes in the psychological contract were of a different magnitude. Here was an organization breaking many of the old assumptions about jobs for life, career development, and skills and attitudes. In both these examples a significant understanding of the nature of people provided a framework for action.

The psychological contract will be transformed if we understand the time dimension of individuals: by respecting and mourning the past; creating a vivid, actively obtained and legitimate understanding of the present; understanding the competitive forces and why change is necessary; building bridges to the future in which individuals are prepared to make the changes and can see the benefits of doing so. Meaning also plays a key role in transforming the psychological contract. Consider the need to think systemically, to understand how meaning is created within the organization, and what process levers can be pulled to reinforce the new contract. This may involve changing the way performance is measured, the way rewards are distributed, and the way training is supported. Finally, changes in the psychological contract are emotional: they are about loss of the past, anxiety about the future, and concern for the present. Successfully changing the psychological contract rests primarily on understanding the emotions of this change, being aware of the emotional capital in the organization and realizing the amount of trust and commitment employees feel. Building trust requires two-way information channels which convey both good and bad news and provide the opportunity for individuals to have their needs and concerns heard, and to actively engage in their future by having a choice about themselves. Fundamental to all this is a management cadre capable and motivated enough to treat people with respect and dignity.

Having considered the third tenet that we have soul, in Part III we bridge from the tenets to the six steps of creating a living strategy.

The six steps to creating a living strategy

The living strategy journey

Bridging from philosophy to action

W e operate in time, we search for meaning, we have a soul – these are the tenets on which the fundamental humanness of organizations is built. To deny them is to create organizations without hope, inspiration or excitement. To acknowledge them brings creativity and inspiration. But how do you bring these tenets to life? The nine capabilities create a broad context, but they are little more than a wish list of broad aspirations. They show the general direction but not the detail of action. The rest of this book shows how the three tenets and nine capabilities can be harnessed to create superior performance through inspired and committed people. It shows traction, what can happen when the rubber hits the road.

My goal here is not to present you with a list of concepts you should consider, or examples from great companies. These examples can only be the result of a complex heritage which, as we saw at Hewlett-Packard, we can admire but not imitate. Rather, my goal is to share with you a journey of decisions and actions which will lead to a living strategy and set of actions with people at the heart. This is a journey I have taken with a number of companies over the past decade, a journey that has been illustrated by insights from the research with the Leading Edge Consortium of companies. I want to describe the journey in two ways, first by reference to what the journey is seeking to achieve, i.e. the *content* of the journey, and then by the path the journey can take that is the *process* of the journey. In doing so I will share the elements which I believe are crucial to the content and process and which acknowledge and build from the three tenets and their related capabilities.

For me, the genesis of the journey to creating a living strategy started many years ago when I began to advise companies on how to do more than simply design the best assessment centres or reward strategies. By doing so we had begun to acknowledge that the alignment between these processes and the business goals would be critical to the success of the organization. But it was no good having the world's most advanced assessment centre if the competencies it profiled and the simulations it created were out of line with the mission of the business. Working with teams at BAT, Unilever, Northern Telecom, Philips and Shell we began to experiment with various ways of bringing life into strategy. At about the same time it became clear to me from the in-depth interviews of the companies in the Leading Edge Research Consortium that generally human resource professionals and their line manager partners felt confused and unclear about what a strategy for people could look like, and how it could be enacted. By articulating this journey I hope to share with you at this early stage the elements which guide my views of both the *content* and the *process* of the journey.

TABLE 4 ◆ The elements for creating a living strategy

With regard to content, the journey should contain the following elements:
◆ a vision of the short- and long-term goals of the business;
◆ an understanding of the current and future capability of the business to deliver to these business goals and an awareness of the extent of the gap;
◆ a cluster of people processes capable of changing the context in which people work.
With regard to process, the journey should take the following path:
◆ it should be capable of building wide involvement across the organization;
◆ it should work back from a vision of the future;
◆ it should be capable of creating alignment between the business goals and the context in which people work;
◆ it should be action orientated and build on the inspiration and commitment of people.

Creating living strategy, the *content* of the journey

To understand the content of the journey, let us consider the three key elements. Let me describe these three elements as a cycle of activity, illustrated in Fig. 20, which shows the link between the short- and long-term vision of the business and the performance of the business.[1]

Bridging from philosophy to action

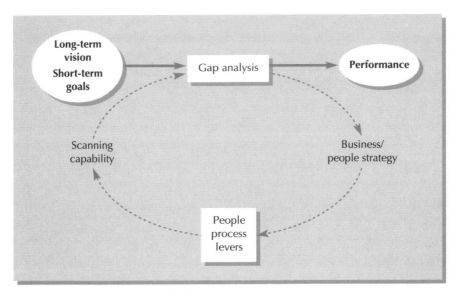

FIGURE 20 ◆ **The elements of a living strategy**

Element 1: a vision of the business

The key to the energy of the system is the first element, a collective under-standing and vision of what the organization is capable of achieving, expressed as *short-term goals* and as a *long-term vision*. This collective understanding and vision has the potential to create a focal point for activity which is engaging and inspirational. At the heart of this is a wide group of people who have shared their view of the future and arrived at a common understanding of what the future could be. It is the energy and inspiration of these goals and visions which drives the whole system.

Element 2: an understanding of current capability

The short-term business goals and long-term vision create a broad strategic agenda and an understanding of where the organization should be heading. But to make these goals a reality there must be a more clearly defined awareness of what has to be achieved. The pathway of action comes from the second element, the *gap analysis*, which creates a deep understanding of the gap between current capability and the desired state. The extent of this gap is the basis for a shared understanding of what needs to be achieved, and potentially the energy for the journey. Therefore, on the left-hand side of the cycle we see the major sources of energy: an articulated and agreed vision for the future and short-term business goals, *scanning of the capability* to deliver to the business goals and vision and, from this, an awareness of the gap between vision and capability. This cycle operates in the short term and in the longer term. In Fig. 21 I have described them as two distinct and separate cycles of activity, to show that their cycle speeds are different. However, in reality those two cycles operate simultaneously. At any one time, managers are grappling with making short-term adjustments to the policies and processes, yet preparing for and implementing changes which will be felt only three or four years hence.

At the top is the long-term cycle, operating over a three- to five-year period. The primary energy pump is the shared articulation of the future vision which is shown by the arrow entering the model. Feeding into the future vision is the scanning of future capability, in a sense the perceived ability of the organization to deliver to this future vision. The gap analysis expresses the degree of alignment between the future needs and likely future capability. The understanding of this gap creates the frame for the long-term people strategy and this highlights those long-term policy and process levers which can be pulled. The short-term cycle is a mirror image, operating on an annual cycle time and focusing on short-term business goals, current capability and short-term people strategy tactics. Here the emphasis is on those levers which have the capacity to create relatively rapid changes in the performance of the business.

When the cycle is viewed in totality it portrays the balance between the short-term and the long-term cycles. These two cycles of activity are seen to be working in tandem. The energy each creates may be different, they may rotate at different speeds, but the energy is balanced. If one cycle assumes greater momentum, the other suffers by losing energy – they are not independent systems. The challenge is to create a strong and vibrant short-term cycle, and an exciting and compelling long-term cycle. Dominance of either cycle breaks this balance and harmony. Balancing the impact of the short-term and the longer-term drivers is critical – an overemphasis on the short-term goals and levers and the organization descends into continuous, iterative, reactive movement without building the capability to meet the longer-term vision.

Bridging from philosophy to action

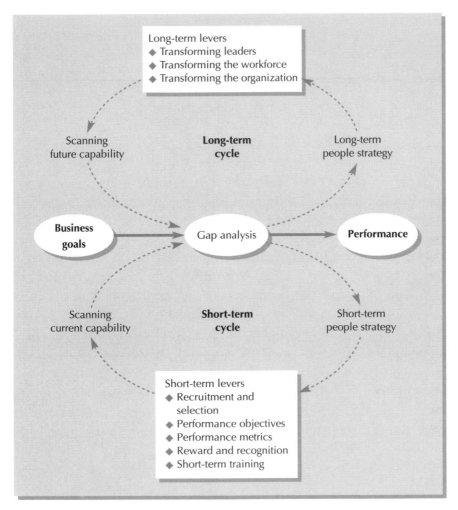

FIGURE 21 ◆ **The people process model**

Next come the issues of implementation. The outcome of the understanding of this alignment is a *people strategy* which describes the key
actions needed to bridge from the present to the future. Part of this strategy will examine the role played by the third element, the key *people process
levers* (e.g. selection, performance management, career development). It
will focus on those levers which are most appropriate to the delivery of the
short-term goals and the long-term strategy.

Element 3: a cluster of people process levers

The cycle described in Fig. 22 simply refers to the key activities, the sequence of these activities and the feedback loops between them. In reality the cycle operates within the context of time, with short-term elements spanning one year and longer-term elements spanning three to five years. For most organizations there is a dominant short-term cycle which follows the annual cycle of business planning – the creation of annual budgets and goals, the communication and commitment to these goals, the monitoring of performance and the annual ritual of agreeing performance-related pay and bonuses. This short-term cycle focuses on the rapid realignment of the business as the needs and aspirations of the business change. All the aspects of the cycle are crucial. Without the driving force of the goals and the vision, the actions lack energy and focus. Without the ability to monitor the current capability and understand the gap between aspiration and reality, actions are simply tactical responses to the most obvious problems, with limited understanding of what could be more profound issues. Without an understanding of the total system and the points of leverage, managers fail to see the bigger picture and the key emerging themes.

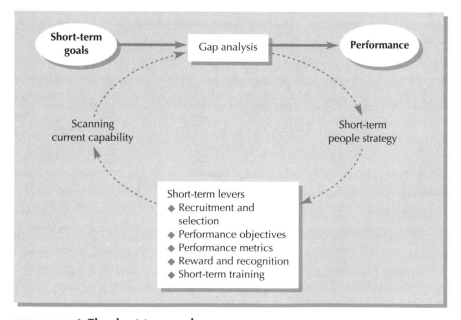

FIGURE 22 ◆ **The short-term cycle**

The energy of the short-term cycle comes from a collective agreement about the goals of the business, and an understanding of the capability of the business to deliver. Organizational capabilities and resources include the skills and motivation of the individual members of the organization, and the capability of the organization to deliver to the short-term business goals. From this understanding comes the short-term people strategy which focuses on those short-term actions that will be necessary to fine-tune the delivery of the goals. We saw earlier how managers at HP use the Hoshin to drive the short-term cycle of the business. In the short term there is limited potential to create systematic leverage. However, there are five possible process levers that can be realigned relatively quickly to meet subtle, annual adjustments in the business goals.

◆ Recruitment and selection

◆ Performance objectives

◆ Performance metrics

◆ Reward and recognition

◆ Short-term training

Recruitment and selection

In the space of one year of the short-term cycle it is possible to refocus the recruitment and selection criteria and processes to rapidly bring and promote the skills, capabilities and behaviours needed by the current business goals. Changing the competency profiles for key roles sends strong messages about what is valued. The recruiting of talent from the external labour market is the most critical first step to building the base of the organization. However, buying talent from outside may plug short-term skills and competency gaps, but the nature of the psychological relationship between these individuals and the organization is likely to be mercenary, where skilled individuals are attracted primarily by the financial contract. They are more likely to move on when a competing firm brings a better offer for their skills. So while the rapid deployment of skills and talent into the organization can have a crucial impact on the delivery of short-term goals, the systematic selection and retention of a stable and committed pool of talent cannot be achieved in the short term. For this we have to look to the longer-term cycle.

The characteristics of selection and recruitment processes which are aligned to the people strategy are:

◆ the basic competency and skill descriptions accurately reflect what is needed for the current business goals (i.e. there is strong vertical alignment) and future business goals (i.e. there is temporal alignment);

◆ the selection methods are capable of accurately identifying the needed competency profiles and skills;

◆ recruiting line managers accurately portray the business goals in the selection process;

◆ the selection process takes place in a manner which is judged to be fair by those participating.

Performance objectives

The first step in providing a context which defines performance expectations is to deploy and agree performance objectives which focus energy and key tasks on delivering the business goals. As we saw earlier, creating this vertical alignment between the business goals and individual performance creates a strong sense of shared meaning. The characteristics of performance objectives which are aligned to the people strategy are:

◆ the performance objectives reflect what is needed to the business goals (i.e. there is strong vertical alignment);

◆ there is a strong shared agreement between the manager and the individual about the nature and extent of the business goals and what has to be achieved to meet these goals;

◆ the objective setting takes place in a way which is judged to be fair and accurate.

Performance metrics

Performance can be realigned around business goals by creating performance metrics which measure, highlight and communicate these business goals.[2] These metrics are the means by which the contribution of the business unit to the organization can be recognized. Moreover, creating a broad understanding of performance is crucial to understanding the 'state of the system' and to leveraging organizational learning. The vertical alignment created between the business goal and individual performance allows managers to monitor the implementation of strategy and to learn either to adapt the strategy or change their behaviour.[3] The characteristics of performance metrics which are aligned to the people strategy are:

◆ the metrics accurately reflect the business goals;

◆ there is an appropriate mix of what has to be achieved (outcomes) and how it is achieved (behaviours);

◆ individuals are given feedback about their performance in an open manner;

◆ the appraisal takes place in a way which is judged to be fair and accurate.

Reward and recognition

What gets measured sends out strong messages and cues about what is important and valued. Realigning the reward processes reinforces the business goals and makes known those behaviours that support the business context. Reward and recognition can be one of the greatest sources of leverage available to a company in its quest to increase organizational performance and effectiveness.[4] There is the strongest potential for leverage when individual and team-based pay is high enough to encourage and reward effort, and when the basis of reward allocation is clear, fair and accepted. Our research shows that while aligning rewards to business goals is moving up the corporate agenda, the use of this potential lever is fraught with difficulties. For some companies the highly competitive environment in which they operate has created razor-thin profit margins, so the overriding focus is on containing costs, which wipes out the potential benefits of performance-related pay. For other companies the overriding perception is that while attempts have been made to accurately measure team or individual performance, the link between pay, job-related performance and business goals is not clear.

The characteristics of rewards which are aligned to the business strategy are:

◆ financial and non-financial rewards and recognition are in line with the implementation of the business goals;

◆ the financial rewards create a sense of shared meaning through their alignment with objective setting and metrics (horizontal alignment);

◆ the non-financial and financial rewards meet employee and organizational needs;

◆ the rewards process is judged to be fair and accurate.

Short-term training

Within a relatively short term it is possible to bring new skills into the organization, to realign the objectives and metrics, and to reshape the reward mechanisms. Within a relatively short timescale it is also possible to increase the skills and competency base through focused, skill-based training and coaching. Short-term business-focused training is a key lever in creating the flexible and multi-skilled workforce crucial to delivering short-term business performance. The speed of response depends on a clear and shared understanding of the skills necessary to deliver to the business goals, the provision of high-quality training, and the diagnosis of individual training needs. Short-term training and development is as much about participating in challenging jobs as off-line training. The characteristics of short-term training which is aligned to the business strategy are:

◆ training and development is capable of delivering to the business goals of the organization;

◆ individual skill needs are profiled and understood;

◆ managers are actively involved and sponsor training and development.

Creating alignment between the people processes of the short-term cycle and changing business goals is critical to organizational success. Without this capacity to realign, the processes remain incapable of selecting, developing and rewarding the skills and performance required of the current business goals and adapting these to align with the future vision. The short-term levers have a key role to play in reinforcing changing business goals and creating a shared sense of meaning about what is important.

The short-term cycle provides the opportunity to make relatively small, incremental, fine-tuned adjustments as the annual business goals emerge. The energy, feedback loops and levers of the cycle ensure the organization is capable of reacting relatively swiftly to changes in the competitive environment.

The long-term cycle

The short-term cycle is capable of making adjustments to meet the needs of changes to the business goals. But the organization also operates in a longer-term cycle, of three to five years, the speed at which more significant changes take place. For example, at Glaxo Wellcome the creation of a team-orientated culture could not occur simply through the realignment of the performance management processes. At Glaxo Wellcome this longer-term vision was supported by organizational restructuring and by re-skilling of the workforce. At Motorola the delivery of the business strategy in China required a fundamental transformation of the way in which the management cadre of the company would be selected and developed.

This longer-term timescale reflects the development of the knowledge base of the company, created through management skills and competencies. It is the timescale for building relationships and sharing through networks and teams, for the development of trust and inspiration. The levers of structural change, leadership development and a basic realignment of skills are not levers which bring instant results. They reflect the human timescale that operates over many years.

The long-term cycle is a mirror image of the short-term cycle (*see* Fig. 23). The energy for the system is created through an engaging and exciting vision. The extent of the gap between the vision for the future and the capability of the organization to deliver to this vision comes directly from scanning future capabilities. The long-term cycle has at the core those levers which are crucial to the organization yet for which the complexity and scale requires continued management commitment over many years. There are three key people processes which support the delivery of a longer-term vision:

◆ the capability to transform the leadership cadre of the organization;

◆ the capability to transform the skills and behaviours of the workforce;

◆ the capability to create organizational structures, roles and responsibilities aligned to the longer-term goals.

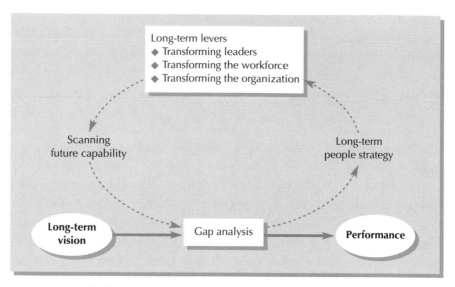

FIGURE 23 ◆ **The long-term cycle**

Transforming leaders

The vision of the future may well paint a picture of a leadership cadre that is very different from the current group. Inevitably, changing business environments need refocused business goals and different leadership skills. In the late eighties and early nineties the key leadership competencies at Glaxo Wellcome were the capacity to understand and analyze complex information, to create plans of action, to delegate these action plans to subordinates and to monitor progress. By the mid-nineties this leadership style was looking increasingly slow, bureaucratic and inappropriate. The decision to realign the business goals to emphasize speed and innovation required a change in leadership style. As one senior manager said at the time:

> 'We really need team players, leaders who can work in teams, who can excite and inspire. It is not sufficient to simply tell people what to do, that is the old style, and it's cumbersome. We need people who can take the bigger picture, who can create networks with their colleagues, who can support the innovation and creativity of their team.'

A raft of developmental experiences and the assignment of a personal coach to the key leaders of the businesses supported the short-term realignment of the leadership cadre at Glaxo Wellcome. Together they agreed those behaviours that would be most appropriate and the coach gave feedback and coaching. In the longer term, the challenge for the senior Glaxo Wellcome team was to realign the developmental experiences of future leaders of the young high-potential cadre from hierarchical to team skills. Historically, high-potential people were identified in their mid to late 20s, participated in a series of relatively short job assignments and received mentoring from senior figures in the business. While this raft of experiences developed their 'management' skills, it did little to develop the networking and team skills which would be so critical for the future. As a consequence, the development experiences were realigned to include longer periods in jobs so that teams could be developed, more cross-functional experiences to support networks and the development of trust and reciprocity, and an emphasis on coaching and development.

The characteristics of leadership development which is aligned to the business strategy are:

◆ the articulation of those leadership competencies that will be crucial to the future;

◆ the capacity to identify young people with the potential to develop these competencies;

◆ a range of developmental experiences capable of supporting these leadership competencies.[5]

Transforming the workforce

The contribution of leaders to creating sustained competitive advantage is well understood. But as companies decentralize and push responsibility through to teams, and as the customer-focusing roles become crucial, so there is increasing awareness of the crucial role played by the inspiration and skills of people in all key roles who have tacit knowledge of the organizational procedures or customers need. Sustained competitive advantage does not simply arise through the skills of the leadership cadre; it comes from the larger pool of people who make up the entire organization. This wider group can play a key role because they are directly involved in production of the product or service and are potentially less mobile, more committed and linked with the fate of the organization.

The process that transforms the skills of the workforce to meet future needs takes many years of management commitment, resources and focus. At the core of this commitment is an understanding of what future skill requirements will be, and a portfolio of development opportunities capable of reinforcing these skills. It is crucial to articulate a broad view of how the key skills in the industry sector are likely to change. Forecasting future skill needs is difficult, particularly in times of rapid change, but without this fundamental agreement the creation of management commitment is simply a dream.

The Leading Edge Research Consortium showed that while this commitment to the long-term development and retention of people with key skills may be vital, the policies and processes which support this commitment are fraught with difficulties. As we saw at BT Payphones, no Western company can now support a policy of lifetime employment. To do so would run counter to the long-term skill flexibility and cost effectiveness that may be central to success. As a result, companies face a paradox – dismantling the structures associated with long-term careers creates flexibility, but it also breaks the old psychological contract which may be crucial to retaining the commitment and motivation of key people. The challenge is to create career paths and development opportunities capable of providing hope for the future and pathways to the vision. The characteristics of workforce transformation which is aligned to the business strategy are:

◆ the articulation of those workforce competencies and skills that will be crucial to the future;

◆ a forecast of how skill needs will change in the industry;

◆ individual members of the workforce being clear about the future needs of the business, understand their present skills profile, and are aware of what they need to do to develop to meet future business needs;

◆ a range of training and development experiences capable of developing those fundamental workforce competencies;

◆ team leaders committed to the development of the workforce and enthusiastic and skilled in mentoring and supporting.

Transforming the organization

The long-term transformation of the organization complements the trans-formation of the workforce and leadership transformation. It provides the context in which work will take place. The organizational context includes the basic structure, the way in which roles and responsibilities are defined, and the use of project teams and task forces. Transformational capability rests with the ability to understand and articulate what will be appropriate in the future. It also rests on an ability to manage the changes associated with transformation. This is dependent on project management and change capability skills among a significant number of managers. The characteristics of organizational transformation which is aligned to the business strategy are:

◆ the articulation of the organizational design which is most appropriate to meet the needs of the business strategy;

◆ the capacity to implement and operationalize organizational design;

◆ change managerial skills to adjust the organizational design parameters as necessary.

Creating living strategy, the *path* of the journey

Creating this harmony between the short term and the long term is at the heart of the new agenda. Harmony plays to the importance of the human time frame; it balances the long-term and the short-term meaning of the organization. The case for a fundamental change in the way we think about people in organizations, creating a new agenda, and balancing the short term and the long term is the basis of much of my work.

Now we move on to the next task of building from the arguments and models to the capability to deliver – moving from the rhetoric of business goals to the reality of high performance. In moving the focus we will con-sider how visioning capabilities are built; how they become articulated through people-centred strategies and plans; and how these strategies and plans become embedded in actions which are capable of realigning the key people processes in a manner which is fair and just to individual members of the organization.

In the short-term and long-term cycles (see Fig. 23), the dynamics are shown in their true state, as a cycle of iteration in which all the elements occur simultaneously. Thus, the articulation of the vision for the future, the scanning of current and future capability, the awareness of the gap between the future needs and current capabilities, and the creation of a people strategy are all elements which are continuously adjusted with changes in the short-term business goals and the longer-term vision.

But in developing a more strategic, long-term and systemic way of thinking about people, inevitably these elements are seen not as a cycle but as a sequence of activities through which a management team progresses. In Part III, we will look at a detailed methodology which has the potential to act as a frame for putting people at the heart of corporate strategy. The roots of this methodology stretch back over a decade when it became clear to me that we would need a step change from the focus then on individual human resource processes such as selection, rewards or appraisal. By the early eighties there was a shared understanding of how these processes worked, and some notions of best practices. In other words, the basic building blocks were in place. What was lacking at that time was a real understanding of how these blocks could be fitted together, how they could be changed over time, and their impact on the performance of the business. Grappling with this problem in the early eighties I spent a couple of years as a member of a team of business strategists at PA Consulting Group. It became clear to me that some of the strategy debate would have real implications for the field of human resources. Henry Mintzberg's views on emerging strategy, the work of Arie du Geus on scenario planning at Shell, and Peter Senge's work on systems thinking all had real implications on the dilemmas we faced in putting people at the heart of corporate strategy.

At the same time, working as an adviser to a number of large, international companies, I was struck by the general lack of depth and the paucity of thinking about the future, particularly in terms of the people side of the business. Some companies did indeed have written human resource strategy documents, but these had been constructed in what appeared to be primarily an intellectual exercise. They were overly complex, contained many unrelated actions and had not gained line management support or commitment. In some cases line managers appeared unaware of their existence. In other companies there was no real debate about the people side of the business, with the majority of time delegated to the consideration of rates of growth and return on equity.

During this time I was able to build my understanding of what a living strategy could look like, of the elements of the journey's path. I believe that with regard to process the journey should take the following path:

◆ it should be capable of building wide involvement across the organization;

◆ it should work back from a vision of the future;

◆ it should be capable of creating alignment between the business goals and the context in which people work;

◆ it should be action orientated and build on the inspiration and commitment of people.

In 1988, I began to experiment with a visioning process in which groups of managers worked together to discuss and agree a vision of the future which had people at its centre. These discussions lasted a couple of days at a time and in some cases they involved people from different parts of the business and from different levels in the organization. Over the next five years I worked with more than 20 companies to help them develop a visioning capability. It became increasingly clear to me that the involvement of a wide group of people was key to the success of the project. Building a guiding coalition was crucial, and this is described in Step 1 of the six-step process. The initial visioning methodology began as a simple idea and remained so. I began to learn that the value came not from the complexity of the technique but from the depth and richness of the dialogue. This simple but powerful technique of visioning is described in Step 2.

I believe the visioning capability on its own can bring real benefits to a management team, and as I have argued earlier, is very much part of the new agenda. However, for these visions to be embedded they need to be grounded and linked to reality. This grounding formed the base of the second development of these ideas, with the creation of the risk matrix. This brings into the debate the concept of risk. Unlike many other areas of managerial concern, people aspects are rarely quantifiable in the same 'hard' terms as finance or markets. Faced with 'soft' information, the tendency is to create lists of possible actions. By introducing the concept of risk, the team is able to quantify the issues they face in relative terms, without having to convert between different realms of information. This simple matrix provides a frame for managers to debate two crucial issues: the key strategic factors for the future, and the current alignment, described through the capacity to deliver to these factors. Together these create a graphic representation of the areas of risk, where the organization is vulnerable, and those factors of high strategic impact and low current alignment. It is these factors of vulnerability which provide the core of the agenda for change. The risk matrix is described in detail in Step 3.

These rich and complex visions yielded descriptions of the future that reflected many facets. Over this time of experimentation I became aware of the need for simplicity and integration. It was not useful for managers to create a list of the 50 key factors for the future – they became drowned in the information and immobilized by its complexity. These were the intricate strategy documents that were going nowhere. The question of simplicity and integration was uppermost in my mind and I devised two ways of dealing with it. First, through prioritization, when managers are faced with the problem of choosing those factors they believe would really make a difference to the performance of the company. Second, I worked with the issues of complexity and integration by using the work of Peter Senge and his colleagues to create systemic maps that allowed us to see how the factors worked together. More importantly, these maps supported the team in their understanding of the dynamics of the system, how the factors influenced each other, how the feedback loops worked, and what would be the impact of changing any elements. The creation of these systems is described in Step 4.

The visioning and risk matrix workshops created energy and interest, but did they create change? In some companies they did, while in others they faded at the expense of yet another 'flavour of the month' exercise. By the late eighties I had worked with a number of large, complex companies to see how a more strategic, long-term approach to people could be created. Of these companies, I have described in some detail the work with the management team of Philips Lighting and will use Philips Lighting as an example of the six steps.

Figure 24 gives an overview of the sequence of steps to create a strategic approach to people. This sequence of activities begins with the building of a guiding coalition which will take the process through the steps that follow. This guiding coalition brings together people from many functions and levels in the organization. It is they who will create a vision

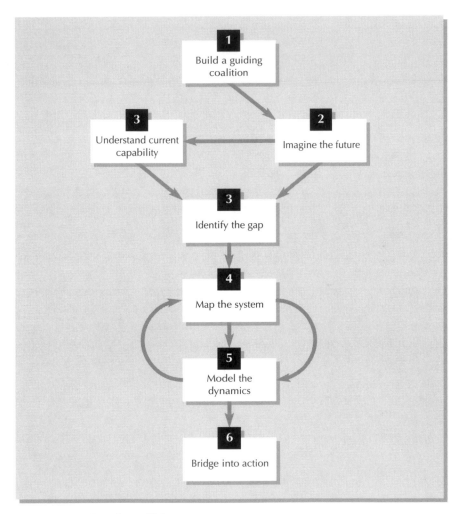

FIGURE 24 ◆ **Creating a living strategy**

for the future and provide much of the energy to actualize that vision. In the second step the vision is created, using as a frame the broad strategic direction of the organization. The visioning process then begins to generate strategic conversations in which the future can be debated and discussed. The third step involves scanning for current and future capability and understanding the gap or alignment between capability and vision. At this stage a dialogue about the people aspects of the strategy becomes more concrete. This understanding is deepened through Step 4 and Step 5 when a map of the system is created, and the dynamics are modelled. This modelling has three aspects: agreement of the broad themes which will be crucial to the delivery of the business goal; a description of the levers capable of delivering these themes; and the modelling of the forces and feedback loops which will form the system. Step 6 is an action step, designed to implement the ideas from the visionary session and risk matrix and gain traction.

Building on this six-step model will support your business in increasing its performance by putting people at the heart of its strategy. For each step I have articulated the guiding principles which led me to develop this step, a description of the tools to support the objectives of the step, and a description of the outcomes you can expect if the sequence is followed.

Building a guiding coalition

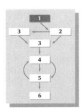 When Motorola invested heavily in building managerial skills and competencies in Chinese nationals; when Glaxo Wellcome refocused the reward policies to reinforce cross-functional and team-working; and when Hewlett-Packard worked to create a high commitment workforce, in each case they went against the norms of the time. Other Western multi-nationals in China relied on bringing in expatriates from their home markets; other pharmaceutical companies invested in building stand-alone research teams; and other computer manufacturers brought people in on short-term contracts and 'let go' of them when their skills were deemed less useful. How did it come about that Motorola, Glaxo Wellcome and HP were prepared to take the unconventional approach?

Each took the risk because there were a group of people in each of these companies who had a shared view of what that company could be in the future, people who were prepared to take the unconventional first step towards a future they found engaging and inspiring – to build a worldwide capability in personal communication; to be at the forefront of creating the next generation of life-saving drugs; to create information products that accelerate the advancement of knowledge and improve the effectiveness of people and organizations. In each case there was not simply managerial rhetoric but a vision and a set of actions against which hard management decisions could be taken.

Bucking the trend, taking the unconventional approach, doing the unexpected demands a shared and articulated view of how the organization will perform – a shared view of what the future could be, of the current reality, and of the steps which could lead from the present to the future.

Bucking the trend demands a shared and articulated view of how an organization will perform. The journey is one made by a group of people with shared hopes and dreams. The journey begins and is renewed through the creation and building of this guiding coalition. The ability of this coalition to sustain the journey rests on one critical guiding principle: the importance of broad involvement of people from all functions and all levels in the business.

The guiding principle

Involve multiple stakeholders

Visions wither and die and people lose interest before the ink on the page of the strategy plan has dried. The path forward that was agreed with such clarity and enthusiasm by the executive group becomes confused and ambiguous by the time it reaches those who are tasked to implement it. Earlier the three options for strategy creation were clearly described: the top-down, rational process; the emergence of strategy through discussions from employees at all levels in the organization; and the emergence of vision aided by a platform of processes designed to build visioning capability (*see* Fig. 9). In creating credible and involving visions we need a leadership cadre prepared to state where they see the organization going, combined with broad involvement of a wider constituency who can bring ideas, inspiration and, ultimately, the energy for action.

The creation of a vision, if it happens at all, is often seen as a managerial prerogative – the capability to visualize comes with age and seniority, wisdom and experience[1]. Certainly this can be true, but age and seniority also bring caution, cynicism ('we've seen it all before and it does not work') and a distance from the needs and aspirations of younger customers in the marketplace. It is the young people of the organization who will bring vitality to the creation and delivery of a vision, who can speak unburdened by years of politics and deals of reciprocity. It is their voice that should be heard when the future of the organization is discussed. We need diversity of views, diverse age groups and diverse functional experience. Without this diversity, the visions of the future are trite and predictable[2].

Tools and techniques

If we believe that learning and involvement are critical, then one of the earliest stages of creating a vision is to build the guiding coalition. We need to understand who the stakeholders are, how they should be involved, and how the visioning process should proceed. These stakeholders are capable of turning the rhetoric of strategy into the reality of action. Yet they are also capable of being the strongest critics of what will follow, and ensuring that it gets no further than rhetoric. It is they who will learn and share their ideas and inspirations. The membership of this guiding coalition can make or break everything that follows. For it is only through broad involvement and identification with the vision that people can have the 'face-offs' about resources that are such a critical aspect of the power and political structures of organizations. Involving people throughout the organization provides an opportunity to create a broad view of the future, to allow the collective dreaming, and to create trust and commitment through engaging and giving a voice to people regardless of grade or status.

Effective guiding coalitions are established when members play a crucial role because they have positional or influential power, have something important to say, or can bring a new angle to the discussion. The visioning exercise is part of what will be a long and tortuous journey. To develop an organization capable of bringing long-term competitive advantage needs strength and focus, courage and fortitude. It needs the active involvement of people who have power or influence within the organization. Creating an organization that is aligned to its business goals involves changing some of the hard wiring in the system, and this requires determination and courage. There are five potential stakeholders in the guiding coalition: senior managers, team or line managers, the front-line operating core, younger members of the organization, and human resource professionals. Each brings a unique perspective and source of energy. Without each of these stakeholders the probability of success will be reduced.

These five stakeholder groups are vital to the whole process. But each plays a particularly crucial role as the steps unfold.

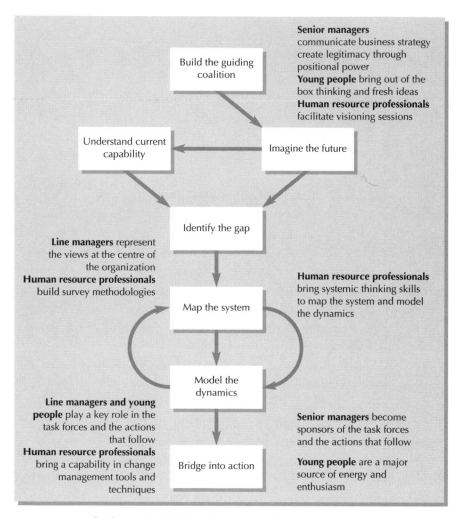

Senior managers communicate business strategy create legitimacy through positional power
Young people bring out of the box thinking and fresh ideas
Human resource professionals facilitate visioning sessions

Build the guiding coalition

Understand current capability

Imagine the future

Identify the gap

Line managers represent the views at the centre of the organization
Human resource professionals build survey methodologies

Map the system

Human resource professionals bring systemic thinking skills to map the system and model the dynamics

Model the dynamics

Line managers and young people play a key role in the task forces and the actions that follow
Human resource professionals bring a capability in change management tools and techniques

Bridge into action

Senior managers become sponsors of the task forces and the actions that follow

Young people are a major source of energy and enthusiasm

FIGURE 25 ◆ **The key stakeholder roles in building a people-centred strategy**

Step 1 in action

Building the guiding coalition at Philips Lighting

Each management team embarks on creating a people-centred strategy in the way they believe is most appropriate for their context. At Philips Lighting, a business of the Philips Company, I have had the pleasure of working with the management team from the early nineties. Since then we have had an opportunity to explore some of our thinking and to refine the steps and tools. I am therefore delighted that the management team have allowed their journey to be used to illustrate the six steps.

The journey began for Philips Lighting late in 1993. In November of that year, John Vreeswijk, head of research and development, gathered together his management team in the company's head office in Eindhoven, Holland, to discuss the performance of the lighting business. At this meeting were Peter Gilsing, Wim Konijnendijk, Rob Peters and Hans Van Reenen. With two members of the human resource group present, the conversation focused particularly on the people capabilities of the business. During that meeting and over the next couple of weeks the management team made a realistic appraisal of the global business. By late November, the review was complete. A note from John Vreeswijk captured the mood.

> '*Our environment is changing. Where lights used to be relatively simple products, and controlling the materials and chemistry were the most important technologies, lamps are now very rapidly becoming parts of larger products. They are integrated with electronics, or in a reflector, or in even larger suppliers, and electronics, design and mechanical product engineering are becoming important technologies next to traditional chemistry and physics. Energy saving was always a driving force for lamp innovation, but is reinforced now by care for the environment and by legislation. Reusing and recycling of materials are now important drivers for innovation. The market in Europe and the Americas is changing, due to the increased demand for excellent logistic service, and our customers are merging and accumulating more power. The market in Asia-Pacific is opening and growing at high rates, and also Eastern Europe has opened up. With the opening of the global market, competition is becoming more intense. Following changes in society, lighting will be seen more and more as a design tool, an element to create impressions and images, a means to express individual identity. The pace of change has been set in Asia-Pacific and will increase considerably.*'

The review showed that with 15 per cent of the world market in lighting, the Philips business was battling it out with its key US competitor, General Electric. The review emphasized the need to keep costs down while creating an innovative and customer-focused product range. The team were well aware that the balance between innovation and customer focus would be crucial. The innovation rate at that time (where only 25 per cent of sales came from products less than five years old) was not sufficient to meet rapidly changing customer needs. But the team were also aware of the need to globalize the company. In 1993, only 10 per cent of turnover came out of the Asia-Pacific area. Yet it was clear that Asia-Pacific would increasingly be a key region in which the competitive battle would be fought. This would require the transformation of an organization that still had the majority of its research and development capability and manufacturing bases in Europe to one with truly global capabilities.

Stretching the innovative capacity of the business, reaching further into Asia-Pacific, and keeping the cost base world competitive would demand a whole new set of management skills, a more global structure, and a quicker pace of reaction. The management team understood that this was an opportunity to build the capability of Philips Lighting by involving and energizing people throughout the business. I began to work with the team late in 1993. At that stage the business and people processes showed a highly centralized, bureaucratic business, paper driven and focused on short-term actions.

Up to that point the senior team had set broad business targets and the human resource function identified the problems and went about solving them. Over the years this had created a short-term, action-based team engaged primarily in problem solving. It was clear that these tactics would not be sufficient to create the leap into the future. Reviewing the current processes and future challenges, the team made two key decisions: they would move from engaging with the present to engaging with the future, and they would move from being top down to being more involving and participatory in their decision making and actions.

This was not an easy decision to take. Up to that point the management team in Eindhoven had taken most of the key managerial decisions and these had been communicated down the line. In our initial discussions we increasingly approached the view that to continue to do so would severely reduce the probability of success – we had to engage a broad group of people and hear their views on the future of the business. Reflecting back to that time, I can appreciate the courage of John Vreeswijk. How much easier it would have been for him to simply repeat old practices, to concentrate on the business of the coming year, develop operational plans, discuss those with the HR team and identify key action plans. But he knew this would not be sufficient. So in 1993 he and his team took a courageous leap to start from the future and to involve a broad group of people. As we discussed at the time, developing visionary sessions would create its own momentum, if we involved people in visionary sessions, they would naturally presume that action would take place. By widening the base of decision making we were well aware that we had created something which would have a life of its own. But we were also aware that the energy and excitement of this group could be crucial to its success.

In building the guiding coalition we decided to involve a wide group of people from different functions and levels in the lighting organization. Over a three-month period 40 people participated in five visioning workshops. As the process evolved, the benefits of this coalition became clear. The younger members of the group in particular, being less shackled with the past, were able to speak about topics others didn't feel able to discuss and bring fresh ideas to the challenges. In my notes at the time I captured some of the views of these early participants.

'It is great to be involved, I really believe in Philips Lighting and appreciate the opportunity to talk about the future' – a young researcher.

'It's about time people from this level were listened to. We are too focused on Eindhoven and those outside do not get an opportunity to put their views across. I am glad that someone is listening to me' – a team leader in Belgium.

As important to the later stages was their enthusiasm and energy. They felt deeply committed to the visions they had created. When the process began to lose momentum, it was often the younger members of the group who pushed forward and wanted to use their skills to keep the momentum going.

In Step 2 we review how this guiding coalition set about visioning the future.

How do you benefit?

Building a guiding coalition is a crucial first step to the process of putting people at the centre of strategy. If a broad range of stakeholders are involved from the very beginning, you can anticipate the following positive outcomes from this first step:

◆ a broad range of views and ideas;

◆ the beginning of a high-quality strategic dialogue throughout the organization;

◆ the opportunity to really engage managers in the people side of strategy, and in particular to participate in the resource 'face-offs' which will be so crucial to later success;

◆ the energy and sponsorship which will propel the actions which follow.

Where do you stand now?

Consider your own process of building a people-centred strategy. How much are a broad group of shareholders involved? Reaping the benefit described earlier requires broad involvement. Test your business by checking these five scenarios. Choose the one which most accurately describes the current situation in your company. Mark your current situation in the profile presented in Section 3 of the Living Strategy Workbook.

Understanding current capabilities

Very broad involvement (very strong)

The strategic direction of the people aspects of the business is discussed by a *broad range of stakeholders* across various functions of the business. This includes senior and middle managers, human resource professionals and people in customer and market-facing roles. Younger members of the business take part in these discussions and their voice is heard. These *groups are actively involved in the task forces* which follow.

Broad involvement (strong)

The people aspects of the strategic direction of the *business are discussed by senior managers, line managers and human resource professionals*. There is some involvement of younger people. There is some involvement of this broad group in the task forces and actions which follow.

Average involvement (average)

The people aspects of the strategic direction are discussed by senior managers, line managers and the human resource function. There is *limited*

---

involvement of younger people and those from wider functions. There is some continued involvement of this group in the implementation phases.

Weak involvement (weak)

The people aspects of the strategic direction of the business are primarily *discussed initially within the human resource function*. These discussions are then reviewed with line managers and colleagues. There is *limited involvement of a broader range of potential stakeholders* such as line managers, operating core or young people. The primary members of the task forces are the human resource function.

Very weak involvement (very weak)

Discussions about the people aspects of the strategy take place in an *ad hoc manner* within the human resource function. There is *very limited involvement* of others in the process either at this stage or at the action stage.

Moving forward

The line manager's role

Looking back to the early experience at Philips Lighting, it is clear to me that the line manager's role is crucial:

◆ first, to have the courage and value set to create broad involvement and start from the future, when narrow involvement and present focus may well be more palatable;

◆ second, to continue to support and sponsor the whole process. In particular at this early stage, to work with the team to choose and brief those who will be involved in the visioning sessions;

◆ finally, to work closely with human resource colleagues to ensure that this is seen as a line management activity and centrally important to the business, not as a one-off, HR-driven initiative.

The human resource role

The senior HR professional has to be part of the business team for this approach to work. This became clear at Philips Lighting where John

Vreeswijk included the professional advice of his HR colleagues and was prepared to work in this multi-functional way. The HR professional has three key roles:

◆ to engage the senior team in the decision about broad involvement;

◆ to work to select a good mix of people to take their place within the guiding coalition;

◆ to ensure that members of the coalition are given sufficient space and resources to participate, and to sell the benefits of the process.

Summary of specific actions

1.1 Identify the broad groups of people from the various parts of the organization. Build a group of 20–40 people.

1.2 From this larger group create smaller working teams of six people who can participate in the visioning sessions.

1.3 Work with each team to identify the likely time and resource involvement. Ensure that this is seen as an important part of their work and sufficient resources are put in place to support them.

1.4 Communicate the broad aims and plans of this process to the wider audience.

Imagining the future

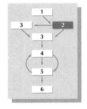 The creation of a shared vision is at the heart of a people-centred strategy. This section explores Step 2, how a visioning capability can be created and become part of the everyday actions of people in the organization, not a one-off activity or a fad for a month, but a way of thinking about the future and about people which has meaning – a way of collective dreaming, raising the excitement level, and focusing on the shared agendas.

We look at how to kick off the hard conversations about what is really important for the future and how these collective dreams can become a reality, capable of balancing short-term with long-term aspirations by creating a 'memory of the future' which is so strong, so powerful and so engaging that the future assumes greater importance. We look at developing a people-centred strategy that creates meaning by building symbols for the future, is understandable, and develops action that propel the organization towards this future.

This approach to imagining the future is based on four guiding principles.

The guiding principles

Guiding principle 1: Look back from the future

To create people-centred strategies we must build on and acknowledge the very essence of humanness: the human relationship to time, the search for meaning, the soul. Understanding the time dimension brings with it the need to operate simultaneously in the present and the future, to build from the future back to the present. The challenge here is to engage with the excitement and vitality of the future and to use this source of energy to propel the plan forward. Focusing on the short-term concerns simply engages the business in a cycle of slow iteration and tactics. Making the big leap needs a break with the concerns and politics of the present. The routes of strategic discussion were illustrated in Fig. 8.

Take Route 2 and begin this process with the excitement and exhilaration of the future.

Discussions about the future will be broad and will continue over the years. We cannot accurately describe the future, but what we can do is build the capacity to discuss it in a way that remains relatively broad and unconstrained. In a sense, what is crucial here is not the goal itself but the creation of groups of people who are energized to build the knowledge and skills to bridge the future.[1]

Effective visions create broad directions which simplify the more detailed decisions that follow, and by doing so co-ordinate the actions which allow people to work independently but still within the frame of the general direction. They are credible yet appealing, creating a picture of the future which is energizing and responsive to current (or anticipated) problems. Engaging visions provide a balance of specificity, allowing people to understand the general direction, yet remain somewhat ambiguous and sufficiently flexible so that people can add their own insights and adapt the vision with changing needs. Visions can be important for various reasons: as directional and signalling mechanisms; as symbols, to provide a point for rallying and identification; and as learning tools, to help individuals understand the events around them.

In Route 2, the long-term implications are clear. But what is the time frame between the future and the present? Should we consider the future to be the coming year, or a decade away? Consider the people process model described in Fig. 21. The short-term cycle operates over an annual timescale and contains processes such as selection, appraisal and rewards which could be realigned over a year. The long-term cycle has within it levers which take many more years to realign, the development of a leadership cadre, the re-skilling of the workforce, the realignment of the basic organizational structure. The people process model suggests that the time frames for the development of people and the organization are a balance between the short-term processes of recruitment, performance management and training, and the long-term processes of leadership, workforce and organizational development. If we plan now for leaders who will take a significant role over the next decade, or describe an organizational structure which may take four years to implement, the vision has to have some capacity to bridge to this future. The time frame of this process should reflect the human time frame. A distance of five years for most companies is sufficiently far out of the present to allow creativity, but not so far as to provoke incredulity.

Guiding principle 2: Keep the process simple

I believe simplicity is crucial. When I began developing the visioning exercise, I experimented with many different approaches and tools. Some were sophisticated, involving the creation of scenarios and based on the collection of large amounts of analytical data. Others were simple, involving managers working together to share their views of the future. What became apparent was that the complexity of the more sophisticated processes was diverting managers' attention. They were so keen to 'get it right', to take all the information into consideration, that they had little energy left to debate the implications of the scenarios and to move on to action. Creating scenarios had an added difficulty in rapidly changing environments such as telecommunications where it is hard to find a single factor (such as the oil price for Shell) on which to hang the multiple scenarios. As a consequence, the early scenario work was relatively unsuccessful, so I began to develop simpler and more transparent visioning processes that encouraged people to debate and converse unencumbered by complex rules and procedures.

It is easy to become embroiled in complex, multi-staged actions that involve the collection and assimilation of a vast array of information about the future and about current capability. Faced with the complexity of such information, management attention focuses on analysis rather than action. Simply participating in the visioning exercise becomes an end in itself, and once completed there is a sigh of relief and a tailing off of commitment and excitement. The visioning stage should be attempted with speed, elegance and simplicity.

Guiding principle 3: Measure success through the richness of dialogue

This whole endeavour will live or die simply on the depth and richness of the strategic dialogue it generates. The process itself has no other real function. Unless people from across the organization begin to debate the future of the company, unless they are invigorated and excited and are prepared to take action, this becomes another piece of managerial bureaucracy which will atrophy as soon as management attention lapses.[2]

Guiding principle 4: Focus on the few themes which will make a real difference

One of my early recollections of working on a visioning exercise with a strategy team is that at the end we identified the 50 actions that could make a real difference to the company. While these were important, the management team drowned in them. If we believe that continuity and consistency are important, and that people create a shared sense of meaning, we have to examine how we describe and communicate the future. Fifty points of action confuse and irritate. The principle here is to identify those three, four or possibly five themes which could really make a difference and with which people can identify and believe in. We need to create a message which is simple but compelling, and has sufficient clarity and focus to remain intact as it moves through layers of communication and interpretation.[3]

The tools and techniques

The broad aim of visioning is to provide a structure and 'permission' for the dialogue about the future to take place. To be successful it has to be engaging and exciting. But it must also clarify the general direction, focus on those key themes that will really make a difference, and identify what could stop the vision from becoming a reality. The initial meetings will create a first draft which will be refined and discussed over the coming months. In time it may be that the group wants to move to a higher level of sophistication, involving the generation of alternative scenarios. But for those for whom visioning is a relatively new experience, the emphasis should be on keeping it simple. In the spirit of simplicity, my entry into the visioning is basic and designed to create a forum for the strategic debate about people to take place.

The visionary step begins with the creation of sub-groups of the guiding coalition. These sub-groups initially spend one day together participating in the visioning process, beginning with a review of the broad strategic goals of the business. This may include, for example, market share, product development or customer base. The group then imagine that these strategic goals have been met and describe their vision of the organization capable of delivering these goals. There are two tools which support the journey of visualization:

◆ visualizing around the five key factors;

◆ prioritizing the vision.

Tool 2.1: visualizing around the five key factors

The exact timescale of the projected visualization depends upon the temporal frame of the organization and its strategy, but is typically five years. In visualizing the future, the group imagines that five years have passed, and each of the company's strategic goals has been achieved.[4] These descriptions of the future are framed by the five broad factors described in Fig. 26. In my experience, these factors are sufficiently broad to allow a wide-ranging discussion to take place.

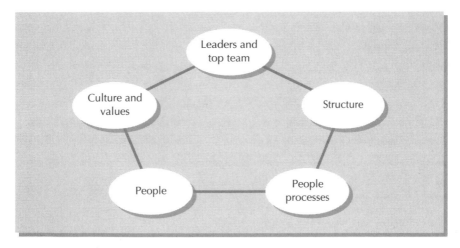

FIGURE 26 ◆ **Visualizing around the five key factors**

There are a number of ways to start the visualization. I tend to approach it in a somewhat playful manner in role play as a researcher. This is what I typically say:

> *'It is five years from now and I am an external researcher who has approached your organization to understand it in more detail and to try to pinpoint with you the basis of its success. I would like you to walk me through this company, to visualize it five years hence.'*

Then:

> *'From this description I would like you to identify the ten strategic factors which are central to your company in the future. Of all the factors that are important, what are the ten that are most central to the vision? From these ten strategic factors, select the three that have the highest impact, the three or four that have medium impact, and assign low impact to the remaining strategic factors.'*

Here are some questions you may want to think about for each of the five factors.

The leaders and top team

◆ Describe the top team. Who are they? Have they grown up with the company or have they been recruited from outside the organization? What is their international experience expertise?

◆ What are their common cognitive frames, experience, aspirations and visions?

◆ What are the key leadership characteristics?

◆ How effectively do the team work together?

◆ Who are the key stakeholders?

The structure

◆ How is the organization structured? What are the key characteristics of the formal and informal structure and processes? What is the balance between centralization and decentralization?

◆ What are the primary co-ordination processes?

◆ What is the primary structure through which work is achieved? How many levels are there and what is the basic organizing unit?

◆ What is the degree of specialization and division of labour?

◆ How are teams used?

◆ What are the key systems and processes of the organization?

The culture and values

◆ What are the culture and values? What are the core beliefs of the organization?

◆ What are the norms of behaviour? What do people value?

◆ What is the management philosophy?

◆ What is the operating style? How do people in the organization operate and interact with each other?

People processes

◆ What are the key mechanisms and criteria by which people are recruited, selected, promoted, inducted?

◆ What are the performance variables for which performance is appraised and rewarded? How are rewards allocated?

◆ What will characterize effective performance?

◆ What is measured and talked about?

◆ Who gets developed? What are the key aspects of development and career progression?

◆ How are leaders developed and succession issues resolved?

The people

◆ What are the motivations and aspirations of people? What is their level of commitment and trust?

◆ What skills and behaviours are necessary to meet the business goals?

◆ What is the dominant psychological contract between individuals and the organization?

The five key factors provide a framework for the group to use brainstorming to visualize the future and explore and share their 'memories of the future', and imagine what their company could be like. This sharing of visions is extremely personal – it needs space and time to foster the opportunities to be able to speak the unspeakable, to expose the sacred cows and to create a feeling of integrity and trust. Energy and excitement is high and there is also tension around whether people are sounding intelligent, whether they are 'on the right track' and whether they are being profound. Think of it as a brainstorm, an opportunity for each member of the group to share their personal vision, talking through what will make them excited and inspired.

The rules of brainstorming are simple: let each member of the team speak, don't interrupt, don't analyze or criticize . . . just let it be. A team of six will have begun to speak about their vision of the future over a period of approximately two hours. The dreams begin to take form, the hopes find a way of expressing themselves, the team begin to create a field of mutual respect, shared ideas, hopes and dreams. The energy of this collective dreaming is vital to the process – it inspires excitement and fosters support and mutuality. People feel privileged to have their voices heard and they find it moving to hear other dreams of the future.

Tool 2.2: prioritizing the vision

The first phase ends with team members recording their many ideas on flip charts. The next phase is about prioritization, consolidation and consensus seeking. The aim is to create broad agreement about the aspects of the vision which are really important. Focusing on ten strategic factors kick off the process of discussing priorities – those which are of highest strategic impact, medium strategic impact and lowest strategic impact:

◆ *High strategic impact*: those factors that have been crucial to the business as it is described in the future. Without these factors, it would be impossible to achieve the business goals and vision;

◆ *Medium strategic impact*: the factors that are important to the actualization of the vision, but are not as crucial as those of high strategic impact;

◆ *Low strategic impact*: those factors that are least vital to the delivery of the vision. However, since they are in the top ten, they remain important.

Clearly this is a somewhat artificial ranking. But the aim is to force consensus and to create pressure for the group to begin the 'face-off' discussions and negotiations which are so much a part of resource allocation. This prioritization is also the beginning of the later emergence of the themes, and forms one of the axes of the risk matrix which will be discussed in the next step. The group has begun the process of refinement into the three or four themes that will form the basis of the plan for action.

This visioning process provides a channel through which people can make themselves heard. It triggers people to develop their knowledge by communicating to the outside world and contributing to the common pool of knowledge from which the shared view emerges. By now the members of the group are beginning to understand each other's vision of the future of the business, and how these differ from their own. They are often surprised to discover that their colleagues in other areas of the business do not share their visions. This exploration of the learning process is the bedrock of the dialogue about the strategically critical factors.

Step 2 in action

Imagining the future at Philips Lighting

In 1993, at Philips Lighting, a number of broad strategic business goals for the next five years were discussed by the senior executive team and agreed on as a frame of reference by the visioning teams:[4]

◆ Philips Lighting business would grow to approximately 25 per cent of the world's market in lighting.

◆ It would be the No 1 premium choice in Europe and the best alternative to the rest of the world.

◆ It would be No 1 in customer satisfaction.

◆ Return on equity would be higher than its key competitors, General Electric and Osram.

◆ The business would be the market leader in energy-saving products and equal to its major competitors in environmental friendliness and customer satisfaction.

◆ With regard to innovation, more than 40 per cent of turnover would be supplied from products less than five years old.

◆ The business would be a lean manufacturer of mature products.

◆ More than 50 per cent of turnover would come from the Asia-Pacific region (primarily through joint ventures and acquisitions). This strong global presence would be supported by strong R&D bases in Asia-Pacific, the US, Europe and Eastern Europe, and strong manufacturing bases in Asia-Pacific, the US, Europe, Eastern Europe and the rest of the world.

This was a demanding and inspirational set of strategic goals. At the time of the exercise in 1993, Philips Lighting held 15 per cent of the world's market in lighting, had 10 per cent of its turnover from Asia-Pacific, had the majority of its R&D and manufacturing bases in Europe, while only 25 per cent of its sales came from products which were less than five years old.

The broad parameters of the vision were clear to many participants in the visioning session. What was less clear was what an organization capable of delivering this vision would actually look like. In visualizing the future, the groups considered many aspects. To give a view of the depth and breadth of the vision I will present the ten areas of strategic importance from one of the early groups.

The group identified two structural factors that would have a high impact on the delivery of the vision: *a structure capable of delivering a market and business creation orientation* and a *network-driven organization*. They visualized an organization structured to meet the needs of customers around the world, with a strong regional orientation and close integration between the research, manufacturing and sales centres. They described these centres as closely linked by real-time networked information and video conferencing. This network structure would be supported through projects running at the level of the plant, with project leaders pulling projects from product creation to local market introduction.

The global nature of the company was described in many of the factors that were assigned medium importance. The *senior management cadre represent the major markets* in which Philips Lighting operates and have a deep understanding of international business, supported by cross-functional and cross-country business expertise. This global management cadre would be mirrored in a *global skill set*, in which individual profiles of skills, competencies and work experience would be shared across the world. This would facilitate getting the right people into the right place, and create movement across the functions and countries. *Knowledge of areas such as miniaturization, integration and product design*, team working and information technology skills are critical. At the centre of this global organization are groups of *high-performing teams*, capable of operating across functional and regional boundaries, and bringing product innovation to the customer. Still on the global theme, but judged of low strategic impact, was *global recruitment*. In its description of the future, Philips had close relationships with universities, particularly in Asia, and these links provided a rich source of recruits and ensured that the population was made up of people representing the major regional markets in which the business operates.

Many people spoke of the importance of performance management in their vision of the future. They visualized an organization with *transparent and clear objectives*, in which individual responsibilities were clear, and individual goals reached through a consensus. As a consequence, employees were motivated to contribute to the business objectives. This clarity of objectives would be supported by a *variable reward package* based on ROE of lighting, and there would be a clear and transparent relationship between the performance of the business and the remuneration of individuals. At least 20 per cent of salary would be directly related to the ROE of the business. These reward mechanisms would be capable of rewarding teamwork and innovation. Finally, judged of lower strategic impact was the creation and development of an *entrepreneurial and innovative culture* which allows failure and provides space to grow and in which people are prepared to take risks and do not give up easily.

How do you benefit?

Imagining the future is a crucial step in building a people-centred strategy. In this step the guiding principles have been the importance of starting with the future and working with and building in human time frames. Both these guiding principles spring from the fundamental tenets of individuals. The other guiding principles are focused on the process itself, the importance of keeping it simple, measuring the success through the richness of dialogue, and focusing on a number of themes.

The visualizing process proceeds through two phases. In the first phase the guiding coalition works in small teams to visualize the future within the frame of five key factors. In the second phase each group identifies the ten strategic factors which they believe will be most critical to success and rates them according to high, medium and low strategic impact.

The Philips Lighting dialogue gives some flavour of the benefits and potential outcomes of Step 2. There are two benefits which are central to this step:

◆ *a deep strategic dialogue about the future*: I believe this is one of the most profound benefits of the six steps. The visioning session provides permission and a frame to explore the future. The dialogue is exciting and rich. It creates the source of energy which will propel much of the subsequent action;

◆ *a shared understanding of the priorities*: broad, unfocused discussions of the future may initially generate enthusiasm and energy, but this is quickly dissipated unless this energy is focused on a number of specific points of action. This step begins the process of prioritization by asking the group to consider the strategic impact of the factors they have discussed. As a consequence they move on to the next step with a clear agenda of those areas which need to be addressed.

Where do you stand now?

Visioning capability is central to the development of a people-centred strategy. It can build around the human time frames and create a shared sense of meaning. Brief descriptions of visioning capability are presented below. Choose the description which most accurately reflects the current visioning capability of your business and mark it on the profile presented in the workbook section.

Understanding current capabilities

Very strong visioning capability

Cross-functional teams work through an ongoing process in which they *discuss the visions for the future*. These visions are described against *a number of key variables, some of which refer to people*. In particular there is debate about the potential structure of the company; the culture; senior management; people; and people processes. These discussions create an understanding of some of the *key people determinants for future success* and how these can be measured and mapped against current capabilities.

Strong visioning capability

Visioning the future is not a well established ongoing process in the organization. However, there are *structured* opportunities for cross-functional groups to meet to discuss long-term business goals and the impact on people issues. A range of key variables is considered. These will tend to be those variables which are most *pertinent to the current situation*, or to problems the teams have encountered in the past. As a consequence there is a *broad understanding of where the organization should be heading with regard to people*.

Average visioning capability

While there are *no systematic processes* in place to facilitate discussions about the future, there are groups of managers who through *ad hoc task forces* meet to consider *one or two people issues* which are considered to have a potential long-term impact on the organization. These people issues are likely to be those which are a *current problem*, and seen to be a problem in the longer term. For these issues the response may well be *strategic rather than tactical*.

Weak visioning capability

There are *no processes to facilitate the discussion* of the people aspects of the future. However, individual managers are *encouraged to plan* for the immediate future. These plans refer principally to *broad targets for numbers and skills sets*.

Very weak visioning capability

There are no *processes in place which encourage or facilitate managers* to meet and discuss their vision of the future and people imperatives associated with this vision. The focus is on the *delivery of current objectives*. As a consequence, there is *very limited awareness* of the alignment between the people requirements of the future and current capabilities.

Plot your position of the six steps in Section 3 of the Living Strategy Workbook.

Moving forward

The line manager's role

The creation of a strong and deep strategic dialogue about people can occur only through sustained management interest and commitment. There are three key roles for line management at this stage of the process:

◆ to present a clear and articulate view of the broad future business goals. These goals should be demanding yet plausible;

◆ to build time for the visioning sessions and encourage the participation of the guiding coalition;

◆ to participate in the visioning session without dominating or letting their views become paramount.

The cues to creating an open and engaging debate in the visioning session will come from the behaviour of the senior managers. If they dominate the discussion or fail to listen to the views of others, it will become clear that the process is a sham.

The human resource role

The role of the human resource professional is to facilitate the visioning session. My advice here is to have a 'light hand' in the proceedings. In fact, the groups need very little facilitation, but two aspects should be kept in mind:

◆ ensure that a single individual (often a senior manager) does not dominate the discussion. If this occurs, it will have a detrimental effect on the subsequent actions. Reminding the group of the brainstorming conventions can be useful here;

◆ ensure that all five factors are discussed. In some groups the preference is to go through each factor and describe the organization of the future. This is useful but should not be the only source of discussion. The group should also visualize in a broader manner.

Summary of specific actions

2.1 Review the plan for the visioning sessions and ensure that commitment has been gained to the time and resource implications.

2.2 Describe the key business goals for the future. Use these as the entry into the visioning session.

2.3 Working with groups of about six, facilitate a discussion about the future using the five-factor model. Ensure that the group has sufficient time to do this. If possible, run parallel sessions so that each visioning group can present and test out their views on members of the other groups.

2.4 Remind the group of the rules of brainstorming and ensure that they record their thoughts on flip chart paper. Once the brainstorm is exhausted, encourage the group to focus their attention on the ten strategic factors and assign them high, medium and low impact.

2.5 If running parallel groups, ask each to present their ten strategic factors as a basis for debate and discussion.

Understanding current capability and identifying the gap

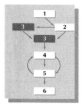

The visioning step creates a clear view of what the company can be and agreement of the strategic factors that will underpin the future. The next step is understanding where the organization is now and the gap between the aspirations of the future and the reality of the present.

The guiding principles

There are two principles which guide this step: the importance of really understanding reality, and the principle of risk analysis.

Guiding principle 1: Create a deep understanding of the current state

Beginning with the future creates a broad aspirational force that energizes and reinvigorates. But to move from aspiration to action requires a thorough and shared understanding of the current reality of the organization. This involves grasping the reality of the way the leaders work together and communicate their vision; the structure of the organization and how ideas are shared and decisions made; the culture of the organization, including the norms of behaviour and the 'unwritten rules of the game'; the way in which the key people processes are embedded and operate deep within the organization; and finally, the commitment, skills and inspiration of people throughout the company. Without this understanding of the current situation it is impossible to truly see the gap between the aspirations of the future and the reality of the present and be able to build the bridges of action from the present to the future.[1]

In this step I have argued that collecting information about the current states is crucial to the six-step process. Actually, much of the information on behaviours and attitudes (e.g. employee satisfaction or organizational health surveys, technical competency, test scores, and even observations of behaviour demonstrated in performance appraisal and customer satisfaction surveys) is often collected by organizations. This information is typically collected at the individual level, although often sampled, rather than universally representative. These measures are typically aggregated for analysis and used to capture snapshots for problem resolution rather than to regularly and consistently track measures for achieved and continued guidance.

Guiding principle 2: Use the risk matrix to identify gaps

All too often an organization takes a cursory glance at the current capability, builds up an idealized view of the future and overestimates the capability to bridge the gap. As a consequence it embarks on a plethora of unrelated and unintegrated initiatives. The result of this over-optimism is cynical employees (they have seen it all before, it is 'death by a thousand initiatives') and frenzied activity followed by managerial disappointment with the lack of speed and outcome. The actions taken are too simple, too unintegrated and too under-resourced. The second guiding principle in this step is the importance of creating a shared understanding of the nature and extent of the risks faced in meeting the vision, and specifically the risks of not changing fundamental aspects of the company. This notion of risk energizes, focuses and channels resources. By concentrating on the risks, the teams begin to understand the two or three themes that will be crucial for the future, which are central to the delivery of the future vision but for which current capability is underdeveloped.[2]

The tools and techniques

There are two tools which aid this step:

◆ understanding current capability;

◆ using the risk matrix to identify the gap.

Tool 3.1: understanding current capability

Diagnosing current capability is far from simple. Like an iceberg, some parts are more visible than others. The most visible aspects of current reality are the written policies about how people will be managed. 'We are employers of choice.' 'We pay for performance.' 'Our training is designed to reinforce customer satisfaction.' These are all policy descriptions in Fig. 27.

But below the surface are the actual mechanics of the people processes and structures, the way performance is rewarded, the extent of training. As our research has shown, there is often a gap between perceptions of the extent of process embedding and the reality. These realities surface only through focus groups, interviews and surveys. At the deepest level of organizational capability are the skills, behaviours and attitudes of individuals. It is these behaviours that drive organizational performance, yet in many companies there is limited understanding of current behaviour.

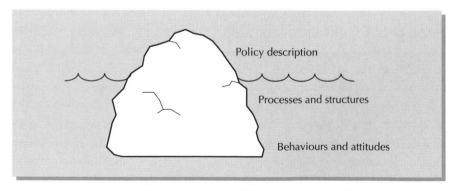

FIGURE 27 ◆ **Understanding current capability: the iceberg effect**

Policy

With regard to the people context, there may well be an agreed statement or policy about what should be occurring. In the case of Philips Lighting, in 1993 there was in place a policy statement about global recruitment which stated that Philips Lighting would strive to recruit people from across the world, and in particular in the key markets of Asia. Such policy statements give information about what managers have agreed is important, what they have communicated, the focus and priority of management action, and where management resources are focused. Therefore a close examination of policy documents is a useful first stage in the analysis of current reality.

However, it would be a mistake to stop at this level of reality. Our work in the Leading Edge Research Consortium showed the extent in some companies of the gap between company policy and the reality of practice. For example, in a number of companies the career development policy stated that career development discussions were a key part of the new employment contract based on 'employability'. When we interviewed managers about career practices, many also believed the career development policy was embedded in managerial action (i.e. managers engaged in career discussions with their team members). However, employee surveys showed that few employees had spoken to their managers about their careers, and many were dissatisfied with their career progress and development. Without the employee survey or employee discussions of practice, our understanding of career development in these companies would have been seriously flawed.

Processes and structures

The descriptions of the future created in the visioning session provide a first analysis of the processes and practices that would frame the vision. For example, at Glaxo Wellcome the vision described a time when cross-functional teams would be rewarded by team-based performance management processes and broad development opportunities. Similarly, in the case of Philips Lighting the teams visualized a strong regional orientation with close integration between research, manufacturing and sales. For both Glaxo Wellcome and Philips Lighting, the visions of the future specified processes and practices in place.

At this second level of analysis, the diagnostic question is whether these processes and practices are already in place in the organization. Answering this demands a more detailed analysis, using employee interviews and surveys. The team at Glaxo Wellcome gained a true notion of the extent of cross-functional working only after running focus groups and surveying a proportion of employees. While diagnostic measures such as focus groups and surveys are time consuming, they provide a more grounded description of reality. They also make it possible to use this information as a benchmark against which change over time can be monitored.

There are questions to be asked about alignment, embeddedness and process justice. Are the processes and structures aligned to the business goals? How embedded are the processes and structures (e.g. performance management processes, training and development)? Are the processes and structure developed and operationalized in a way that provide employees with a voice and choice?

Behaviours and attitudes

The greatest analysis is of the capabilities, behaviours and attitudes of the workforce. Understanding this is important since it is these behaviours that will drive performance. At Philips Lighting, the group described a future in which senior managers had comprehensive international understanding, and specific employee groups had a well developed knowledge of miniaturization, integration and product design, with employees behaving in an entrepreneurial and innovative manner.

There are three key questions here. What are the attitudes and values of the workforce (e.g. trust, commitment, attitude to innovation, team working)? What are the skills and competencies of the workforce (e.g. competencies of team working, leadership; skills in specific areas)? What is the competitive level of performance and how does it compare with other companies (e.g. profit per employee)?

There are a number of possible diagnostic tools for creating a realistic and shared understanding of the current capability:

◆ *Benchmarking*: to provide a view of how the policy and practice shape up to the best in class.

◆ *Employee surveys*: can add 'hard data' on the reality of practice (e.g.

how often do you speak to your manager about your performance?) or 'soft data' (e.g. how satisfied are you with performance management?). A crucial source of data, but needs industry sector norms and longitudinal data before any real conclusions can be drawn.

◆ *Focus groups*: small groups of employees brought together for an open debate on specific issues. Useful for collecting 'softer' data about values, meaning and culture (e.g. what is the climate of innovation around here? What do you value about your job?).

◆ *Employee interviews*: can be useful to gain insight into the reality of practices (e.g. what happens when your manager speaks about your performance?) and employee attitudes and values (e.g. what is the most enjoyable, exciting aspect of your work?).

◆ *360°/collegiate feedback*: formal, questionnaire-based feedback elicited from colleagues, peers, subordinates and customers. Particularly useful in gaining information about behaviour (e.g. my manager treats me with fairness and respect).

◆ *Self-perceptions*: self-administered questionnaires – particularly useful for self-diagnosis of current knowledge base and skills, and future skill needs and aspirations.

Tool 3.2: using the risk matrix to identify the gap

Understanding the gap between future needs and current capabilities energizes the group, focuses their attention and begins the hard, sharp discussion about priorities and resources. Without this agreement about the size and extent of the gap there is little clarity about the reality of the current situation, and what is important for the future. The notion of risk arises from two axes: a description of the importance of the factor to the vision (the greater the importance, the higher the potential risk), and the current alignment of the factor (the higher the alignment between the aspiration for the factor and the current reality, the lower the risk). Together these two axes produce a matrix on which the degree of potential risk can be described (*see* Fig. 28 overleaf).

The visioning stage finishes with an understanding of the factors of strategic impact, which describe the vision for the future. Having estab-

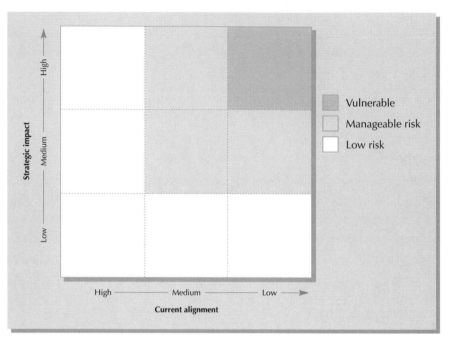

FIGURE 28 ◆ **The risk matrix**

lished this vision, and the people implications, we now return to the present. Taking each of the strategic factors in turn, the task is to arrive at a consensus about current alignment. The alignment of the factor is literally the 'alignment' between the projected situation five years hence, which has just been visualized, and the present situation vis-à-vis the particular factor. In particular, we must consider where the organization is now and how far it has gone to achieve these factors.[3]

The risk matrix has two axes against which the strategic factors of the vision can be described. The vertical axis is the *strategic impact of the factor* to the creation of the vision. The horizontal axis describes the *current alignment* of the factor – the gap between what is required for the future and current capabilities. Again this is described at three levels:

◆ *High alignment*: indicates that for this specific factor, the alignment between the needs of the vision and the current reality is high. So for these factors much has already been achieved, and there is no gap between the present and the needs of the future.

◆ *Medium alignment*: suggests that although the factor is not completely aligned, the group is confident of the company's ability to do so. There are sufficient policies and practices in place, and sufficient resources and commitment, to ensure that the company is on track to deliver this factor within the timescales.

◆ *Low alignment*: indicates that not only is the company some way from creating alignment for this factor, but the present situation may actually militate against this alignment. In other words, the group is not confident of the business's ability to achieve this factor unless major changes are made and resources and energy focused on this factor.

By using the risk matrix, it is possible for each group to plot all the strategic factors according to each factor's rating upon strategic impact and alignment. This allows an immediate understanding of the relative risks attached to the strategic factors, and hence to the delivery of the business strategy, since each part of the matrix is defined in terms of risk. The matrix illustrated in Fig. 28 can act as a 'shared map' to stimulate discussion of the risks attached to the vision of the future.

The strategic factors are categorized by three levels of risk:

◆ *Vulnerable*: those factors in the top right of the box in Fig. 28 are factors of greatest risk and illustrate those factors for which maximum leverage could be gained through refocusing resources. Factors in this category are of high strategic impact; any failure to implement these factors will put the delivery of the vision at severe risk. At the same time, these factors are of low alignment, and hence will need considerable management attention and resources if they are to be realized. Factors in this category figure prominently in the group's discussion. Those factors in the vulnerability category are ones from which managers expect to gain the greatest leverage if they can succeed in implementing them.

◆ *Manageable risk*: an area of medium to high strategic impact, medium to low alignment; factors in this category clearly must be given attention and resources, but the risks are acceptable. The three boxes within the category can indicate, in order of priority, factors where high strategic impact clearly ranks above those with medium impact.

◆ *Low risk*: describes the remaining categories. Factors in these categories are either of low strategic impact, in which case their successful implementation is relatively less important, or they are of high alignment, in which case they do not require additional resources.

It should be remembered that every factor in the matrix has been agreed by the group to be of importance to the realization of the vision. The strategic impact ratings on the matrix are a relative estimate. The purpose of the risk matrix is to indicate the relative risks attached to these factors and hence to the vision itself, since these factors were derived from the projected vision. The strategic impact as it can be seen has a benefit axis: higher strategic impact brings greater benefit. The alignment axis brings with it a sense of time: high alignment represents the present, low alignment the future. Present benefit represents the lowest risk, future benefit the highest risk and most likely sources of leverage.

Step 3 in action

Scanning for capability and identifying the gap at Philips Lighting

The consolidation of the visioning exercise at Philips Lighting had identified a number of key strategic factors and their level of impact. Each group was then set the task of scanning for current capability against each of the strategic factors to determine alignment. For the first of the Philips groups, the perceptions of current alignment are shown in Table 5. The strategic factors are the nine factors this group believed were critical to their vision of the future. The group's perceptions of the impact of each factor is shown in the second column (high, medium and low).

The measures the group used to identify current capability for each of the strategic factors are shown in the third column. Some refer to policy statements (for example, the policy on pay); others to the diagnosis of skills and attitudes (for example, through employee survey results and collated country information). In the fourth column the findings of the group for each strategic factor are shown, with the group's perception of current alignment (high, medium or low alignment).

Understanding current capability and identifying the gap

TABLE 5 ◆ Philips Lighting: impact and alignment

Strategic factor	Strategic impact	Measures	Current alignment	
Leaders and top ten				
Nationality of leaders representing major markets	Medium	Career history of key managers	Relatively low number of non-European managers	Medium
The structure				
Market and business creation orientators	High	Current structure of the organization	Structure functionally dominated	Low
Network, project-based organization	High	Number of projects Number of career moves across countries and business Employee survey items on networking and projects 360° feedback on team skills	Some technical projects are running successfully Limited reward for project skills	Medium
High-performance teams	Medium	Employee survey items on team skills	Some teams performing well Project management training in place Limited team-based training	Medium
Culture and values				
Enterpreneurial and innovative culture	Low	Employee survey items on risk taking and innovation Innovation measure: percentage of products less than five years old Number of creative ideas	Many creative ideas generated Limited links across functions reduces the impact of these ideas Not-invented-here syndrome is strong	Medium
People processes				
Global skill sets	Medium	Policy on skill development Process to support exchange	Global skill development in its infancy	Medium
Transparent objectives	Medium	Employee survey on clarity of business objectives	Business objective not clear to all employees	Low
Variable reward package		Pay policy/ remunerative process	Limited performance-related pay Dominated by European recruitment	Low Medium
Global recruitment	Low	National recruitment figures	Recent attempts to strengthen Asia recruitment	

At Philip's Lighting, as in many companies with whom I have worked, the discussions of the alignment between the needs of the future and the reality of the present show clearly the lack of understanding of current reality. While managers are aware of current return on investment, profitability or return on capital employed (ROCE), many are unclear about culture, values and people. One of the longer-term outcomes of this process is that more effort is put into understanding the current situation. In this case, there were some factors for which the group were confident that they had made an accurate diagnosis of current capability. For example, in the case of transparency in objective setting, the annual Philips employee survey asked employees if they understood the business goals of their business, and if they were clear about their personal objectives. For other strategic factors the group were less confident in their accuracy. Markets and business creation orientation was of high strategic importance but the group found they could not accurately rate the market orientation of the organization without further diagnostics.

The risk matrix in Fig. 29 summarizes the outcome of the discussions of Group 1. There were no strategic factors for which current alignment

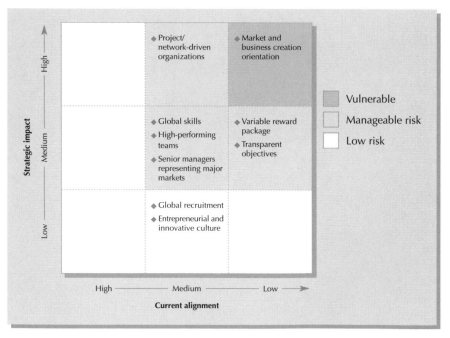

FIGURE 29 ◆ **Risk matrix – Philips Lighting Group 1**

Understanding current capability and identifying the gap

was judged to be high. Three factors were judged to be of low current alignment: *market and business creation orientation, variable reward package,* and *transparent objectives.* Market and regional business creation orientation was judged to be the factor of high risk and therefore major vulnerability, with high strategic impact and low current alignment. In 1993, the regional organizations, particularly in Asia-Pacific, were not fully realized. As a consequence the senior team had limited knowledge of the customer needs and business opportunities in the local markets.

The variable reward package of performance management was seen as an area of manageable risk. Creating strong vertical alignment between the business goals and individual objectives would be key in a company with such clear global aspirations. However, the employee survey showed that many employees' *transparent performance objectives* were not in place and they were unclear about what they had to do to achieve the business goals. This vertical linkage was further weakened at the level of remuneration, with few employees receiving performance-related pay through *variable reward packages.*

The *project/network-driven organization* was seen to be an area of manageable risk. At that time there were a number of successful projects in operation, but these were mainly technically orientated and dominated by research and development. Project management was not seen as a normal business procedure and the reward and training processes did little to reinforce these skills. This was mirrored in two other strategic factors: the creation of *high-performing teams* and the *global skill set.* It was well understood that the movement of business from Europe to Asia would necessitate closer links with the universities of Asia, and the sharing of information about employees across the globe. These were both seen as medium alignment. Links with universities were very strong in Europe and the skills of the workforce were beginning to be documented and shared. However, outside Europe these links were much less developed and represented a real risk to the strategic goal of internationalizing manufacturing and R&D.

By this stage of the process the teams have visualized the future, begun to understand current capability, and are increasingly aware of the gaps between their aspirations for the future and current reality. Typically, the groups leave this phase energized and excited. Now comes the challenge of assimilating all the visions and moving into action.

How do you benefit?

Understanding where you are now is a key organizational capability. Recall John Golding's metaphor of the speeding car. For him, leading Hewlett-Packard in Europe is like driving a speeding car along a winding road. Who knows what will be around the next corner? Therefore some broad visioning for the future is crucial. But driving a high-speed car also requires continual feedback about the car and its environment. What is its speed? How much petrol is left? How far is it to the left? How far to the right? In fact, this metaphor is so strong at Hewlett-Packard that they have created a mock-up of a jet plane which includes a range of information to reinforce the importance of speed and feedback.

Too often the senior team are driving a high-speed car with little idea of how much petrol is left or whether it is going to the right or the left. Creating the capacity to understand where you are now is crucial for developing a people-centred strategy. But it also has broader benefits to the management team. A full understanding of current capability is crucial to managing change over time.

◆ *A deep understanding of current reality* is highly important because without a sense of reality the gap between rhetoric and reality can become dysfunctionally wide. Earlier we considered the importance of meaning in organization. This comes essentially from the alignment between personal and organizational values and realities. These organizational values arise from the day-to-day behaviour of managers, the way in which decisions are taken, the focus and themes of the key people processes. Without an understanding of the reality in organizations, the rhetoric of policy continues apace, with limited understanding of reality. Subsequently a gap between rhetoric and reality breeds cynicism and distrust. It leads to a feeling that management are out of touch, that they do not have their hands on the tiller. Understanding and bridging the gap can occur only when reality is understood.

◆ *Potential courses of action become clear* when a diagnostic capability, particularly using the risk matrix, is built. The analysis of risk begins the discussion of priorities, where action should be taking place, and what has to be achieved.

Where do you stand now?

Scanning and alignment capabilities are explored in these brief descriptions. Consider each description in turn and identify the one which most accurately fits with current reality in your organization. Mark it on the profile presented in Section 3 of the Living Strategy Workbook.

Understanding current capabilities

Very strong diagnostic capability

The current policies, processes and people of the key aspects of the organization are understood. The behaviour competencies, skill sets, aspirations and motivations of the workforce are *accurately measured and benchmarked against industry equivalents* (e.g. through systematic and annual surveys of aspirations and motivations), and appraisal and training needs analysis to identify capabilities and skill sets. These diagnostic data are *collected, recorded and systematically provided to business managers.* There is an understanding of the alignment and gap between the needs of the future scenarios and current capabilities.

Strong diagnostic capability

Attempts are made to *collect some data on skill sets, motivations and aspirations.* Available information is systematically collated and *communicated across the relevant HR teams and to business managers.*

Average diagnostic capability

Some systematic collection of data (e.g. one-off surveys, data on some skill sets). *Ad hoc* attempts are made to share information *across the HR teams and with business managers.*

Weak diagnostic capability

No systematic collection of information about capabilities, competencies, skills sets, aspirations and motivations. However, *ad hoc impressionistic* information is collected and shared *across the HR community* and with business managers.

Very weak diagnostic capability

No systematic collection of information about capabilities, competencies, skills sets, aspirations and motivations. Ad hoc information which is collected *is kept within the immediate HR team* or business group.

Moving forward

The line manager's role

Building a long-term diagnostic capability is crucial for a rapidly evolving organization. Line managers and human resource professionals have a key role to play, both in building long-term capability and in engaging in dialogue about the strategic factors and the extent of alignment.

Line managers play three key roles: to provide the resources to support the process and to actively engage themselves in the dialogue; to be prepared to face up to the mirror of reality; and to work to build over time a diagnostic capability.

◆ The first of these, resources and engagement, is crucial to this stage, setting up the personal resources to actively participate in the risk matrix workshop and the broader resources to support the creation of a diagnostic capability.

◆ Facing up to the mirror of reality is tough. It means acknowledging the impact of the mistakes of the current organizational structure and the extent of low commitment and inspiration, or the low level of skills. Faced with these realities it is possible to deny the quality of the measurement tool ('we just have not measured commitment properly') or to bury the results ('we cannot do anything about it so why collect the evidence?'). Both result in a fast-moving organization steered by blind people. Facing up to reality is difficult, particularly if reality is far from rhetoric, but it is a crucial part of building strategies which have people at their heart. The role of the manager is to have the courage and conviction to look reality in the face and to be prepared to understand and work on the gap between current capabilities and future aspirations.

◆ Finally, as the senior Philips team found, working on the risk matrix can illustrate the depth of current diagnostic capability. It became clear to the Philips team that there were a number of factors which would be key for the future but for which they had relatively sketchy diagnostic data.

The risk of creating a diagnostic capability is to measure and analyze everything. To drown in data and facts, to create an overly complex process which rapidly becomes stultified, another piece of organizational bureaucracy. The challenge is to build a number of long-term diagnostic measures (skills, attitudes, culture) and to create a diagnostic capacity (focus groups, in-depth interviews) which can rapidly measure key factors. Building these long-term measures and fast diagnostic capabilities requires resources and management attention.

The human resource role

The human resource professional has three key roles to play in this step. First, to continue to help the teams to think about the future and current capability. Second, to bring professionalism and best practice to building the diagnostic capability. Third, to act as the advocate for employees to ensure that their voice and concerns are heard at this stage.

◆ The facilitation capability, which was so important for the visioning step, continues to be important here. The HR professional needs to help the group to consider the current alignment and the risks they face, but is also required to take a view of confidence levels, to consider the accuracy of perceptions of the current situation, and to work with the team to agree in which areas deeper diagnostic capability is required.

◆ The second role of the human resource professional is to help the group understand current reality, and also what the reality may be in competing companies. It could be that the team are either unclear or complacent about what is happening in the company. The role here is to bring data from outside to illustrate reality across the competitor landscape. Allied to this notion of best practice is the importance of creating diagnostic capabilities which are strong, valid and reliable. Here, skills in survey design and analysis, focus group and in-depth interviewing will be of paramount importance.

◆ The final role of the human resource professional is to ensure that at this crucial step the voice of the employees is heard. Building realistic and strong bridges to the future requires a firm grasp and grounding in the reality of employee skills and hopes, competencies and aspirations. Reflecting this reality, being an advocate for employees will be a key capability for this step.

Summary of specific actions

3.1 Each group takes each factor of strategic impact and debates the alignment between the aspirations for the future and the present capabilities. Alignment is rated as high, medium and low. It is also useful at this stage to gain a view of the confidence of the group in their ratings. Low confidence indicates that the group cannot confidently report on the current capability of the factor, and further diagnostic scanning is required to increase the confidence of the ratings.

3.2 Following from the group work, revisit the confidence levels and identify those factors where the group cannot accurately rate current alignment. It may be necessary at this stage to loop back into a more detailed analysis of current capability. Three levels of analysis are appropriate: the policy level, the process level, and the level of behaviours and attitudes.

3.3 Once the group is confident in their analysis of current capability, move to framing the risk matrix and discussing the areas of vulnerability.

Creating a map of the system

 A fundamental characteristic of humans is the search for meaning, the active interpretation of the events, the creation of coherence and integration. Earlier we saw the efforts of the team at Citibank to realign key people processes to create cohesion of meaning around customer networks and thinking globally. For them the creation of integrated meaning meant a move from sequential, ad hoc decisions about separate parts of the organization to an integrated, cohesive map of the system. In this step we consider how this integrated approach can be developed and become part of the way a people-centred strategy is created. The emphasis here is on those tools which support and reinforce the capacity to think systemically, to see organizations as integrated, complex wholes, to understand the inter-relationships within the system, and the impact that change will have on any part of the system.

The development of this fourth step is based on three guiding principles.

The guiding principles

Guiding principle 1: Organizations are dynamic systems

The dynamics of an organization are felt by individual members every day of their working lives. Processes such as selection or reward, organizational structures, management behaviours are all independent factors. Yet they are perceived by members of the organization in their totality and if a shared sense of meaning is to be created, this totality of experience must be reinforcing and aligned to the basic strategic thrust of the business.

This need for alignment and reinforcement immediately suggests that while these factors can be built independently, to do so is to potentially create misalignment and a lack of clarity. These factors work together in a complex system of inter-relationships. Changes in one aspect will create changes in others, some of which are unintended. So in creating visions for the future, great sensitivity is needed on the issues of alignment, synergy and reinforcement. Systemic thinking and modelling the relationships leads to a strong tool to view the complexity of the organization.[1]

Guiding principle 2: Systemic thinking creates a way of framing dynamics

In my experience, there are three key aspects of systemic thinking which are capable of framing these conversations: the notion of themes and the clarity around these themes; the modelling of the inter-relationship between the themes; and the creation of dynamic models to understand how the organization is likely to change over time.

Visions are engaging and exciting, they build enthusiasm and commitment, and they create momentum. But the excitement of a vision can pass like a dream, half remembered in the cold light of day. To become more than a dream, visions have to become solid, understandable and actionable. The risk matrix tool goes some way to distilling the essence of the dream and identifying those areas of the dream which need action. But many risk matrices pulled together begin to look like a shopping list, and become about as inspiring. The challenge here is to move from sequential thinking to dynamic thinking.

The development of these maps of the system plays a crucial role by allowing participants to share their views on the key elements of the system, to model causality and the inter-relationships between these elements. In doing so this process allows the team to move away from static and sequential thinking to broader systemic thinking. These models of causality are crucial for distinguishing between means and ends. They clearly demonstrate the impact of failing to act on any one of these areas.

There are two challenges in modelling the people aspects of the organization. First, to understand the broad themes which are capable of bringing a unity of meaning to potentially disparate factors. Second, to model the inter-relationships between the key elements of the system, in particular the key levers, and to describe how the processes and interventions affect behaviour and attitudes. The emphasis here is on developing a map and a story line that is provocative, memorable, and capable of eliciting a rich imagery. These maps should be capable of creating a *Gestalt*, where the final map is greater than the sum of the parts. They should express the simplicity of the system in a single diagram in a manner which is internally consistent and understandable.

Guiding principle 3: Identify the blind spots

The map of the future is a diagrammatic representation of what is in the minds of those who participate in the visioning session. By reflecting their aspirations it is authentic and able to create commitment. But as a representation of the collective viewpoint it also contains the blind spots and myopia of the group. The description of the vision arises from past experience; the final principle of the mapping stage is the principle of overview and review. Be aware that you are likely to over-emphasize the tried and tested levers and under-emphasize the new or the novel. This viewpoint should be questioned and analyzed before the action phase begins.

The tools and techniques

There are four sequential techniques to creating a map of the system, as shown in Table 6.

Tool 4.1: identify the themes

Visions of the future have many facets. The challenge here is to create broad themes of meaning capable of creating simpler, more holistic ways of thinking about these complex data. These broad themes show the direction in which the company should be travelling, and bring simplicity and coherence. By concentrating on broad themes, action is focused and the path shaped from current reality to the future vision.

TABLE 6 ◆ **Creating a map of the system**

Identify the themes	*For example*
◆ Four or five key themes	◆ Customer orientation
◆ Assimilate areas of strategic impact	◆ Innovation and entrepreneurship
◆ Reflect future business goals	◆ Globalization
	◆ Market share
Model the levers	
◆ Levers which have the potential to create change	◆ Short-term levers include recuritment, objective setting, reward and short-term training
◆ Capable of short-term or longer-term impact	
◆ Importance of focusing on key levers	◆ Long-term levers include organizational development through structure change, changes in leadership behaviour through leadership development and changes in employee behaviours through employee development (*see* people process model)
Model the end states	
◆ Desired outcomes, the behavours and culture which will deliver long-term business goals	◆ Behavioural end states include skills, competencies and performance
◆ Occur as a result of the application of levers	◆ Cultural end states include attitudes and values
Model the dynamics	
◆ The relationships between the levers and the end state	◆ The primary relationship between the lever of short-term training and the outcome of increased competence and performance
◆ Some are primary relationship in the sense that they are capable of directly influencig the real point	
◆ Other are reinforcing relationships, in the sense that they work with other levers	◆ The reinforcing relationship between short-term training is innovation and the realignment of reward systems to increase innovative behaviour

The visioning tools described earlier yield numerous flip charts of factors that are believed to be descriptive of the future organization. Each group has reduced these factors to the ten they consider most important to their vision of the future, and has ranked these strategic factors as high, medium and low impact. In the subsequent risk matrix the groups considered each factor and its current reality to gain a view of the alignment with future needs. As these workshops are run with different groups in the organization, so there begins a shared view of what is important for the future.

The flip chart information and the lists of strategic factors are essentially sequential – they are a shopping list. These items simply reflect the sequence in which they were discussed. Now is the time to transform this linear definition to a systems view of the organization and to understand how these separate factors relate to each other.

The first step in the creation of a systems map is the identification of the themes that will form the frame. These themes should have three basic characteristics:

◆ there should be *no more than five themes*. Any more and the framing becomes overly complex and simplicity is lost; less than four and the framing is too simplistic;

◆ the themes should be capable of capturing the *major business outcomes and goals* that define the vision. In a sense they reflect the cornerstone of the company in the future, and by doing so define the broad sense of direction;

◆ the themes should be strongly linked to the future business goals, so it is clear what has to be achieved to meet these goals. They are expressed in a manner that is *credible and integrated* with the business. For example, customer focus, innovation, growth and profitability all provide a credible glimpse into the business of the future.

Tool 4.2: modelling the levers

The factors clustered around the theme are of two types. Some are *levers* – factors which if changed or built could be capable of supporting the development of the business around the themes – while others are *end states*, the specific aspects of the themes. For example, in the globalization theme, global recruitment is a potential lever which could build on an end state of globalization. Similarly, in the innovation and entrepreneurship theme, skills in miniaturization is a lever which could potentially impact on innovative and entrepreneurial culture.

The emphasis here is on levers, those aspects of the system which have a disproportionate impact on the total system and the ability to deliver the vision and create momentum. Focusing on a small number of key levers is important since it is unlikely that all the processes can change simultaneously. As we saw earlier in the people process model (Fig. 21), the short-term process levers, such as changing the recruitment criteria, reshaping the objectives, building new performance metrics and feedback loops, rewarding specific aspects of performance, and designing new training processes, are all capable of leveraging action within a timescale of one or two years. In the longer term, redefining the development of future leaders, changing the structure and roles within the organization, and re-skilling the workforce will all affect the organization over the next five years.

Looking again at the model of the themes at Philips Lighting it becomes clear that the strategic factors and themes can be divided into two major categories: end states and levers. *Levers* represent those processes and systems that are capable of leveraging change, while *end states* are the desired outcomes, for which many actions may have to be taken. The desired end states represented in this model include the three major themes: customer orientation, globalization, and entrepreneurship and innovation. Other end states are the delivery of total lighting solutions, an entrepreneurial culture, market and business creation orientation, and cross-functional team working. Each of these specifies a desired end state, but not how these could be leveraged or achieved. Most of the levers in this model are long-term ones, in the sense that they will take some years to bring about any change.

Customer orientation will be leveraged primarily through the creation of a local/regional structure in which more responsibility and autonomy is devolved from the corporate centre to the regions, allowing the voice of the local customer to be heard. It will also occur through the creation of research and development capabilities closer to the customer base, particularly in Asia. The theme of globalization will be leveraged through people processes that include the development of a global recruitment capability, a global skill portfolio, and the encouragement of cross-country career moves. The creation of an innovative and entrepreneurial culture is more problematic. For this theme most of the cluster describes end states (a culture of innovation, work is fun, risk-taking encouraged) rather than the levers that would create this culture. Later in this process we explore the dynamics of this theme in more detail.

Tool 4.3: reviewing the map

The map is a pictorial representation of the collective vision of the group. It is likely to emphasize what has worked in the past, and under-emphasize untried practices and processes. It may also have 'blind spots', aspects which are outside the experience of the group. In reviewing the map at this stage, two questions should be asked:

◆ What are the 'blind spots' and what have we failed to consider in this map of the future?

◆ What more can be done to deliver on the key business themes?

Step 4 in action

Identifying the themes at Philips Lighting

At Philips Lighting, five groups participated in the visioning sessions, which ensured representation from all key functions and levers. At this stage there were more than 50 strategic factors and many pages of back-up flip-chart information. The challenge was to move the thinking from a sequential perspective to considering these factors from a systemic perspective. This was achieved through an initial content analysis and clustering of all the information which represented the future for the company. It became clear through this clustering that three major overlapping business themes dominated the vision for the future.

Success for Philips Lighting in the year 2000 would necessitate a stronger focus on *customer orientation* with a cross-business perspective supporting this orientation; a perspective which was *global*, with particular emphasis on Asia-Pacific; and the creation of an *innovative and entrepreneurial culture*. This would be underpinned by a structure and culture that encouraged high-performing teams and highly developed performance management processes. These three themes captured in a simple manner the thoughts that were in the minds of the people who had participated in the visioning exercise.

This first attempt at mapping the system (*see* Fig. 30) shows the three major themes that have emerged and the factors that could be categorized with them. For example, the broad theme of innovation and entrepreneurship has been clustered with the strategic factors of skills in miniaturization and integration, the development of an entrepreneurial culture, and the encouragement of risk taking. Customer orientation could be clustered

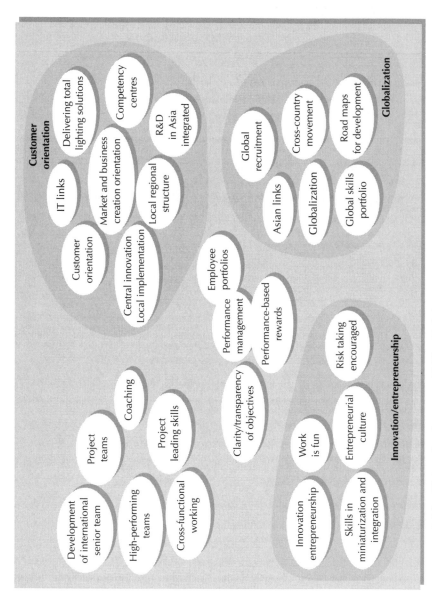

FIGURE 30 ◆ **Identifying the themes at Philips Lighting**

with the delivery of total lighting solutions, the creation of regional research and development competency centres, and a local structure. Globalization was a key theme; people described the global recruitment processes, the provision of global skills portfolios, and road maps for development, with strong links into the universities and labour markets of Asia.

The map includes a set of factors around team performance and performance management which have implications for all three major themes: the clarity and transparency of objectives, the provision of performance-related pay, the development of employee portfolios, the creation of high-performing teams, skills in project leading, and structures which reinforce cross-functional working.

Modelling the levers at Philips Lighting

The challenge here is to consider the factors of the vision for the future and to describe those which are end states in the sense that they will be outcomes, and the levers which are likely to influence the development of these outcomes. The first attempt to understand and model the levers and outcomes at Philips Lighting in 1993 is shown in Fig. 31.

As the map shows, there are a number of levers that would create a real impact on the delivery of this vision in the longer term. A key longer-term lever would be the creation of a *local/regional structure*. As the relationship arrows show, this would facilitate the creation of integrated project teams as it would result in greater customer orientation, since the research, development and manufacturing sites would be closer to the customer and would support the globalization of the business by developing skills in the local markets. The second longer-term lever is the development of an *international senior team*. As the arrows show, this would aid the globalization of the business by providing opportunities for local managers to grow into senior roles, and a team based around the world would be more likely to work in the virtual and integrated projects which would be crucial to the future. The final long-term lever is the creation of an *employee group* whose skills are shared on a global basis. While these longer-term levers will take time to be developed and their effects felt, it is imperative that immediate action is taken to begin the structural, leadership development and skill set changes.

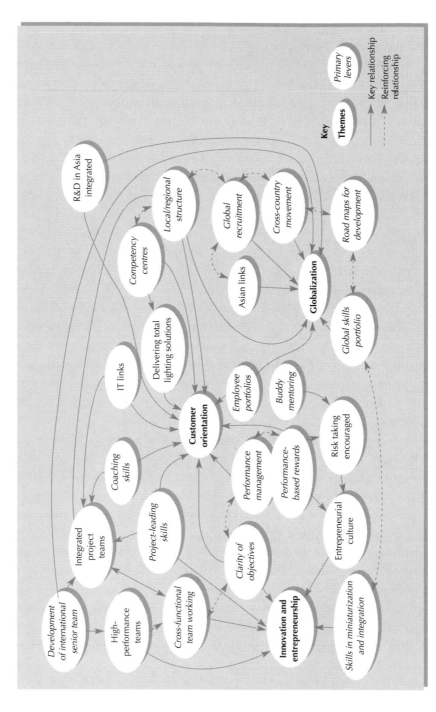

FIGURE 31 ◆ **Modelling levers at Philips Lighting, 1993**

The model also shows the key short-term levers capable of creating change within a couple of years. *Clarifying objectives*, building *performance-based reward* mechanisms and developing *employee portfolios* can all leverage innovation and customer orientation. Embarking on *global recruitment* and setting up mentoring and buddy processes for nationals will have an immediate impact on globalization. Training in *project-leading skills* and coaching will create stronger teams and therefore greater customer focus and innovation. Finally, the globalization theme would be leveraged through a group of processes including *global recruitment* the creation of a global skills portfolio, and the facilitation of job moves across countries.

Reviewing the map at Philips Lighting

The Philips team took a critical approach to the map of the future. They identified three areas which needed further consideration. First, innovation and entrepreneurship was a business theme with many desired outcomes (entrepreneurial culture, risk taking encouraged, high-performing teams) but limited understanding of how this innovative, entrepreneurial culture would be developed. Interestingly, in focusing on skills in miniaturization and integration, the team were simply emphasizing the technical capability which had been the hallmark of Philips in the past. What was needed now was a deeper understanding of how innovation and entrepreneurship could be developed.

Second, the team became aware that many of the major levers to develop customer orientation were structural – the creation of a local/regional organizational structure, the development of local and regional competency centres, the integration of research and development in Asia. In the past the business had relied on restructuring to push behavioural change, with relatively limited success. The question here was whether the structure levers could be strong enough to create customer focus.

Finally, the group reviewed the performance management levers (performance-based rewards and clarity of objectives). This had historically been something of a holy grail at Philips – long hoped for but rarely achieved. The group debated whether other levers would be necessary to support performance management.

How do you benefit?

There are two major outcomes of doing this step well. First, a pictorial representation of the future, and second, a framework for debating this representation.

◆ *The pictorial representation* is an enormously powerful outcome. Shopping lists of actions fail to grasp the imagination or convey the complexity of organizations. The map begins to represent this complexity, and as a pictorial representation it has the power to engage the imagination and to provide a frame within which further dialogue can take place.

◆ *The creation of the relationship arrows* begins the dialogue about cause and effect. In modelling the potential relationships the groups are drawn into the world of reality – where taking one action effects another action, and where there may be both intended and unintended consequences. The map allows the groups to begin the hard conversation about the possible course of action.

Where do you stand now?

Systemic capabilities are explored in these brief descriptions. Consider each in turn and indentify the one which most accurately fits with the current reality in your organization. Mark it on the profile in Section 3 of the Living Strategy Workbook

---

Understanding current capabilities

Very strong systemic capabilities

There are *well understood and developed systematic thinking* capabilities across the organization. Decisions are taken on the basis of the impact on the total system. Systemic data on behaviour and performance are collected and analyzed to allow *causal linkages* to be established.

Strong systemic capabilities

There are *pockets of the organization* where systemic thinking is used to model the people systems. These maps are shared and influence deci-

---

sions about actions to take. There is *broad awareness of the impact* of certain actions on the behaviour and performance of employees.

Average systemic capabilities

Some understanding of the *vertical and horizontal linkage* between business goals and processes. There is an awareness of the *impact of managerial actions* and some understanding of the possible unintended consequences.

Weak systemic capabilities

There is some attempt to establish *linear linkages*, i.e. 'if we do A then B will occur'. However these are not seen within a broader consequence and there is *limited awareness* of the potential unintended consequences.

Very weak systemic capabilities

Management actions take place on an *ad hoc and unintegrated basis*. There is no attempt to understand how changes in one process may affect changes in others. The *impact of changes in processes and structure* on attitudes and behaviours is not understood or discussed.

Moving forward

The line manager's role

The line manager's role here is to:

- ◆ keep engaged and involved in the process. The mapping is a crucial step and needs commitment and focus;

- ◆ be prepared to debate how these relationships could work. This involves bringing past experience to predict potential relationships and being open to the critique of the map to distinguish and discuss other sources of leverage and relationship.

The human resource role

The human resource professional has two key roles to play in Step 4.

◆ First, to bring the skills of systemic thinking to mapping the relationships. It has been my experience that without this skill it is very difficult for people to have the confidence to proceed with this step. Systemic thinking is considered a crucial skill in any change management role. It is certainly of central importance at this step.

◆ Second, to have the breadth of business experience to lead the analysis of the map. It is critical at this step that the HR professional understands how the core people processes work and is familiar with the other levers, such as structure, and outcomes, such as culture.

In many ways Step 4 is the point at which the HR professional can potentially add real value. But to do so requires preparation of systemic thinking skills and a broad awareness of how change occurs in complex, dynamic organizations.

Summary of specific actions

4.1 Gather all the flip chart information from all the groups and create an initial content analysis by themes. Identify the most prevalent, select the top four or five and label them in a manner that has meaning to the business.

4.2 Create a first cut of the system showing the key themes and all the factors that could be categorized under these themes.

4.3 Work with the groups to identify the levers (those processes and procedures which could create change) and the end states.

4.4 Refine the map by sketching both the primary and the reinforcing relationships between the levers and the end states.

4.5 Review the map and risk matrix. Consider what more could be done.

Modelling the dynamics of the vision

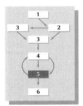

Visioning the future, understanding the key strategic factors and themes, identifying the risks and building systemic descriptions are all essentially cerebral activities. Groups across an organization could participate in all these activities without actually doing anything. In my experience this may happen – they remain in the world of dreams and discussions, of rhetoric rather than reality. The challenge is to create a bridge from the dreams of the future to the realities of the present. The strength and construction of the bridge will be crucial to the success of the endeavour – too weak and the ideas and excitement will fade, the documents will gather dust, and the visioning experiences will be a fond, lingering memory.

The challenge at this stage of the process is to build excitement and commitment to the road ahead. This commitment begins by understanding what may happen as ideas turn into action. There are two guiding principles for this step: first, leverage with processes and behaviours and values will follow, and second, understand the forces for and against change.

The guiding principles

Guiding principle 1: Leverage with processes and behaviours and values will follow

At the centre of organizational life is the striving to create meaning, to interpret and to understand. People are immensely sensitive to cues and signals and aware of the gaps between the rhetoric of policy and the reality of actions. Yet while this creation of meaning occurs primarily for individuals, all are members of groups with shared patterns of beliefs. The creation of this meaning provides insight into the sequence of the actions on the journey. If individuals search for meaning and this meaning is created through everyday actions, then attempting to create change initially at the level of values and culture will lead merely to cynicism and disbelief.[1]

In Step 4 we distinguished between levers and outcomes. Values and culture are not levers for changes but outcomes, the accumulation of actions taken every day by individuals in organizations. If we believe that the creation of meaning is important in organizations, we should concentrate first on understanding the behaviours and actions that together will create this future. This can be achieved by focusing initially on the potential short-term levers – recruiting the people who espouse the vision, and exiting those who do not, creating performance management processes which provide feedback and reward these new ways of performing, providing short-term training to accelerate the development of the skills which will be crucial for the future. When people are provided with clear messages that innovative behaviours are important and rewarded for being innovative, when the structure in which they operate supports the sharing of ideas, when they see risk taking encouraged, then a creative culture and context will emerge.

There will certainly be strong resistance to embarking on the journey to the future. People may be comfortable with their routines and committed to the status quo, there may be strong political dynamics that are acting to block change. However, there will be less anxiety about the journey if processes and channels are built throughout the organization which lead to comprehensive conversations about the vision and which engage groups to become skilful observers of the business environment and where knowledge is shared by a critical mass of people who are capable of creating action on the basis of their consensus view.

In the preceding steps a map of the future has been created and those levers identified which will be crucial to the delivery of this vision. In considering the action to bridge to the future, we must take account of the dynamic, systemic nature of the organization, and the strong forces acting for and against changes.

Guiding principle 2: Understand the forces for and against change

There are a number of basic principles of physics that provide some illumination of how the system could work. These are drawn from Newton's Third Law of Motion, and the notion of homeostasis. The Third Law of Motion states that for every action there is an equal and opposite reaction. So within an organization, as the forces for change increase so the resistance to change increases proportionally. Movement is created by working at both forces simultaneously, to increase the forces for change, and to decrease the forces operating against change.[2]

At the same time, homeostasis is the tendency of a system to maintain internal stability through the co-ordinated response of its parts to any situation that disturbs its normal condition or function. In an organizational context, inertia and resistance to change grows primarily through a gradual accumulation of resource commitments and institutional routines and therefore leads to a commitment to the status quo. This reflects the organizational values, the structure of the organization or the way in which people have been rewarded or developed. Over time this inertia grows. More detailed and routine policies and procedures are created around the way in which performance is measured, around reward and development and around the structuring of roles. These are primarily created to increase reliability, but over time they become institutionalized. Resistance to change and renewal arises in part because it is increasingly more time consuming to abandon these complex activities. As current and prior commitments become more difficult to change, and as administrative mechanisms are put into place and satisfactory results are more predictable, managers are motivated to work with what they have inherited.[3]

So what of the forces for change? In part they increase as the current state of affairs is perceived to be unsatisfactory. They reflect the imperfection people can see in organizational reality and strategic goals and the environment in which they operate. Accumulating dissatisfaction and stress are likely to lead more people in the organization to perceive the benefits of change. At the same time there may be more tangible forces that would support the change. For example, there may be organizational structures and embedded skill sets that would have the potential to become forces for change. Understanding the forces for and against change establishes a frame for beginning to model the dynamics.

The tools and techniques

Building a dynamic map of the system requires a clear and agreed description of those forces which are operating for and against change and an awareness of how the forces for change can be increased and the forces against change decreased. This can be achieved only with an open discussion of the barriers in moving to the vision. Without this openness, and unless all the impediments are taken into account, it is impossible for the group to adopt a realistic plan to bridge from the realities of the present to the vision of the future. This means that issues that are normally hidden, because they are threatening or embarrassing, must be brought to the surface. This capability for open dialogue is crucial. Without it the team cannot arrive at a shared diagnosis of what needs to be achieved, and without this shared diagnosis, they cannot craft the steps to arrive at the journey to the common vision.

Tool 5.1: forcefield analysis

In my work I have used a process termed 'forcefield analysis' to bring out the forces operating for and against change. An overview of this is given in Fig. 32.

1   Define the desired outcome

2   Brainstorm the dynamics, the forces operating for and against change

Forces for change   ⟶   ⟵   Forces against change

3   Cluster similar forces

4   Work on creating action

Actions to increase forces for change   Actions to decrease forces against change

FIGURE 32 ◆ **Overview of forcefield analysis**

The forcefield analysis is basically a group process which frames a debate about the desired outcomes. It takes place within groups of about six people. My preference is to use the same stakeholder team that participated in the earlier visioning session. However, in this step, self-selected groups to work on specific topics are more appropriate, i.e. people have an opportunity to work on a topic that is important to them or of which they have prior experience. The selection of group members is important since they may well become members of the task forces which follow in the next step. The basis of the forcefield analysis then, is the outcome from the previous stage. For example, at Philips Lighting this could be an entrepreneurial culture, or the encouragement of risk taking. Here, forcefield analysis can be a useful tool for making a critical analysis of the levers associated with an outcome. Forcefield analysis can also provide greater insight into the levers and the likelihood of them having an impact.

There are four key phases in the forcefield analysis tool:

◆ *Define the desired outcome.* Each group works with one end state or lever. They begin by defining the desired outcome, in other words, 'How would you know when you have achieved this?' The emphasis here is on clarity and measurability. This is a crucial first stage. If the description of the desired outcome is unclear or immeasurable, the subsequent discussion is less focused and useful.

◆ *Brainstorm the dynamics, the forces operating for and against change.* Next, the group enters a brainstorming phase in which each member describes what they believe are the forces operating for change, and the forces of inertia and resistance. These are noted on a flip chart. This discussion should be as open and honest as possible in order to identify some of the 'blind spots' and to discuss the previously undiscussable.

◆ *Cluster similar forces.* Following the brainstorming phase the group move to a period of consolidation and clustering. Forces with similar themes are drawn together to identify the underlying forces operating for and against change. The clusters may include technical sources, political sources and cultural sources of resistance.

◆ *Work on creating action.* Finally, taking each force in turn, the group consider the actions to increase the forces for change and the actions to decrease the forces against change.

Step 5 in action

Modelling the dynamics of the vision at Philips Lighting

Following the visioning work, the teams at Philips Lighting worked through many forcefield analyses to help them understand the nature and dynamics of the key themes they had identified, and the levers which would impact on these themes. By way of illustration I have chosen a forcefield analysis which focused on the development of an international senior team. The initial discussion of the forces for and against change is shown in Table 7.

TABLE 7 ◆ Forcefield analysis, Philips Lighting 1993

Forces for and against developing an international service team	
Driving forces ⟹	⟸ Restraining forces
◆ Awareness of the need for change	◆ No consistent, communicated road plan to increase internationalization of senior team
◆ Awareness of rapid need for Asian presence	
◆ Senior team has talked about internationalization	◆ Career planning occurs within rather than across countries
◆ Some examples of transfer of senior managers to Asia-Pacific region	◆ Top management dominated by functional experience, primarily gained in Europe
◆ Philips brand in Asia capable of attracting top people	
◆ External pressure: benchmarking of competitors shows that some are moving rapidly on internationalization of the senior team	◆ Limited management commitment to cross-business or cross-national development
	◆ Top echelons dominated by Europeans
◆ Visible shift from functional to business thinking	◆ Lack of management awareness of importance of building global teams
◆ More managers have experience working in the US, general mobility has increased	◆ Local/regional resource needs are not clear
◆ Common language spoken across Philips Lighting	◆ Failure in the past to attract and retain significant numbers of non-Europeans
◆ Sense of urgency to deliver in Asia	◆ No HR systems to support multi-functional and multi-national senior teams
◆ Acquisitions and joint ventures have created local senior talent in Asia	◆ Fear of the unknown
◆ Networks and exchange programmes have laid the foundation for younger people	◆ Centralistic thinking in the European HQ in Eindhoven

As the table shows, in discussion the Philips team identified a number of forces that were operating to support the change to a more international management cadre. They were aware that some members of the senior management team had publicly proclaimed their support and commitment to a more international group. In its key emerging markets in Asia and South America, Philips was fast developing an international brand name, which would make it a more attractive recruitment proposition outside its home territory. The lighting business had grown in the past and was predicted to grow in the future through a combination of organic growth and growth through acquisitions and joint ventures. This rate of organic growth and acquisition strategy, particularly outside the European home market, had the potential to establish more international roles, some of which could be filled by managers from the key emerging markets.

However, as the group discussed the theme, it became clear that the end state they had described would not be achieved unless some basic forces against change were confronted. These forces reflected in part the country-based, decentralized business structure of Philips Lighting in 1993. While this structure had the advantage of decentralizing decision making and taking it closer to the country level operations, it had also created organizational structures, career planning processes and an HR function which were country-based and highly independent. This independence reduced opportunities for people to move across countries, and had reinforced the 'country barons', who were unwilling to lose their best people or to accept others.

In considering the actions necessary to overcome the forces operating against change, the team had to strike a difficult balance – to build on the benefits of autonomous country operations while creating cross-country and business line networks and structures capable of facilitating cross-country recruitment and career development. This would require building on the forces for change, particularly through harnessing senior management commitment and establishing a corporate human resource development function and additional budget.

A broad analysis of the key forces for and against change against the three business theories is presented in Figs 33A and B. Many of the restraining forces shown in Fig. 33A are focused around the structure of the organization. The strong functional organization in 1993 was restraining the creation of a global company, and the internal layers and

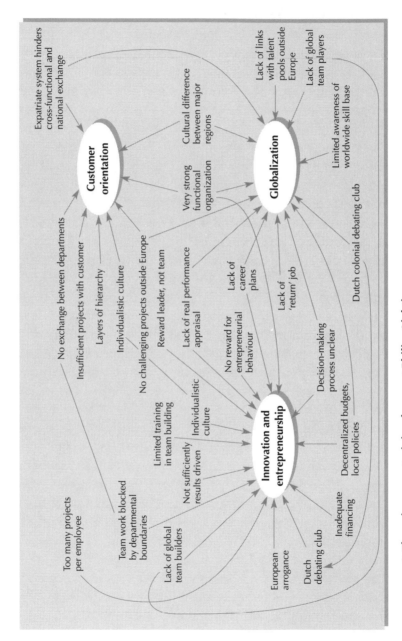

FIGURE 33A ◆ **The primary restraining forces at Philips Lighting**

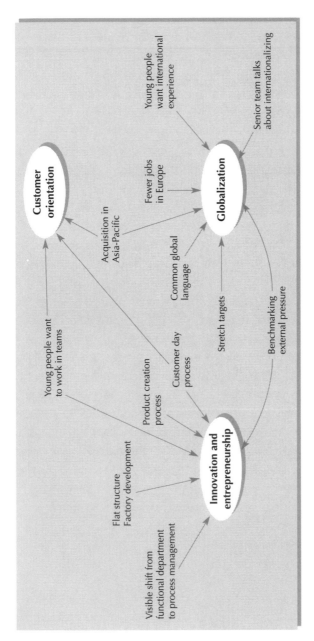

FIGURE 33B ◆ **The primary driving forces at Philips Lighting**

departmental boundaries and lack of project working were impacting on globalization, innovation and customer orientation. Other forces restraining the vision included the people processes – reward mechanisms favoured individual rather than team performance which would be so important for the future. There was limited training in team building and project management skills. The expatriate career system restricted the creation of the global vision by hindering cross-functional and national exchange and by failing to provide jobs for people when they returned from positions outside their own country. There were also broad cultural forces operating against change. For example, the perceived insularity of the European team and strong cultural differences across the regions hindered the development of the global business.

However, there were driving forces that could be built and capitalized upon. The Philips Customer Day, a day in which the employees spend a day with customers, fostered innovation and customer orientation and it was widely believed that more could be done to capitalize on this. The structure was shifting from functional to cross-functional teams, and could be accelerated. Interestingly, many of the younger people in the teams saw themselves as forces for change – they were keen to work in teams and wanted international experience.

Over time the teams worked with each of the themes building a shared awareness of the forces operating for and against change. These discussions had two major benefits. At the level of content they encouraged the groups to discuss what was really happening at Philips Lighting, and create a more detailed and realistic picture of what would need to change if the business was to become more customer focused, innovative and global. But these discussions also developed teams of people who revealed and shared their hopes and fears for the organization. Plotting the driving and restraining forces helped to create a more complex picture of the system.

How do you benefit?

There are two major outcomes of doing this step well. First, a strategic dialogue across the organization about the future, and second, a shared view of the reality of the forces which could accelerate or impede this vision of the future.

◆ Throughout the six-step process I have argued that what is important is the dialogue, not what is written down in a strategic plan. Nowhere is this more apparent than at this stage. It is the debate about the forces for and against change and the collective modelling of the dynamics that creates a shared sense of meaning. Like the visioning dialogues, these dialogues are capable of bringing to the fore subjects which are not usually discussed, identifying power and politics within the organization, and providing collective agreement and acknowledgement of the forces which have to be overcome.

◆ Second, there is a surfacing of those factors which could potentially impede the actions which follow. My experience is that these may not be acted upon. But the mere process of bringing them out ensures that they remain in the circle of what can be discussed, and the team may well return to them when the time is right.

Where do you stand now?

Here we explore the modelling of the dynamics of the system. Consider each description in turn and identify the one that most accurately fits with current reality in your organization. Turn to Section 3 of the Living Strategy Workbook and plot your findings.

Understanding current capabilities

Very strong modelling capability

The dynamics within the systems of the *organization are understood.* Managers have a shared perception of the links between process levers and outcomes and the way in which these will change over time. Possible changes are modelled and there is collective knowledge about forces operating for and against change formed out of strategic dialogues across the organization.

Strong modelling capability

There is some understanding of the dynamics of the system. *Managers have some perceptions of the links between processes and levers.* This knowledge is held within teams rather than shared collectively.

Average modelling capability

There is an understanding that the *organization will change over time*. This change is seen within a broader context of the organization and the forces that operate within it.

Weak modelling capability

There is some understanding that the organization will change over time. However, this consists of *individual forces* rather than as part of the wider system.

Very weak modelling capability

There is no understanding of the *organization as a system* or the manner in which it could change over time.

Moving forward

The line manager's role

The forcefield analysis tool is a helpful frame to the strategic dialogue. The role of the line manager here is to keep committed and remain part of the process, entering into the forcefield discussion in an open and honest manner.

The human resource role

Here the facilitation skills of the human resource professional come to the fore:

◆ to continue to use the skills of systemic thinking to model the end states and the forces for and against change;

◆ to use facilitation skills to ensure the forces for and against change are captured and to guide the group to clustering those forces and building deeper understanding.

Summary of specific actions

5.1 Identify the key end states from the themes.

5.2 Assign a group to work on each end state. Identify the forces for and against change, building on the forces for change, reducing the forces against change.

5.3 Assimilate all groups forcefield analysis to identify the underlying forces.

5.4 Begin to identify the actions, the timescales and the responsibilities for action.

Bridge into action:
the journey continues ...

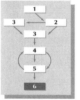

There is no great strategy, only great execution. The challenge now is to move from the rhetoric of themes and systems to the reality of implementation and action. At the beginning of this book I proposed that creating a strategic vision for people in organizations takes place within a wider context of change and transformation. This concept of revitalization is at the heart of the new agenda.

How can organizations move from the rhetoric of a great strategy to the reality of strategic action? In Step 4, the first three phases were described: in the first phase the basic themes of the future vision are identified, in the second phase we identify the processes and behavioural levers which are capable of creating a context for the future vision, in the third phase the map of the system is reviewed. In Step 5, the next stage was described, of modelling the dynamics using the forcefield analysis tool. An understanding of the forces for and against change develops a deeper awareness of the specific actions that must be taken for the vision to be realized. Some of these will be short-term actions that can be taken very quickly, others will require sustained resource focus over several years.

It is appropriate at this time to put these actions into a broader change context. The people process model and the visioning, alignment and gap analysis create the dynamism and momentum within the model. It describes the creation of a vision for the future, an understanding of current capabilities, and the gap between the two, as well as the identification of a number of themes around which the system should be realigned. In doing so, it refers fundamentally to ongoing renewal, adaptation and revitalization.

This is a crucial stage in some of the companies I have observed. The excitement of the visioning and risk matrix phase fades rapidly as the bleak reality of the magnitude of the gap between current capability and future aspirations becomes clear. Faced with the enormity of what has to be achieved, managers retreat rapidly, leaving it to the human resource function to ponder how it can work. For those companies which are committed to making it work, the reaffirmation of management commitment at this stage is crucial. I believe the strength of the journey rests on five guiding principles: the continued involvement and enthusiasm of the guiding coalition; the ongoing building of the capacity to change; the capacity to remain focused on the initial business themes; the development of performance measures; and the realization that the journey is one of emotions and will.

The guiding principles

Guiding principle 1: Continue to build guiding coalitions

The continued involvement of broad groups of people is crucial – to build management learning through involvement in the visioning process; to map the causal relationships; and to become involved and committed to making the journey. I believe the energy of the journey can be sustained through the creation of cross-functional teams whose initial task is to make recommendations, and later to move to action. The role of these task forces is clear: to create a more detailed description of what must be achieved; to identify the early targets and stretch goals; and to begin to identify how the progress of the theme could be monitored over time, the critical success indicators. These task forces are temporary structures designed to create a greater understanding of the current reality and to make specific recommendations for the short- and long-term actions.

In creating these plans for action task force membership is crucial. In particular, the people involved should take an active part in the implementation of the process as early as possible. The credibility of these task forces depends on their level of innovation and creativity and their ability to make their ideas work. Involving the most creative people and those with a good network will go some way to ensuring this. The seriousness of the task force is judged in part by the standing and power of those involved. The members must be credible and act as a role model as the recommendations are put into action.

The emphasis here is on the ability to continuously realign. These groups of people are certainly dealing with concrete and immediate business issues, but they are also focusing on how learning relationships and knowledge sharing produce the answers they seek. This process simply becomes the vehicle for new ways to co-operate, to learn and to share knowledge. The focus shifts from tackling work issues to generate one-off benefits, to creating the ability to generate benefits continuously. The emphasis here is on seeing these groups not as a response to crisis but as part of a constructive process of choice, learning and growth.

Guiding principle 2: Build the capability to change

Business goals change as customer needs develop, as the business broadens its markets, and as technologies advance. The challenge here is not to see this as a one-off process with a finite life but as a continuous adaptation to changing conditions. This six-step process is about creating genuine adaptation, developing an organization which is permanently adaptable and flexible and is involved at both the individual team and organization levels, with a collective wish to move forward.[1]

The metaphor of the process of unfreeze, change and refreeze may have been appropriate for stable businesses in stable environments. But in dynamic environments, refreezing should be deliberately avoided – the organization should remain in a fluid state where realignment takes place on a continuous basis. This six-step process is designed to build organizational capability by aligning individuals with a vision of what the business could be, realigning key processes around this vision, forming cross-functional teams responsible for the continuing success of the project, creating centres of excellence to cultivate learning and ensure the renewal of the processes and measures, and finally, creating learning loops and learning events to capture and embed best practices.

Think back to Glaxo Wellcome, where the team decided that sweeping changes were required in its drug delivery operations. Re-engineering has taught us that a horizontal process view of the company helps to identify and remove barriers to efficiency, flexibility and effectiveness. In the past this would have generated competitive advantage, but today it produces only parity, and only for a while. For Glaxo Wellcome it is not enough to be able to change. The real pay-off is embedded capability. Here the primary focus is not on the work to be done but on groups of people and the need for new patterns of skill and knowledge. In these final steps of putting people at the centre of corporate strategy, the groups of people working on these projects are vital to developing the capacity to learn and adapt.

Guiding principle 3: Keep focusing on the themes

The broad themes of the journey act as a focus for action. This overview plays a crucial role in bridging from the present to the future. Perhaps most importantly it is a vehicle for communication, both across the teams and to the wider group which will be involved. In a succinct and clear way the themes communicate the key strategic goals, the themes of action which will bridge from the present to the future, and the specific actions necessary to bridge the gap. They show clearly where actions and resources should be focused. The overview ensures consistency of action across the organization and between functional and departmental plans.

Guiding principle 4: Build performance measures

This provides a crucial feedback loop between the aspirations captured in the systems map and the themes and the reality of the actions. In Step 3 we saw some of the diagnostic measures available to understand current capability and monitor action. The challenge here is to create a set of performance measures which create awareness of the impact of the master plan and the actions associated with it, to select a relatively small number of key measures which really capture what is crucial to the theme and therefore the long-term vision of the organization, and which focus on attributes that shed light on these key themes.[2] A cornerstone of this continual change and adaptation is a small number of performance measures capable of signalling where the organization is in its journey. Recall that at Hewlett-Packard, these performance measures were critical to John Golding as he steered what he called 'the high-performance car'.

The challenge is to focus on creating performance measures which revolve around those human performance measures most tightly connected with the business goal. Some measures will be leading, some living, and some lagging (*see* Fig. 34). Let us return to the business performance model.

◆ *Leading measures.* Leading measures show whether the required behaviour is actually taking place. Looking back to the Glaxo Wellcome realignment around multi-functional teams, tracking dimensions of ability (e.g. team members' perceptions of team skills) and motivation (e.g. employees' perceptions of the importance of cross-functional team working to the success of Glaxo Wellcome), it is possible to predict whether the old functional behaviours will be replaced. The second source of lead measures is the effectiveness of the key people processes which have been chosen to lever change. At Glaxo Wellcome the effectiveness of team-based performance management and 360° appraisal feedback would give a good indication of whether the context was likely to be realigned. In Step 3 we considered how a realistic view of the people processes could be gained.

◆ *Living measures.* These are the real-time measures that show performance and the delivery of new levels of value. These living measures include employee behaviour or other key performance outcomes – actual costs, measures of customer satisfaction, or perceived value. At Glaxo Wellcome, the actual behaviour of team members included the time spent in cross-functional teams. Measures of perceived value included the speed of product realization from the laboratory to the salesperson, the cost of creating the drug, and customer satisfaction.

◆ *Lagging measures.* These capture the impact of the behaviours on the performance of the business. They include, for example, relative performance, ROE, capital market measures, market share, and shareholder profit.

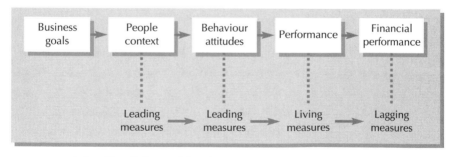

FIGURE 34 ◆ **Leading living and lagging measures**

Guiding principle 5: Remember the journey is one of emotions

Trust and commitment are crucial to the journey, so it is important that the emotional pulse of the organization is established and understood across business units and across time. Understanding the soul of the organization and building trust and commitment is crucial to ongoing adaptation and change. In the cycle of despair and hope (Figs. 17 and 18.) I proposed that building trust and respect was crucial to enabling individual members of the organization to have the courage and determination to change their behaviour. Without this trust and self-esteem, individuals stay within the status quo while their behaviour becomes increasingly inflexible and inappropriate. The adaptability and flexibility that will be crucial to the journey come with people who feel committed to the organization. Listening to and acknowledging the voice, giving people a choice, and treating them with dignity will be central to creating the goodwill that builds revitalization and flexibility.

The tools and techniques

Tool 6.1: building through multi-disciplinary task forces

The multi-disciplinary task forces are the major structure through which the people-centred strategy will be operationalized.[3] Some members of the task force will have been present through the initial steps of visioning and forcefield analysis. To this initial team will be added specialists and people to represent the business areas in which action will take place. The composition of each task force should include:

◆ a *senior manager sponsor* who will drive through the actions. It may also be that they will pilot some of the ideas in their own business. While the sponsor may not be actively involved in all the task-force meetings, they will monitor progress;

◆ an *expert in the area*. For example, an individual capable of reviewing the organizational development and structure. This person could be from within the organization or an adviser from an external consulting practice;

◆ a number of *line managers* who represent the businesses which are likely to be affected. They will be there to articulate the views of the business, and to provide commitment and resources to the subsequent phases;

◆ involved and interested *young people*. This is an excellent opportunity for involving young, talented people who can bring fresh ideas and energy to the subsequent roll-out of the plans. It can also be a crucial part of their personal development.

These task forces are created around each of the themes. Their remit is to build on the forcefield analysis work, to broaden the view of the field by benchmarking other companies, and to prepare goals and actions which are stretching yet plausible.

Tool 6.2: developing an action phase for each theme

The map of the system and subsequent forcefield analysis have led to an understanding of those themes that will be central to success in the future. They have also begun to explore the levers and actions which could be taken to bridge from the present into the future. Now begins the task of bringing order and discipline to these actions.

Effective implementation demands a co-ordinated set of critical success indicators, stretch goals, activities and tasks. Figure 36 shows how these fit together, matching the business theme with intentions and actions.[4] Many of the business themes will take several years to achieve. To affect individual behaviour, they must have intermediate stages – annual goals which bring the larger goal closer to reality. At Hewlett-Packard we saw how the CEOs have used the Hoisin process to create stretch goals to push performance of the entire corporation. Every year they articulate a number of stretch goals which are demanding, important and clearly stated. For example, during the late seventies Hewlett-Packard's performance data indicated warranty failure rates of about 2 per cent per year. In 1980 the CEO, John Young, announced that the firm would aim for a tenfold decrease in the failure rate of HP hardware products. Six years later, frustrated by the time it took to get new products into the market, Young announced a new corporate-wide stretch goal: to cut time to market in half. In both cases, employees rose to the challenge and met Young's demanding goals.

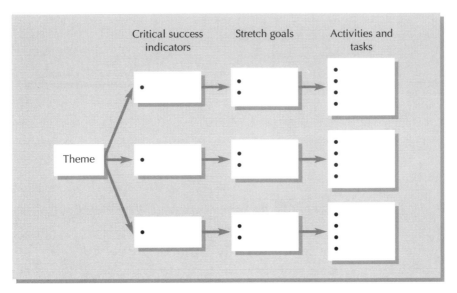

FIGURE 36 ◆ **The flow chart of action**

Key themes describe the three or four themes which summarize the organization's key strategic goals. These are the crucial aspects which will improve performance in the short and longer term. They are identified through the visioning tools described in Step 2.

Critical success indicators directly align intent with action and are there for everyone can see and respond to. To John Young, these few key measures are like the instruments on the dashboard – they tell you when to adjust the steering wheel, what the temperature of the engine is, how the petrol consumption stands. Too often indicators are lagging indicators such as pre-tax earnings, which explain little about the customers, employees or the processes that drive the business. In Fig. 34 we considered live and lagged indicators. The emphasis here is on creating live indicators.

Stretch goals are ambitious, highly targeted opportunities for breakthrough improvements in performance. As we saw at HP, successive CEOs have used them to transform the company. Great stretch goals come from deep discussion within the company, and from collaboration within and across the task forces. This dialogue creates an environment of objectivity in which alternative stretch goals are shared and rationally analyzed. As I have argued throughout this six-step process, this dialogue creates commitment to the goals and actions that follow.

Activities and tactics then need to be developed by the task forces for achieving the goals. These activities and tactics in turn have their own measures.

Step 6 in action

Building task forces at Philips Lighting

By the spring of 1994, there was broad agreement about the key issues at Philips Lighting. In a note to the wider management team and workshop participants, John Vreeswijk described the themes for action. He also promised to take rapid short-term action wherever possible. I believe this was an important intermediary step and signalled that the voice of the people had been heard and understood. By March, a draft document had been prepared which had broad circulation across the business. In this document John laid out the thinking to date. He emphasized the changing nature of the environment and the base for the visualization of the lamps business in five years' time.

He then described the outcomes of the vision sessions, the broad themes which had emerged, and the seven project tasks. For each project the team described the motivation, the assignment, the activities, and the management aspects (timescales, resources, organization including the steering committee, project leader, and project team and passive risks). Many of these seven project teams involved the initial members of the visioning teams. Their mandate was to review the forcefield analysis data and action in more detail, develop a set of recommendations that would be capable of kick-starting the journey to the vision, make more specific action recommendations, and drive the actions forward. The key task forces and the associated themes are shown in Fig. 35.

Initially the task forces focused on creating short-term leverage. In particular, the analysis of the primary restraining forces had shown that the current selection processes were not capable of recruiting talent from around the world, and did not target the new sets of skills in miniaturization and integration. A task force primarily composed of research and development people worked to forecast the skills mix required over the coming five years and reviewed the current skills against these targets. They created a specific plan of action about the new skills requirements and began to establish closer links with those universities developing that skill base.

The analysis had also shown that the dream of globalization would never be a reality unless more talented people were recruited from outside Europe, establishing a global base of skills. This team was made up of younger people and managers representing the European, Asian and US markets. Working initially through video conferencing, and telephone conferencing, they began to review the recruitment and development practices, to benchmark against companies which recruited globally such as Motorola and IBM, and to take advice from experts in the field.

The second major short-term levers to be reviewed were the performance management practices and processes. As the systems map presented in Fig. 31 shows, objectives, metrics and rewards would be crucial to leveraging the innovation and entrepreneurship in the business, and to creating stronger customer orientation. This task force reviewed the situation and benchmarked companies such as Hewlett-Packard and Intel with strong performance management processes and cultures of innovation. It became apparent to the task force that the performance management processes had worked well in the past for Philips Lighting but were too inflexible and

FIGURE 35 ◆ Philips Lighting: key task forces

bureaucratic for the innovative and entrepreneurial culture which would be so crucial to the future. Realignment to the vision would require stronger team-based performance processes, more flexibility of benefits to attract and retain entrepreneurial skills, and a greater emphasis on pay for performance rather than grade or length of service.

Creating strong bridges to the future vision by emphasizing global recruitment, sharing skills across the globe and reorienting reward processes would be critical to the journey. But as the analysis of Philips Lighting had shown, there were structural and cultural barriers with the potential to decouple these early sets of actions. Five task forces were created to address these longer-term levers.

First, they undertook an examination of the relationship between creativity and mobility, with an emphasis on the role of project team working and secondments, defining the pathways for personal growth and development. This group was given the task of working on the earlier forcefield analysis on high-performing teams. Second, a task force worked to create a training policy and plan which reinforced team working and project management, developing a coaching policy and practice for young engineers. Third, another group looked at mapping those skills which would be needed in the future, building from the globalization and innovation themes to a new set of potential career paths that would encourage people to work on innovative projects early in their careers and to gain early experience outside their national country. Fourth, a task force looked at creating entrepreneurial and team behaviours by reviewing the forcefield analysis and creating a set of policies and processes to stimulate and support entrepreneurial behaviour and team performance, reviewing in particular performance management and performance-related pay. Finally, a task force took an overview of the organization and communication infrastructure to build on the visioning exercise and explore the possible scenarios for the location and structure of the research and development laboratories, production facilities and the sales and marketing groups. The visioning exercise had revealed that there was no consensus about how these groups could be structured, particularly around the global-local axis. The role of this task force was to continue the discussion and debate and to create a number of scenarios which would allow the business managers to explore in more detail the structural dilemma they faced.

Developing action plans at Philips Lighting

The challenge here is to create key success indicators which can be rigorously measured. Detailed activities and tasks were created around each of the themes. Let me share one theme – the globalization of talent. At Philips Lighting the globalization task force identified the ways in which the success of globalization could be measured. First, they considered the basic national mix: the proportion of the senior team of non-European nationality, the proportion of the identified 'high-potential' talent of non-European nationality, and the national mix of the key global projects. Next, they looked at how non-Europeans felt about working for Philips Lighting, and the performance of international teams. Finally, they considered the ranking of Philips as an 'employer of choice' in Asia.

For each of these critical success indicators, stretch goals and an associated time frame were agreed. The task force examined the diagnostic capability of Philips to keep track of the indicators. Where necessary they ensured that metrics were put into place. Finally, the task force worked on the activities which would deliver to the stretch goals. For example, ensuring 40 per cent of the senior team were non-European by 2003 would require active identification of high-potential non-Europeans, the active recruitment of senior managers from Asian competitors, and the review of mid-career hiring policies to ensure that once recruited these new employees stayed with Philips. The indicators, stretch goals, activities and tactics are shown in Fig. 37.

By 1995 the senior team of Philips Lighting had gone through one cycle of the development of a people-centred strategy. The task force outputs became the plans that guided the resources of the group over the next couple of years.

The sequence of activities at Philips Lighting is shown in Fig. 38. The first step, in 1993, began with the creation of a management team given the task of developing a vision for the year 2000. The flow diagram shows the main sequence of events and the feedback loops established. The growing commitment of the management team to the process is shown in the feedback loop between the visioning exercise and the involvement in the task forces. This continued involvement ensured that the people who began the strategic conversation continued to be involved in the tough decisions about priorities and actions. The second feedback loop links the diagnostic and alignment phase to the rolling people strategy document. It

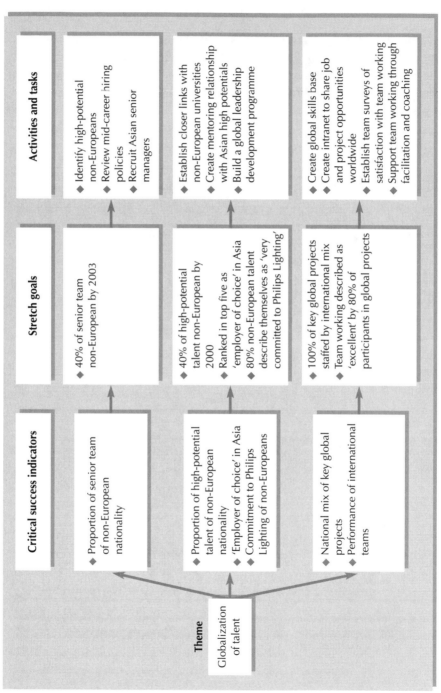

FIGURE 37 ◆ **Building the globalization theme at Philips Lighting**

Bridge into action: the journey continues ...

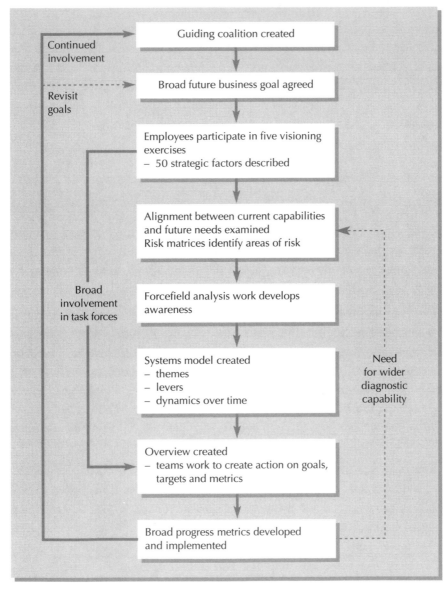

FIGURE 38 ◆ **The sequence of activities at Philips Lighting**

became clear at the diagnostic phase that wider diagnostic capability was required if the team at Philips Lighting were to really understand what was happening, particularly around innovation and entrepreneurship. The third feedback loop shows the iterative nature of the process. The results of the task force and of the subsequent people strategy document feed into the description of goals and ensure that the tension is maintained between current capabilities and future aspirations.

How do you benefit?

Without a bridge into action, the visioning and maps can remain inspirational but unproductive. This final step is crucial to the process. There are three outcomes from doing the step well: first, broad involvement across the business, second, action within the themes, and third, a capacity to continue the journey.

- *Broad involvement across the business.* The process has established from the beginning the importance of involvement from people across the business. Building this broad base of commitment and involvement increases the likelihood of ideas turning into action. The sponsorship of the senior team ensures resources are made available and monitoring takes place. Business line managers bring experience and the potential to use their businesses as sites for pilots. Young people bring ideas and the energy to drive the actions forward.

- *Action within the themes.* The broad business themes continue to provide loose coupling and integrate the actions of the task force. It is impossible for the senior team to actively manage all those projects at the same time. Here the continual commitment to the vision and the broad business goals becomes a guiding principle. The role of the senior team becomes one of leading the overall effort and providing sufficient information and feedback to mechanisms to allow the task force teams to co-ordinate among themselves.

- *Capacity to continue the journey.* The dialogue and commitment created through the task forces fuel the energy to continue the journey. The task force members have created sufficient depth and breadth in interest to keep the interest of this community of action.

Where do you stand now?

Understanding current capabilities

Very strong change capability

People within the organization are adept at *interpreting and communicating the need for change*. There is *involvement of a broad group of people* and a shared awareness of the breadth of the journey. The *performance measures are in place* to mark the passage of the journey and these are communicated and understood.

Strong change capability

There is a shared understanding and agreement of the *adaptive nature of change* in the organization. Task forces are brought together to work *on the shared agenda* and they see their role as creating energy and involvement. There are a small number of *'live' measures* which provide a shared understanding of the current state of the business.

Average change capability

There is *some understanding and agreement* of the adaptive nature of change in the organization. This is essentially a *top-down process*, which rarely involves multi-disciplinary teams. There are *one or two live measures* and those are used, though their use is not embedded throughout the business.

Weak change capability

There is some attempt to create a *systematic approach* to change and adaptation. However, this takes place with *groups of interested managers* and is not shared. Measures are *lagging financial measures*; there are no commonly agreed or used human performance measures.

Very weak change capability

The organization lurches *from one set of tactics to the next*. There is *limited shared awareness* of where the organization is going. Measures are *lagging financial measures*; there are no commonly agreed or used human performance measures

Bridging into action is explored in the brief descriptions above. Consider each description in turn and identify the one that most accurately fits with the current reality in your organization. Turn to Section 3 of the Living Strategy Workbook to plot your findings.

Moving forward

The line manager's role

The key line management role continues to be one of sponsorship and resource allocation. Negotiating the membership of the task forces, ensuring that the members are given sufficient time to work on issues, and providing resources are all crucial to this step.

Many of the actions will require line management commitment and involvement through the provision of sites for pilot work, personal involvement and the capacity to role model and guide the new behaviours.

The human resource role

The human resource professional continues to play a key role in facilitating the task forces. They can also give support through providing opportunities to observe best practice and ensuring that task-force members have a broad understanding of how other companies tackle these issues.

Much of the monitoring of the actions will become the responsibility of the human resource group. It is their role to ensure that the actions take due account of the three tenets: we operate in time, we search for meaning, and we have a soul.

◆ It is my belief that the human resource professionals are 'guardians of the future' – it is their role to ensure that the plans for behavioural change are given sufficient time and resources to take place. Too often initiatives are abandoned before they have had sufficient time to come to fruition. It is the role of this group to educate and communicate the importance of the human time frame.[5]

◆ With regard to meaning, the role of the function is to strive for alignment between the people processes and the goals of the business and by doing so to create a shared sense of meaning. The task forces will be working in a semi-autonomous manner and their recommendations and actions may be independent. The role of the HR professional is to ensure that these actions continue to be aligned with the broad business goals.

◆ The soul of the organization is also crucial in this step. In the cycles of despair and hope we saw how the emotional capital of the organization can be destroyed by unjust actions. The success of these actions in creating a new meaning and vision will depend in part on the way in which the actions take place. Emotional capital is built through providing employees with a choice about how they are treated, giving them a voice and listening to their needs, and by treating them with justice and dignity. The HR professional has a key role to play here.

Summary of specific actions

6.1 Ensure that the guiding coalition remains involved and excited by the events as they unfold. Build a clear communication strategy for them.

6.2 Build the notion that this is a dynamic set of activities, not a one-off annual event. Communicate the need to support the capacity to change.

6.3 Work on the emerging themes. Ensure that they have credibility and people are committed to them.

6.4 Build a multi-disciplinary task force around each theme with senior management sponsorship, functional expertise and line management involvement. Ensure that the membership includes young people.

6.5 For each theme develop a set of critical success indicators, stretch goals and activities and tasks.

A call to action

A message to leaders and the human resources community

Many of us work in businesses that were born when financial capital was king, access to the financial markets was restricted and success came from this rare financial resource. Alternatively, we are part of organizations stamped by technology that has created the patents, ideas and innovations that brought success. This heritage is shown in the jobs we value, the way we develop our highest potential people, what we measure and how we reward success. But while this past has been essential to our success, it will not bring sustainable competitive advantage for the future. To do this we have to build the potential of people in our organizations, the knowledge they bring, and their commitment and enthusiasm. Throughout this book I have argued that building human potential demands a new agenda, a new set of challenges for leaders, and a redefined set of managerial capabilities. This new agenda also provides the human resource professionals in the organization with its greatest challenge, in the way in which processes and practices are developed, and in the competencies and mind sets of the members of the HR community. This new agenda creates a set of expectations of the leader and of the human resource community.

The message for leaders

Expectation 1: dream collectively

Create a time and a process in which you and your colleagues take time out to dream about the future, to engage in collective dreaming, and to create an enthralling picture. Imagine the organization in the future, walk around it, discuss it, understand it. Create enthusiasm and excitement and a vision of the future capable of drawing people towards it. Exchange your ideas about the future and what is important. Be prepared for the face-offs and the disagreements, negotiate what is really important, and be prepared to stand behind your decision.

View the present as a pathway to the future and build channels and roads capable of bridging from the realities of the present to the visions of the future. Create broad visions that simplify the detailed decisions and work to co-ordinate action, allowing people to work independently but still within the frame of the general direction. Be aware of the areas in which the delivery of the vision is vulnerable, and identify those areas that are a crucial part of the future but where current actions are insufficient to bridge the gap.

Delivering the vision will require action on many fronts. View these actions systemically rather than sequentially. Identify the major themes for action, and remember that any more than five is too many. Be aware that you cannot manage all the actions. Instead lead the overall effort, help others to engage in the vision, and leave most of the managerial work to your teams.

Expectation 2: balance the short term with the longer term

Think in the past, the present and the future. Understand the heritage of the organization, the present reality and the future dreams. Create plans of action that reflect human timescales and sequences that are capable of building over several years a capacity in human potential. Think in terms of years, months and days, be aware of the human scale of change, and build a vision of the future that engages people and allows them to understand the role they can play in that future.

Expectation 3: build an organization that values people

Remember that we want to be treated with respect, we want our ideas to be taken seriously, and we to believe we can make a difference. Our emotions and feelings about work influence our ability and propensity to give ourselves and our knowledge and skills. If we feel uncommitted, not respected, or treated unfairly we can choose to withhold our knowledge and skills.

Be aware that upward communication is highly problematic in many organizations and work to create communication channels with employees. Build management reward structures which emphasize and reward people's development. Allow people to remain in jobs for longer than two years so that they can build their human capital as well as that of others. Demonstrate your commitment to them by supporting metrics around people management skills. Expect to receive performance feedback from team members and colleagues.

Treat people with politeness, respect and dignity and in doing so create a strong role model for others to follow. Building a reputation of fairness gives you a buffer against the times when the policy is wrong, or you behave badly.

Expectation 4: understand the reality of the organization

Create a deep and shared understanding of the current state of the business, understand the knowledge base and emotions, and be aware of the changes in this base. Examine your metaphor of the organization and be aware that for many people the dominant metaphor is of the organization as a machine, with interchangeable parts and a 'black box'.

Put the building of a highly committed workforce at the centre of your strategy to create and sustain competitive advantage. Regeneration and revitalization demands people who are emotionally strong, are capable of finding new ways of working and are prepared to experiment and take risks. People with low self-esteem and despair block these changes and retreat into the comfort zone of the status quo. Understand the profound implications of destroying trust in the organization.

Remember that the heritage of the company may have created bureaucracy and paternalism, but revitalizing the business will demand empowered employees who are prepared to take control of their lives. Do not underestimate the difficulty of balancing the sweet and the sour, creating the cycle of hope rather than the cycle of despair. Without energy and hope the organization sinks into a neverending cycle of cost reduction and in doing so destroys any long-term advantage it may have.

Build your understanding of trust and commitment, without which a company is as bankrupt as one with reduced financial capital. Build a model for your organization around what causes high levels of trust and inspiration. Consider the organization against these key influences: do people understand the context in which they operate and the competitive threats and challenges the business faces? Are employees confident about the ability of the organization to adapt? Are they involved in decisions about themselves and the organization? Create a transparent organization in which roles and responsibilities are clear, thus signalling your willingness to trust people. Treat each person as unique and consider individualizing processes and policies.

Develop an understanding of process fairness. Look at what constitutes justice and where this is being violated within the organization. Be certain where your company stands on perceptions of fairness, and understand employees' perceptions of integrity, consistency and pride.

The message for the human resource community

Expectation 1: build the business case for people

Work with the senior team to create a shared understanding of people's role in creating sustainable competitive advantage. Develop a portfolio of measures that accurately reflect the emotional health of the organization. Provide strong feedback loops so that these measures are understood and become part of the strategic dialogue.

Build a strong business case for people so that hard business decisions can be taken in the light of this understanding. Develop the models to show the relationship between the 'soft measures' such as trust and commitment and the 'hard measures' such as company performance. Help the senior team understand the implications of decisions on these core measures. Create an understanding of human time frames, of the importance of the soul and of meaning. Argue strongly for balancing the short-term with the longer-term needs of the business.

Expectation 2: create a compelling people strategy

Build visioning capabilities within the HR team and within the line management group. Encourage the top team to create the time and opportunities for visioning. Create processes in the organization that encourage dialogue and discussion. Support the importance of strategic dialogue in creating flexibility, adaptability and learning capacity. Create a language that engages groups to become skilful observers of the business environment, and communicate this information in such a way that the organization is able to act upon it.

Build a guiding coalition, involving people from different parts of the company and with different viewpoints. Consider involving the young members of the company to bring fresh ideas and to identify the sacred cows. Be aware that these guiding coalitions will be crucial when the subsequent actions become tough and meet resistance. Create a critical mass of people who are able to create action on the basis of their consensus view. This should be embedded, not a new management fad or an episodic activity, but a way of thinking that penetrates the institutional mind.

Create people-centred strategies that enable the senior team to discuss the future, to develop time lines with a human element, to understand where they need to make significant investments for the future, and to maintain inspiration through engaging in visions. Powerful visions come from a deep and rich understanding of what is possible within the organization, and from the wider context outside the organization.

Creating a compelling vision requires an understanding of how the world might change. Build the processes to scan for broad future trends, and communicate an understanding of these wider trends throughout the company.

Expectation 3: view the organization as a complex system

Learn to think systemically; consider bullet points and 'shopping lists' as old speak. Build an understanding of the complexity of the organization and the changes necessary to move from the present to the future. Be aware of the leverage points; differentiate those levers capable of short-term action such as selection and performance management, and the longer-term levers such as the design of the structure and the reward and career development processes. Consider the creation of meaning, and the role of symbols. View the organization as cognitive systems, made up of people who see and interpret the world around them, and strive to create values they can pursue.

Consider what the company espouses through its strategic aims, and the meaning and understanding of these aims as created and shared by employees. Consider the unwritten and the written rules of the game, keeping conscious of rhetoric and reality and the potential gap between the two.

Expectation 4: create alignment and meaning across the people processes

Understand precisely the messages and cues that the people processes are giving about what is important around here, what is valued. Build in focus groups and surveys to keep an eye on the way in which meaning is being construed within the organization. Be sensitive to mixed messages. Think about the people processes as the hard wiring of the organization, and ensure they have integration and cohesion. Understand the heritage of these processes, when and where they were created and what they are reinforcing.

Expectation 5: create just and fair practices

Place a strong emphasis on creating a just and fair working environment. Support managers in understanding that a just and fair organization is created by providing people with a choice, listening to the voice of the people, and providing an adequate explanation of why decisions are made.

Emphasize the importance of managers' actions in creating justice and fairness. Remember that dignity is underpinned with managers who are interpersonally skilled and who listen to people and treat them in a dignified manner. Review role models, create metrics around interpersonal skills, build in strong feedback loops, and ensure this behaviour is noticed and rewarded. Communicate the importance of justice and fairness, help others to understand that this pool of goodwill allows the company to build trust and creates a reservoir of emotional capital. Understand the psychological contract between the organization and the individual. Be aware of times when the contract has been violated, and how it can be rebuilt.

Expectation 6: create a capacity to revitalize

Develop a coherent view of how revitalization takes place, the sequencing of transformational activities, and what makes for successful transformation. Build change management capabilities across the organization. Be aware that processes ossify over time and become resistant to change through an accumulation of resource commitments and institutionalized routines that create commitment to the status quo. Understand that managers may resist change because it becomes increasingly time consuming to abandon complex activities. Be aware that the critical issues of change are motivating constructive behaviours in the face of the anxiety created with change, and actively managing the transitional state.

Understand the key levers that could really make a difference to the themes of the vision. Identify those levers that will bring change in the short term (selection, objective setting, metrics and rewards) and those that will bring change over the longer term (workforce, leadership and organizational development). Understand the themes in their context, consider the forces that will be operating for change and those that will be blocking change. Create plans of action that will build on these forces.

Create cross-functional task forces around the key themes. Use the ideas and thoughts of line managers to bring insight and build commitment. Understand what the task forces have to achieve and build milestones and timescales to track performance. Understand where the actions are going, and create a small number of key metrics that capture what is crucial to the theme. Monitor these metrics over time.

PART IV

The living strategy workbook

The living strategy workbook

n the living strategy workbook I have produced exercises and discussion pieces to take you and your team through a set of experiences. These are designed to create a richer understanding of the people side of the business, to engage in discussions about the future, and to create clarity around the steps which have to be taken to build from the present into the future.

The exercises follow the flow of the book and are in three sections.

◆ *Section 1 – The new agenda*: *putting people at the heart of corporate purpose*. The first section is designed to enable you and your colleagues to gain a deeper insight into the way in which people are viewed in your organization. The discussion points will help you to increase your understanding of the heritage of the business and how this heritage will influence your business in the future.

◆ *Section 2 – The three tenets*. The second section is designed to enable you and your colleagues to understand your company's perspective on time, meaning and soul. This is a discussion piece, which increases your understanding of the three tenets and helps you identify the areas where the business is failing to capitalize on the potential of the three tenets to create a context in which human potential can flourish.

◆ *Section 3 – The six steps to creating a living strategy*. The third section contains a diagnostic tool designed to enable you and your colleagues to profile the current capability of your business against the six steps to creating a living strategy. This is followed by a discussion of three possible profiles, the symptoms of these profiles, and the possible actions you can take.

Section 1 – The new agenda: putting people at the heart of corporate purpose

This is designed to enable you and your colleagues to gain deeper insight into the way in which people are viewed in your organization. You can expect this part to:

◆ enable you to examine and understand the forces driving your business;

◆ provide an opportunity for you to plot the impact of these forces on your industry, and to project how they will change in the future;

◆ help you plot the current context, identify the future context, and establish the challenges associated with the future.

The industry drivers of competitive advantage

This focuses on the broad drivers within the industry and the forces that have shaped the means by which firms within the industry have sought to compete.

Working on your own or with colleagues, consider the sources of competitive advantage which have historically driven your industry and the business. Sources of competitive advantage may include access to markets or financial capital, specific patents or technologies, knowledge and skills. Recall that sources of competitive advantage have three attributes:

◆ they are of *value* to the business in the sense that they have the ability to create superior company performance;

◆ they are *rare*, i.e. they are found in a minority of firms;

◆ they are *imitable*, i.e. they have characteristics which are difficult for competitors to imitate.

Consider this set of questions:

◆ Which sources have historically been most important?

◆ What sources do you consider most important now, and which will be the most important in the future?

◆ How have these affected the industry and how are they affecting your business or company?

For each source of competitive advantage you identify, consider the impact it has had on the 'way you do things around here'. Does the influence still affect your business or company, and in what way?

In Table 9, list the sources of competitive advantage that have defined the industry in the past, those that are dominant today, and predict the emerging sources of competitive advantage that will dominate in five to ten years from now.

The heritage, the dominant paradigm

Companies are born and thrive by their initial ability to create competitive advantage through resources that are valuable, rare or imitable. The nature of these resources, be they access to markets or financial capital, technology or knowledge, profoundly influence how competitive advantage is seen. It is vital that a company understands its heritage to recognize how current managerial thinking and constructs are influenced by the past.

Review what you know about your company's past, note the two or three sources of competitive advantage on which it was built, and identify the dominant view.

Implications

1 What has been the influence of the dominant sources of competitive advantage on the way the organization is managed?

2 How will the changing forces affect your business in the future?

TABLE 9 ◆ **The drivers of competitive advantage in your industry**

Five years ago	Today	Five years from now

Section 2 – The three tenets:
the philosophy of the living strategy

If the current or future source of competitive advantage in your business is people, then the next question is, how well adapted is your company to actively build human performance? In Section 2 we consider each of the three tenets: we operate in time, we search for meaning, we have a soul. For each of these tenets there is a set of questions designed to increase your insight into the current state of your business with regard to each of the tenets. This is designed as a discussion piece, to increase understanding of the impact of the three tenets and to identify the areas where the business is failing to capitalize on their potential to create a context in which human potential can flourish.

Tenet 1: we operate in time

When it comes to time, there is something very special about people. Unlike financial or technical capital, people operate in time. The past, the present and the future are vital aspects of how we see the world. And the timescales for human capital are measured in years rather than minutes, hours or months. The questions that follow highlight some of the key aspects of time. They aim to provide a frame for a broader discussion about how time is viewed within your business.

The relationship between the past, the present and the future

1   How strong and compelling is the vision for the future? How committed are individuals to this vision?

2   Are there policies and practices in place to prepare individuals for the future and which acknowledge the future for individuals?

3   How are managers appraised? Are there reward mechanisms in place to reinforce building future competence?

4   How long do people remain in a role? Is the 'unwritten rule of the game' that the people with the highest potential stay less than two years in a role?

5   Do the short-term processes such as performance management dominate resource allocation? How much emphasis is there on the aspects of the 'longer-term' cycle, particularly workforce and organizational development?

The time for changes in performance

1   What are the dominant time frames for setting objectives and measuring performance in the company? Are there measures of performance which are greater than the annual cycle?

2   Is there an understanding that implementing projects about people will take a number of years? Are there project plans in place which acknowledge this?

3   Are the core people processes relatively stable or are they frequently changed in a relatively ad hoc manner?

4   Do you feel that short-term tactics overwhelm longer-term considerations?

On the scale shown in Fig. 39 the time dimension runs from short-term dominance to a balance between the longer term and the short term. Plot on the time axis where you believe your business is currently and where it should be in the future. In considering the future you should be particularly sensitive to the way in which the sources of competitive advantage will change.

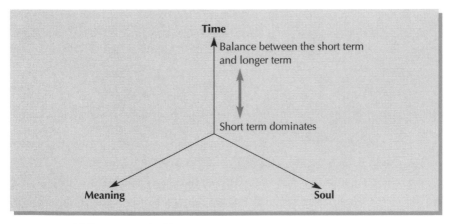

FIGURE 39 ◆ We operate in time

Tenet 2: we strive for meaning

If human potential is a source of competitive advantage now or in the future, this has a profound impact on how meaning is created within your business. We as individuals search for meaning, we want to be part of something that has a purpose, in which we can engage and where we feel inspired. The following questions are designed to deepen your insight into the meaning of your business.

The meaning of the place

1 What do you believe are the fundamental 'unwritten rules of the game' in your business? What do people believe is important around here? How close do you judge these 'unwritten rules' to be to the stated aims and purpose of the business?

2 What are the symbols, myths and stories of the business? Again, how close is the evocation of these myths and symbols to the stated aims and purpose of the business?

3 What is the 'dominant logic' of the place? How shared is this across groups of people? How close is the dominant logic to the stated aims and purpose of the business?

The alignment to meaning

1 Consider the key short-term people processes in the business, the way in which people are appraised and rewarded. Are the cues and meanings of these processes aligned to the purpose of the business, and to each other?

2 Consider the key long-term people processes, the development of the workforce, of leaders and of the organization. Are these processes aligned to each other and to the longer-term purpose of the business?

3 Do people feel inundated with mixed messages, with 'flavour of the month' activities?

4 In your view, how large is the gap between corporate rhetoric and the experiences of individual members of the organization?

5 Are there processes, practices and policies in place which were central to success in the past but which are now no longer appropriate?

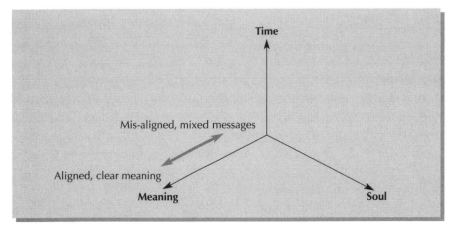

FIGURE 40 ◆ We strive for meaning

In Fig. 40 the meaning dimension runs from misaligned to a meaning that is clearly aligned with the purpose of the business. On the meaning axis, plot where you believe your business is currently and where it should be in the future.

Tenet 3: we have a soul
Diagnosing your company's perspective on soul

There is something fundamentally different about people, call it emotion, call it a soul. But we want to be treated with respect, dignity and pride. The following questions are designed to deepen your insight into the soul of your business. The first group looks at whether there is the capacity within the business to create a deep understanding of the soul, while the second focuses on the attitudes to emotions.

Measures of soul

1 How deep is the awareness of emotions in your business? Are the results of employee surveys on areas such as commitment, pride and inspiration understood and communicated?

2 Do managerial objectives contain any 'soft' measures? Are their performance metrics around the development of human inspiration or commitment?

Attitudes to emotions

1 Do the corporate values refer to people and emotions? Is this received as another piece of rhetoric, or is there real commitment to it?

2 Are discussions dominated by references to financial capital, with limited reference to people and emotions?

3 Is there any understanding in the business of the potential impact of emotions, such as trust, on the bottom-line profitability of the business?

4 When discussing potential tactics and strategies, is the impact on trust or inspiration brought into the calculations?

5 Does untrustworthy, undignified or unjust behaviour influence the promotion prospects of an individual?

On the scale shown in Fig. 41 the soul dimension runs from low emotional capital to high emotional capital. Plot on the soul axis where you believe your business is currently and where it should be in the future.

The three tenets: summary

You have now had an opportunity to debate the three tenets and to consider where your company is now and where it should be in the future.

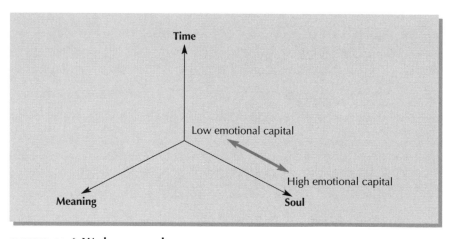

FIGURE 41 ◆ **We have a soul**

Consider Fig. 42 and consider the following questions:

◆ How much are the three tenets acknowledged in your company?

◆ What is the impact of this on the perceptions of employees and the way change is orchestrated?

◆ Do you see the acknowledgement of the three tenets changing in the future?

◆ What will be the impact of these changes.

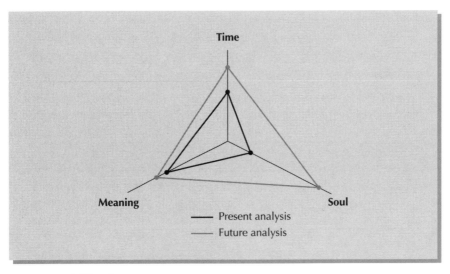

FIGURE 42 ◆ **The three tenets: summary**

Section 3 – The six steps to creating a living strategy

In the first half of this workbook we considered the context of people, the fundamental beliefs within the organization and how those beliefs influence the tenets of individuals: we operate in time, we search for meaning, we have a soul. In the final part of the workbook, we look at the current capacity of the organization to build a living strategy. The objectives of this diagnosis are to:

◆ explore the six steps and their associated capabilities which build a living strategy;

◆ enable you to identify specific characteristics of your organization that can be leveraged or adapted to build a people-centred strategic capability.

There are six steps with associated capabilities.

◆ *Step 1 – Build guiding coalitions.* The capability to involve a broad range of stakeholders who represent the broad functions of the organization. To involve senior managers, middle managers, human resource professionals and people in customer and market-facing ideas. To involve younger members of the organization. The capability to continue to use this guiding coalition through the stages of the process.

◆ *Step 2 – Imagining the future.* The capability to engage people from across the organization in dialogue about the future. To imagine the business in the future, its structure, culture, people, leaders and processes.

◆ *Step 3 – Understanding current capability and identifying the gap.* The capability to accurately build a picture of the current state of the organization. In particular, the context in which people work, their behaviour and key performance measures. This is built over time, benchmarked against industry equivalents, and shared with business managers.

◆ *Step 4 – Mapping the system.* The capacity to understand and develop systemic thinking capabilities across the organization. To ensure that decisions are taken on the basis of their impact on the total system. To build a sufficiently deep understanding of the business to begin to understand causal linkage.

◆ *Step 5 – Modelling the dynamics.* The capability to understand the dynamics within the system. To create a shared perception of the links between process levers and outcomes and the way these will change over time.

◆ *Step 6 – Bridging into action.* The capability to interpret and communicate the need for change through the involvement of a broad group of people. To create a shared understanding of key performance measures which mark the passage of the journey.

For each of these six steps, a set of descriptions has been created to help you diagnose the current level of organizational capability. These are presented at the end of each step description.

On Fig. 43 plot your organization as the business is now and how it should be in five years' time.

Profiling the ability to create a living strategy

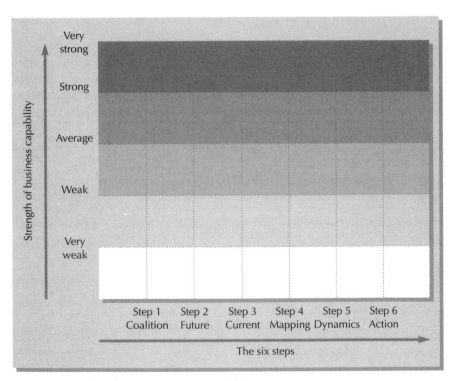

FIGURE 43 ◆ **The six steps to creating a living strategy**

The current capabilities

Your profile may look something like the three profiles presented here. Choose the profile most like your own and consider the symptoms and the action points.

1   Are there steps which have been well developed in the business? How has this happened? What has been the impact on your ability to meet the goals of the business? What, if any, has been the impact on the past, present and future business performance?
2   Are there steps where the business has been unable to create capability? How has this happened? What has been the impact on your ability to meet the goals of the business? What, if any, has been the impact on the past, present and future business performance?

Profiling the six steps: the acid test

Chronic underperformance

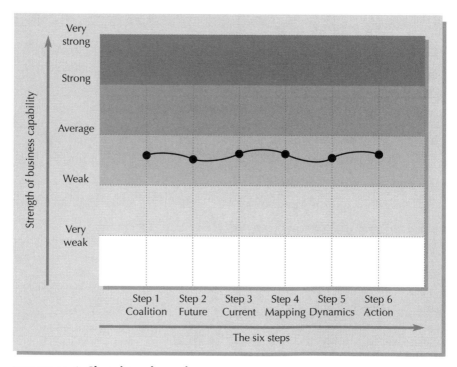

FIGURE 44 ◆ **Chronic underperformance**

The symptoms are:

- a tactical, problem-centred approach to people in your organization;
- short-term, fire fighting with limited longer-term building of capability;
- people issues are for the HR function, not line managers;
- a gradual deterioration in the health of the business, which will accelerate when the competitive environment becomes harder or new competitors enter the marketplace;
- the deterioration in health will feed through to bottom-line performance, resulting in financial underperformance.

Consider the following:

- engage the business in a debate about the link between people and financial performance;
- benchmark against best-in-class competitors, both within and outside the sector;
- find/become a champion and pilot the six-step process in one part of the business where there is a strong sponsor;
- concentrate initially on engaging managers in visualizing and ensure that one or two task forces are followed through;
- monitor the capabilities of the HR function. Recruit or develop specialists in visioning and change management.

Tactical, action-led performance

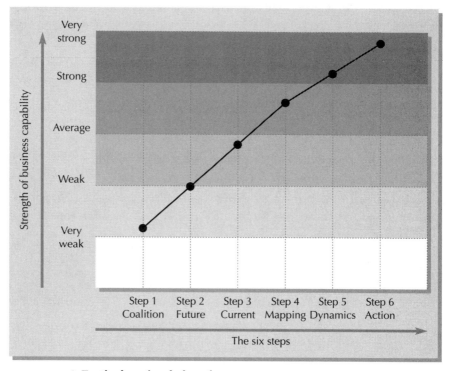

FIGURE 45 ◆ **Tactical, action-led performance**

The symptoms here are:

◆ much action around the people side of the business, probably some task forces, some measurement, lots of activities;

◆ the action orientation is likely to be focused on resolving short-term issues, and as a consequence longer-term issues may well go unnoticed;

◆ probably driven by a small team, led by the human resource function and a number of people-centred managers;

◆ a general feeling that 'people really matter' but an uncomfortable view that all this activity may not be paying off;

◆ when times get tough, the first cut is in the people arena, particularly the training and development budget.

Consider the following:

◆ engage a wide group of people in thinking about the people aspects of the business. Run visioning workshops to engage this group;

◆ begin to balance the short-term tactics with the longer term. Make the case for the human time frame;

◆ train key members of the HR function in visioning and systemic thinking;

◆ pilot a futures workshop, engage people in a debate about the future. Use experts and industry analysts to provide a view of how the industry sector will change.

Aimless visioning and presentation

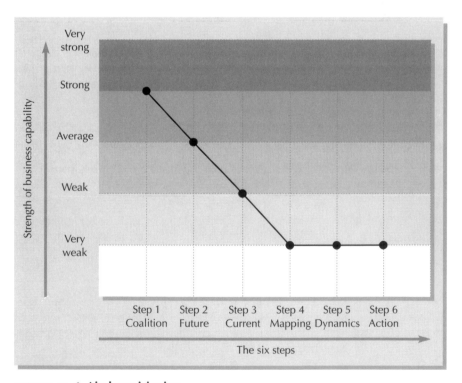

FIGURE 46 ◆ **Aimless visioning**

The symptoms here are:

◆ discussions about the future which seem to rapidly run out of steam. Workshops around scenarios and the future result in debate but limited action;

◆ a general feeling of cynicism about new initiatives. Futuring/visioning perceived as yet another 'flavour of the month';

◆ the 'converted' come along to the events. The non-converts remain on the sidelines, ready to scupper any action;

◆ poor process discipline, a general malaise about the capability of the organization to make things happen. Frustration with lack of progress on some key business issues.

Consider the following:

◆ focus less on diagnosing the issues, more on making them happen;

◆ take a number of themes and create multi-functional task forces around them. Build strong metrics to measure progress. Communicate the state of progress;

◆ take a wider view of process discipline within the organization. Look at how the best practice is embedded within the business;

◆ train key members of the HR function in change management and project management.

Conclusion

Using the workbook you have had an opportunity to consider the philosophy and practice of a living strategy. Part III presents diagnostics and tools designed to help you consider your options for action to build a living strategy. Now is the time to move into action.

Creating action

1   Having read *Living Strategy* and reviewed the workbook, take a moment to summarize the current situation in your company, and the problems and opportunities you face in your quest to build a living strategy.

2   Using this, consider the specific action you will need to take to improve the business.

3   For each action:

♦   note the desired outcome you want to achieve;

♦   consider the forces for and against change which will be operating around the desired outcome;

♦   consider the obstacles and how these can be reduced;

♦   identify the forces for change – the people or situations which could support you.

Involve as many people as possible in the actions and consider the guiding coalition and how they can best be used.

Coventry University

Notes

Preface

Note 1

The data collected in 1992 from the Leading Edge Consortium have been described in Gratton, L., Hope Hailey, V., Stiles, P. and Truss, C. (1999) *Strategic Human Resource Management: Corporate rhetoric and human reality*, Oxford University Press, London.

The new agenda : putting people at the heart of corporate purpose

Note 1

The role of human performance in creating competitive advantage has been extensively described in many papers and books over the last decade. The books that I have found most useful are Jeffrey Pfeffer's (1994) *Competitive Advantage through People: Unleashing the power of the workforce*, Harvard Business School Press, Boston, MA. Pfeffer, J. (1998) *The Human Equation: Building profits by putting people first*, Harvard Business School Press, Boston, MA. Fits-Enz, J. (1990) *Human Value Management*, Jossey-Bass, San Francisco. Kaplan, R.S. and Norton, D.P. (1996) *The Balanced Scorecard*, Harvard Business School Press, MA. Swanson, R. and Gradous, D. (1991) *Forecasting Financial Benefits of Human Resource Development*, Jossey-Bass, San Francisco.

There have been many articles about the particular aspects of human performance that creates competitive advantage. See for example Aaker, D. (1989) 'Managing assets and skills: The key to sustainable competitive advantage', *California Management Review*, Winter, pp. 91–106. Barney, J.

(1991) 'Firm resources and sustained competitive advantage', *Journal of Management*, 17, pp. 99–120.

Note 2

The Glaxo Wellcome case was developed as part of the Leading Edge Research Consortium. Bill Proudlock and Anne Pritchard have both been enormously helpful in providing their own insights into the cases. I prepared the 1993/4 case and my research colleague Philip Stiles prepared the 1996/7 case.

Note 3

The Hewlett-Packard case was developed as part of the Leading Edge Research Consortium. The UK management team, in particular John Kick and John Golding both brought insights and wisdom to our understanding of the company. My research colleague Veronica Hope Hailey wrote the cases.

Note 4

I learned about Motorola in China from a case prepared for the Global Business Consortium at London Business School in the Hong Kong module of 1996.

Note 5

There is growing interest in the relationship between the human resource practices adopted by a firm and its competitive positioning. There are three groups which have commented on this relationship. Jeffrey Pfeffer has identified a number of core practices that impact on financial performance. In his 1994 study he identified the five top-performing firms in each industry sector. He reports that all had a set of high-commitment work practices such as employment security, selectivity in recruitment, high wages, incentive pay, employee ownership, information sharing, participation and empowerment, team and job redesign and cross-training.

Jeffrey Pfeffer (1998) *The Human Equation: Building profits by putting people first*, Harvard Business School Press, Boston, MA. Mark Huselid's work has put wealth creation figures on this impact. See Huselid, M. (1995) 'The impact of HRM practices on turnover, productivity and corporate performance', *Academy of Management Journal*, vol. 38, no. 3, p. 645.

Note 6

In the UK, teams at the Sheffield Effectiveness Programme and London School of Economics have striking longitudinal data on the financial impact of high-commitment work practices. See Patterson, M., West, M., Lawthom, R. and Nickell, S. (1998) *Issues in People Management 22: The impact of people management practices on business performance*, Institute of Personnel and Development, London.

Note 7

The central role of people and processes is explored in the resource-based view of the firm. For a theory-grounded argument on why resources must be scarce and firm specific, see Petraf, M.A. (1993) 'The cornerstone of competitive advantage: a resource-based view', *Strategic Management Journal*, no. 14, pp. 179–191. Barney, J. (1986) 'Strategic factor markets: expectations, luck and business strategy', *Management Science*, vol. 32, pp. 1231–1241.

First tenet: we operate in time

Note 1

The concept of managerial short-termism in the companies we studied in the Leading Edge Research Consortium is discussed by my colleague Pat McGovern in the chapter entitled 'HRM policies and managerial practices' in Gratton, L., Hope Hailey, V., Stiles, P. and Truss, C. (1999) *Strategic Human Resource Management: Corporate rhetoric and human reality*, Oxford University Press, London. For a wider description of the argument see Marsh, P. (1990) *Short-termism on trial*, International Fund

Managers Association, London. Demirag, I., Tylecote, A. and Morris, B. (1994) 'Accounting for financial and managerial causes of short-term pressure in British companies', *Journal of Business Finance and Accounting*, vol. 21, no. 8, pp. 1195–1213. For a wider discussion on the impact of managerial short-termism see Hamel, G. and Prahalad, C.K. (1994) *Competing for the Future*, Harvard Business School Press, Boston, MA.

Note 2

I explored the potential negative impact of fast track career schemes in 'The development of empowering leaders: the anatomy of a fast track' in Thomas, H., O'Neal, D. and Kelly, J. (eds) (1995) *Strategic Renaissance and Business Transformation*, Wiley, London.

Note 3

The importance of 'leaving space', of allowing synchronicity is explored by Joe Jaworski in his (1996) book *Synchronicity: The inner path of leadership*, Berrett-Koehler, San Francisco.

Note 4

At a number of points in this book I speak about the ABB factory in Baden, Switzerland. ABB is a member of the Global Business Consortium at London Business School. The philosophy of the programme is that we spend one day in a site of each Consortium member. In 1996 and 1997 the ABB site was the Baden site in Switzerland. The site manufactures power turbines, parts of which are assembled by highly complex robots. Watching these almost human robots brought home to me how similar and yet how different we are from the technology we create.

Note 5

Perceptions of time have been described by Gert Hofstede. See for example, Hofstede, G. (1984) *Cultures and Organizations*, McGraw-Hill, Maidenhead.

Note 6

The concept of a memory of the future comes from Arie de Geus in his (1997) book *The Living Company: Growth, learning and longevity in business*, Nicholas Brealey, England.

Note 7

My colleague Philip Stiles prepared the case of BT Payphones for the Leading Edge Research Consortium. Our particular thanks to Bob Mason, Personnel Director, and Patricia Vaz, CEO of BT Payphones at that time.

Note 8

This 'classical' approach fails to take account of organizational realities. For a richer discussion of the failures of the rationalistic approach see Henry Mintzberg's (1994) *The Rise and Fall of Strategic Planning*, Free Press, New York.

Note 9

The elements of the 'process school' have been described in some detail by Kees van der Heijeden in his (1996) *Scenarios: The art of strategic conversation*, Wiley, England. He describes his own experience at Royal Dutch/Shell's Business Environment Division. A colleague of Kees, Arie de Geus, has described some of these processes with great subtlety and insight using his own metaphor of the living organism in (1997) *The Living Company: Growth, learning and longevity in business*, Nicholas Brealey, England.

Note 10

This view of process is built on a foundation of thought that goes back to Chris Argyris. He designed an educational experience that instructed management teams in competitive analysis and strategy formulation, as well as the skills for discussing the undiscussable barriers to strategic implementation. See for example, Argyris, C. (1990) *Overcoming Organisational Defenses*, Alynn and Bacon, Boston, MA. Since then others have provided a more comprehensive road map for engaging employees in developing an organization that is aligned with strategy and values. See Beer, M. and Eisenstat, R. (1996) 'Developing an organization capable of implementing strategy and learning', *Human Relations*, vol. 49, no. 5, pp. 597–619. Mohrman, S.A. and Cummings, T.G. (1989) *Self-designing Organizations: Learning how to create high performance*, Addison-Wesley, Reading, MA. Nadler, D.A. and Tushman, M.L. (1989) 'Organizational frame bending: principles for managing re-orientation', *The Academy of Management Executive*, vol. 111, no. 3, pp. 194–204. Daft, R. L. and Weick, K. (1984) 'Towards a model of organizations as interpretative systems', *Academy of Management Review*, vol. 9, pp. 284–295.

Second tenet: we search for meaning

Note 1

See Scott-Morgan, P. (1994) *The Unwritten Rules of the Game*, McGraw-Hill, New York. This provides a deeper understanding of how these rules are created and the basis by which they are sustained within the organization. The methodology described in the book was part of the triangulated methodology created for the Leading Edge Research Consortium and many of the individual quotes in this book are elicited by this in-depth, anthropological method.

Note 2

John Kotter uses the analogy of the elastic bands in his (1996) book *Leading Change*, Harvard Business School Press, Boston, MA. I have used it here because I think it simply, but profoundly, captures the notion of alignment.

Note 3

The notion of cognitive mapping and personal constructs has been described by a number of writers. In particular Weik, K. (1979) *The Social Psychology of Organising*, Addison-Wesley, Reading, MA.

Note 4

The Citibank case was developed as part of the Leading Edge Research Consortium. Thanks in particular to Gillian Arthur for her insights. The core was prepared by my colleague, Philip Stiles.

Note 5

The notion of vertical and horizontal linkage has been well established in the literature and is widely acknowledged as a crucial part of any strategic approach to the management of people. See for example, Dyer, L. (1984) 'Linking human resource and business strategies', *Human Resource Planning*, vol. 7, no. 2, pp. 79–84. Mahoney, T.A. and Deckop, J.R., (1986) 'Evolution of concept and practice in personnel administration/human resource management', *Journal of Management*, vol. 12, no. 2, pp. 223–241. Schuler, R.S. and Jackson, S.E. (1987) 'Linking competitive strategies with human resource practices', *Academy of Management Executive*, vol.1, no. 3, pp. 207–219. Truss, C.J. and Gratton, L. (1994) 'Strategic human resource management: a conceptual approach', *International Journal of Human Resource Management*, vol. 5, no. 3, pp. 663–686. Labovitz, G. and Rosansky, V. (1997) have explored aligning business goals and human performance in some depth in *The Power of Alignment*, Wiley, New York.

Note 6

This quote comes from Packard, D. (1995) *The HP Way: How Bill Hewlett and I built our company*, HarperCollins, New York.

Note 7

The moderating role of HR practices is described in Wright, P., McMahan, G. and McWilliams, A. (1994) 'Human resources and sustained competitive advantage: a resource-based perspective', *International Journal of Human Resource Management*, vol. 5, no. 2, pp. 301–326.

Note 8

For an overview of systems thinking see Senge, P. (1990) *The Fifth Discipline: The art and practice of the learning organisation*, Century Business, New York. De Geus, A. (1988) 'Planning as learning', *Harvard Business Review*, March–April, pp. 70–74. Huff, A.S. (ed.) (1990) *Mapping Strategic Thought*, Wiley, Chichester.

Note 9

The issue of adaptation and flex is fascinating. See for example, Huff, J., Huff, A. and Thomas, H. (1992) 'Strategic renewal and the interaction of cumulative stress and inertia', *Strategic Management Journal*, vol. 13, pp. 55–75.

Third tenet: we have a soul

Note 1

In this section I have spoken about the soul of the organization and of the importance of emotions. The notion of the role of emotions in the performance of the individual and the organization is receiving increasing attention. At the level of the individual, the notion of emotional intelligence has been described by D. Goleman in his (1995) book *Emotional Intelligence*, Bantam, New York. Descriptions of emotions at the organizational level can be found in Hochschild, L.E. (1983) *The Managed Heart: Commercialization of human feeling*, University of California Press, Berkeley, CA. For recent and relatively comprehensive reviews of the role of emotions in organizational functioning and performance, see Fineman, S. (ed.) (1993) *Emotions in Organisations*, Sage, London. See also Quy Nguyen, Huy (1999) 'Emotional capability, emotional intelligence and radical change', *Academy of Management Review*, vol. 24, no. 2, pp. 325–345.

Note 2

The organization as a living entity is at the heart of de Geus, A. (1997) *The Living Company: Growth, learning and longevity in business*, Nicholas Brealey, England.

Note 3

The relation between the commitment and inspiration of employees and business revenues is receiving increasing attention. Individual businesses have begun to create an awareness of the relationship in their own company. See for example Pfeffer, J. (1998) *The Human Equation: Building profits by putting people first*, Harvard Business School Press, Boston, MA. Ulrich, D., Zenger, J. and Smallwood, N. (1999) *Results-Based Leadership*, Harvard Business School Press, Boston, MA.

Note 4

The concept of the 'sweet and the sour' is explored by Ghoshal, S. and Bartlett, C. (1997) *The Individualized Corporation: A fundamentally new approach to management*, Harper Business, New York.

Note 5

For a detailed description of the impact of self-esteem on the ability of individuals to grow see Branden, N. (1998) '*Self-esteem at work: How confident people make powerful companies*', Jossey-Bass, San Fransisco.

Note 6

In my own thinking about trust I have been influenced by Fukuyama, F. (1995) *Trust: The social virtues and the creation of prosperity*, Free Press, New York. Here he speaks particularly about trust at the level of society, but his message has equal meaning for individuals and organizations.

Note 7

The importance of procedural justice became increasingly apparent to us as the research from the Leading Edge Research Consortium progressed. During this time my colleague Joanna Zaleska and I have explored this issue in some depth. The work on procedural justice was supported by a grant from the Economic and Science Research Council. The literature on procedural justice continues to grow. A managerial overview is provided by Kim, C. and Mauborgne, R. (1997) 'Fair process: managing in the knowledge economy', *Harvard Business Review*, July–August, pp. 65–75. In our own thinking on the subject we have been influenced by Folger, R. and Cropanzano, R. (1998) *Organisational Justice and Human Resource Management*, Sage, London.

Note 8

For a discussion of the psychological contract, see Rousseau, D.M. (1995) *Psychological Contracts in Organisations: Understanding written and unwritten agreements*, Sage, London. See also her earlier paper, Robinson, L. and Rousseau, D. (1994) 'Violating the psychological contract: not the exception but the norm', *Journal of Organisational Behaviour*, vol. 15, no. 3, pp. 245–261.

The six steps to creating a living strategy

Note 1

I first described the short- and long-term cycle in Gratton, L. et al. (1999) 'Linking individual performance to business strategy: the people process model', *Human Resource Management*, vol. 38, no. 1, pp. 17–33.

Note 2

The key role played by performance management processes in firm performance is well understood. Within this discourse both John Purcell and John Child have made important contributions. Purcell, J. (1995) 'Corporate strategy and its links with human resource management' in Storey, J. (ed.) (1974) *Human Resource Management: A critical text*, Routledge, London. Child, J. (1974) 'Managerial and organisational factors associated with company performance', *Journal of Management Studies*, vol. 11, pp. 13–27. The 'softer' performance measures such as employee and customer satisfaction continue to be more complex to measure than 'hard' financial measures. This point is made strongly by Ulrich, D. and Lake, D. (1990) *Organisational Capability: Competing from the inside out*, John Wiley & Sons, New York. Descriptions abound of the weak integration between business goals and performance metrics. See in particular Butler, J., Ferris, S. and Napier, N. (1991) *Strategic and Human Resource Management*, South-Western, Cincinnati, OH. Walker, J. (1980) *Human Resource Strategy*, McGraw-Hill, New York.

Note 3

For a deeper debate on the role of feedback on organizational learning see Argyris, C. (1977) 'Double loop learning in organisations', *Harvard Business Review*, Sept–Oct, vol. 55, no. 5, pp. 115–125.

Note 4

Ed Lawler has written extensively about the potential role of rewards and recognition in leveraging organizational performance. See, for example, Lawler, E.E. (1990) *Strategic Pay*, Jossey-Bass, San Francisco. The complexity of aligning rewards to business goals was certainly a recurring theme in our own Leading Edge research, a point made forcibly by Hambrick, D. and Snow, C. (1989) 'Strategic reward systems' in Snow, C. (ed.) *Strategy, Organisational Design and Human Resource Management*, JAI Press, Greenwich, CT.

Note 5

Leadership development is of enormous importance to practitioners and academics. Most recently there has been renewed emphasis on the role played by significant work experience and mentoring. See Kotter, J. (1973) 'The psychological contract: managing the joining-up process', *California Management Review*, vol. 15, no. 3, pp. 91–99.

Step one: building a guiding coalition

Note 1

Nonarka in his own visioning work at Asahi Chemical Industry went even further, by engaging only younger people. This is how he argues: 'The Project specifically excluded the elder managerial staff members from the vision creation process as they tend to adhere to their own manner, which was effective in the past. It is highly probably that younger middle managers will work passionately to realize the visions they actually create and propose under their own name.' Nonaka, I. (1988) 'Self-renewal of the Japanese firm and the human resource strategy', *Human Resource Management*, vol. 27, no. 1, pp. 45–62 and (1988) 'Towards middle-up-down management: appreciating information creation', *Sloan Management Review*, vol. 29, no. 3, pp. 9–18.

Note 2

See for example, Quinn, J. B. (1980) *Strategies for Change: Logical incrementalism*, Irwin, Homewood, IL. The term guiding coalition was used by John Kotter in his (1996) book *Leading Change*, Harvard Business School Press, Boston, MA. See also Schein, E. (1969) *Process Consultation: Its role in organisational development*, Addison-Wesley, Reading, MA.

Step two: imagining the future

Note 1

Peter Schwartz in (1991) *Art of the Long View: Planning for the future*, Doubleday, New York, describes his own journey as a futurologist. He particularly focuses on the networks, wide reading and conversations as a way of gaining insight into the broader long-term context.

Note 2

The central importance of visioning and the richness of the dialogue emerged initially from the work carried out at Royal Dutch/Shell. A number of the Shell strategy groups have written of their experiences. I gained much insight from van der Heijden's (1996) book *Scenarios: The art of strategic conversation*, Wiley, England. Similarly, Arie de Geus's earlier article (1988) 'Planning as learning', *Harvard Business Review*, March–April, pp. 70–74, gives real insight into the processual aspects of strategy. I have also been privileged to work extensively with Joe Jaworski who served as head of the scenario team at Royal/Dutch Shell. His insights into the role of dialogue have been very influential in my own work. He also writes about this in his (1996) book *Synchronicity: The inner path of leadership*, Berrett-Koehler, San Francisco.

Note 3

Faced with many options a key process for managers is the prioritization of actions. This is a point made forcibly by John Kotter in his (1996) book *Leading Change*, Harvard Business School Press, Boston, MA.

Note 4

For a description of a wide range of strategic tasks see Beer, M. and Eisenstat, R. (1996) 'Developing an organization capable of implementing strategy and learning', *Human Relations*, vol. 49, no. 5, pp. 597–619.

Step three: understanding current capability and identifying the gap

Note 1

Researchers have focused on both the internal and external environment. See for example, Hambrick, D.C. (1982) 'Environmental scanning and organisational strategy', *Strategic Management Journal*, vol. 3, pp. 159–174.

Note 2

I first described the Risk Matrix in Gratton, L. (1994) 'Implementing strategic intent: human resource process as a force for change', *Business Strategy Review*, vol. 5, no. 1, pp. 47–66.

Note 3

For a broader description of the Risk Matrix process used across a number of companies see Gratton, L. (1996) 'Implementing a strategic vision: key factors for success', *Long-range Planning*, vol. 29, no. 3, pp. 290–303.

Step four: creating a map of the system

Note 1

The issue of organizations as dynamic systems has received increasing interest. Chris Argyris has talked about the notion of organizational learning as an aspect of the dynamics within an organization. See for example his early article, published in 1977, 'Double loop learning in organisations', *Harvard Business Review*, Sept–Oct, vol. 55, no. 5, pp. 115–125. See also Eden, C. (1990) 'Cognitive maps as visionary tool: Strategy embedded in issue management' in Dyson, R. (ed.) *Strategic Planning: Models and analytical techniques*, John Wiley & Sons, Chichester.

Step five: modelling the dynamics of the vision

Note 1

The role of processes as levers for change has been described by a number of people. See for example, Ghoshal, S. and Bartlett, C. (1995) 'Changing the role of top management: beyond structure to processes', *Harvard Business Review*, Jan–Feb, pp. 87–96. Schuler, R. and Jackson, S. (1987) 'Linking competitive strategy with human resource management practices', *Academy of Management Executive*, vol. 1, no. 3, pp. 207–219. Butler, J., Ferris, F. and Napier, W. (1991) *Strategy and Human Resource Management*, South-Western, Cincinnati, OH.

Note 2

The forcefield analysis was first described by Kurt Lewin in his (1947) article 'Frontiers in group dynamics', *Human Relations*, vol. 1, pp. 5–41. Lewin argued that the nature and pace of change depended on the balance of driving and restraining forces in relation to a particular change. See also Lewin, K. (1951) *Field Theory in Social Science*, Harper and Brothers, New York.

Note 3

It is well understood that individuals and the organizations of which they are a member resist change. Chris Argyris makes the point forcibly in his 1990 book *Overcoming Organisational Defence*, Alynn and Bacon, Boston, MA. Stress and inertia are also central to Huff, J., Huff, A. and Thomas, H. (1992) 'Strategic renewal and the interaction of cumulative stress and inertia', *Strategic Management Journal*, vol. 13, pp. 55–75.

Step six: bridge into action: the journey continues ...

Note 1

Much has been written about the call to action. Some of the frames I found most useful are: Quinn, J.B. (1980) *Strategies for Change: Logical incrementalism*, Irwin, Homewood, IL. Beer, M. and Eisenstat, R. (1996) 'Developing an organisation capable of implementing strategy and learning', *Human Relations*, vol. 49, no. 5, pp. 597–619. Brown, S. and Eisenhardt, K. (1997) *Competing on the Edge: Strategy as structured chaos*, Harvard Business School Press, Boston, MA. Kotter, J. (1996) *Leading Change*, Harvard Business School Press, Boston, MA.

Note 2

There is a useful description of the role of performance metrics in Labovitz, G. and Rosansky, V. (1997) *The Power of Alignment: How great companies stay centered and accomplish extraordinary things*, Wiley & Sons, New York.

Note 3

The use of task forces to bridge into action is at the centre of the process as management learning. This point is made forcibly by Kolb, D. (1984) *Experiential Learning*, Prentice-Hall, Englewood Cliffs, NJ. It is also at the centre of much of the work of Argyris, see for example, Argyris, C. and

Schon, D. (1978) *Organisational Learning: A theory of action perspective*, Addison-Wesley, Reading, MA. For Weick action is central, see Weick, K. (1977) 'Enactment processes in organisations', in Staw, B. and Salanchick, R. (eds) *New Directions in Organisational Behaviour*, St Clair Press, Chicago, IL. The role of teams in creating organizational change is described in Orsburn, J., Moran, L., Musselwhite, E. and Zenger, J. (1990) *Self-Directed Work Teams: The new American challenge*, Business One Irwin, Homewood, IL.

Note 4

This model has been described by Labovitz, G. and Rosansky, V. (1997) *The Power of Alignment: How great companies stay centered and accomplish extraordinary things*, Wiley & Sons, New York.

Note 5

This is what Dave Ulrich refers to as Change Agent in his quadrant model of the role of the HR professional in Ulrich, D. (1997) *Human Resource Champions*, Harvard Business School Press, Cambridge, MA. For a broader discussion of the roles and challenges of the HR function see Ulrich, D., Losey, M. and Lake, G. (1997) *Tomorrow's HR Management 48: Thought Leaders call for Change*, Wiley & Sons, New York.

Bibliography

Ackermann, K.F. (1986) 'A contingency model of HRM strategy. Empirical research findings reconsidered', *Management Forum Bond*, 65–83.

Adler, N.J. and Shoder, F. (1990) 'Human Resource Management: A global perspective' in Pieper, R. (ed.) *Human Resource Management: An International Comparison*, Berlin: De Gruyter.

Alpander, G.G. and Botter, C.H. (1981) 'An integrated model of strategic human resource planning and development', *Human Resource Planning*, 4, 189–298.

Amit, R. and Schoemaker, P. (1993) 'Strategic Assets and Organizational Rent', *Strategic Management Journal*, Vol. 14, 33–46.

Argyris, C. (1989) 'Strategy implementation: An experience in learning', *Organizational Dynamics*.

Barney, J. (1995) 'Looking inside for competitive advantage', *Academy of Management Executive*, Vol. 9, No. 4.

Beer, M., Spector, B., Lawrence, P.R., Mills, D.Q. and Walton, R.E. (1984) *Managing Human Assets*, New York: Free Press.

Boxall, P.F. (1993) 'The Significance of Human Resource Management: A reconsideration of the audience?', *International Journal of Human Resource Management*, 4 (3), 645–664.

Brignall, S. (1992) 'Performance Measurement Systems as Change Agents: A Case for Further Research', *Warwick Business School Research Papers* 72.

Butler, J.E., Ferris, S.R. and Smithcook, D. (1988) 'Exploring some Critical Dimensions of Strategic Human Resource Management' in R.S. Schuler, S.A. Youngblood and V. Huber (eds) *Readings in Personnel and Human Resource Management* (3rd edition), 3–13.

Chan, Kim W. and Mauborgne, R. (1997) 'Fair Process: Managing in the Knowledge Economy', *Harvard Business Review*, July-August, 65–75.

Dierickx, I. and Cool, K. (1989) 'Asset stock accumulation and Sustainability of Competitive Advantage' *Management Science*, 35, 1504–1511.

Fombrun, C.J. and Devanna, M.A. (1984) *Strategic Human Resource Management.* Wiley.

Gratton, L. (1996) 'Pathways to Strategic Intent: The Role of People Processes.' *Long Range Planning* (in print).

Gratton, L. (1996) 'Short-term and long-term business strategy through people processes: a description of the model', *Centre for Organisational Behaviour, Working Paper Series.*

Gratton, L., Hope-Hailey, V., McGovern, P., Stiles, P. and Truss, C. (1996) 'Delivering short-term and longer-term business strategy through people processes: A description of the findings', *Centre for Organisational Research Working Paper Series,* London Business School.

Guest, D. (1987) 'Human Resource Management and Industrial Relations', *Journal of Management Studies,* 24 (5), 503–521.

Guest, D. (1988) 'Human Resource Management: Is it Worth Taking Seriously?', *First Annual Seear Fellowship Lecture,* London School of Economics.

Guest, D.E. (1990) 'Human Resource Management: Its implications for industrial relations and trade unions' in J. Storey (ed.) *New Perspectives on Human Resource Management,* London: Routledge.

Hamel, G. and Prahalad, C.K. (1989) 'Strategic Intent' *Harvard Business Review,* May-June, 63–76.

Hamel, G. and Prahalad, C.K. (1990) 'The Core Competence of the Corporation' *Harvard Business Review,* May-June, 79–91.

Hendry, C. and Pettigrew, A. (1986). 'The Practice of Strategic Human Resource Management', *Personnel Review,* 15 (3), 3–8.

Jackson, S.E., Schuler, R.S. and Rivero, J.C. (1989) 'Organisational Characteristics as Predictors of Personnel Practices' *Personnel Psychology,* 42, 727–786.

Katz, D. and Kahn, R.L. (1978) *The Social Psychology of Organisations.* New York: Wiley.

Kees Van Der Heijeden (1996) *Scenarios: The Art of Strategic Conversations,* Wiley.

Kochen, T.A. and Dyer, L. (1993) 'Managing Transformational Change: The Role of Human Resource Professionals', *International Journal of Human Resource Management,* 4 (3), 569–590.

Johnson, G. (1987) *Strategic Change and the Management Process,* Oxford: Basil Blackwell.

Johnson, G. and Scholes, K. (1992) *Exploring Corporate Strategy* Wiley.

Lundy, O. (1994) 'From Personnel Management to Strategic Human Resource Management', *International Journal of Human Resource Management*, 5 (3), 687–720.

McGovern, P. (1995) 'Learning from the Gurus: An analysis of the unwritten rules of the game', *Business Strategy Review*, 6 (3), 13–25.

McGovern, P., Gratton, L., Hope-Hailey, V., Stiles, P. and Truss, C. (1996) 'Tilting at Windmills: Devolution of Human Resource Management', *Human Resource Management Journal*.

McLaughlin, D.J. (1985) 'Reinforcing Corporate Strategy through Executive Compensation' in Beer and Spector (eds) *Readings in Human Resource Management*.

Meyer, A.D., Brooks, G.R. and Goes, J.B. (1990) 'Environmental jolts and industry revolutions' *Strategic Management Journal*, 11, 93–110.

Noon, M. (1992) 'Human Resource Management: A map, model or theory?' in P. Blyton and P. Turnbull (eds) *Reassessing Human Resource Management*. London: Sage.

Pettigrew, A. and Whipp, R. (1991) *Managing Change for Competitive Success*. Oxford: Blackwell.

Porter, M. (1985) *Competitive Advantage*. New York: Free Press.

Purcell, J. and Ahlstrand, B. (1994) *Human Resource Management in the Multi-Divisional Company*. Oxford: OUP.

Purcell, J. and Sisson, K. (1983) 'Strategies and Practice in the Management of Industrial Relations' in G. Bain (ed.) *Industrial Relations in Britain: Past Trends and Future Prospects*. Oxford: Blackwell.

Quinn Mills, D. (1985) 'Planning with people in mind', *Harvard Business Review* 63, July-August, 97–105.

Senge, P. (1990) 'The Fifth Discipline: The Art and Practice of the Learning Organisation' *Century Business*.

Stiles, P., Gratton, L., Hope-Hailey, V., McGovern, P. and Truss, C. (1996) 'Flattering to Deceive: Performance Management in Leading Edge Companies', *Journal of Management*.

Storey, J. (1989) 'Introduction: From Personnel Management to Human Resource Management' in J. Storey (ed) *New Perspectives on Human Resource Management*. London: Routledge.

Tichy, N.M., Fombrun, C.J. and Devanna, M.A. (1982). 'Strategic Human Resource Management', *Sloan Management Review*, 23 (2), 47–61.

Tylecote, A. (1995) 'Policy revitalisation: managerial objectives, short-termism and innovation', 11–13 September *British Academy of Management Annual Conference*. Sheffield.

Truss, C. and Gratton, L. (1994) 'Strategic Human Resource Management: A Conceptual Approach', *The International Journal of Human Resource Management*, 5 (3), September, 663–686.

Truss, C., Gratton, L., Hope-Hailey, V., McGovern, P. and Stiles, P. 'Strategic Integration and the Employment Contract: New forms of human resource management.' Leading Edge Forum Project Working Paper No. 1, *Centre for Organisational Research Working Paper Series*, No. 45, London Business School.

Tyson, S. and Fell, A. (1986) *Evaluating the Personnel Function*. London: Hutchinson.

Ulrich, D. and Lake, D. (1990) *Organisational Capability, Competing from the inside out*. New York: John Wiley and Sons.

Wright, P., McMahan, G. and McWilliams, A. (1994) 'Human Resources and Sustained Competitive Advantage: A Resource Based Perspective', *International Journal of Human Resource Management*, 5 (2), 301–326.

Index